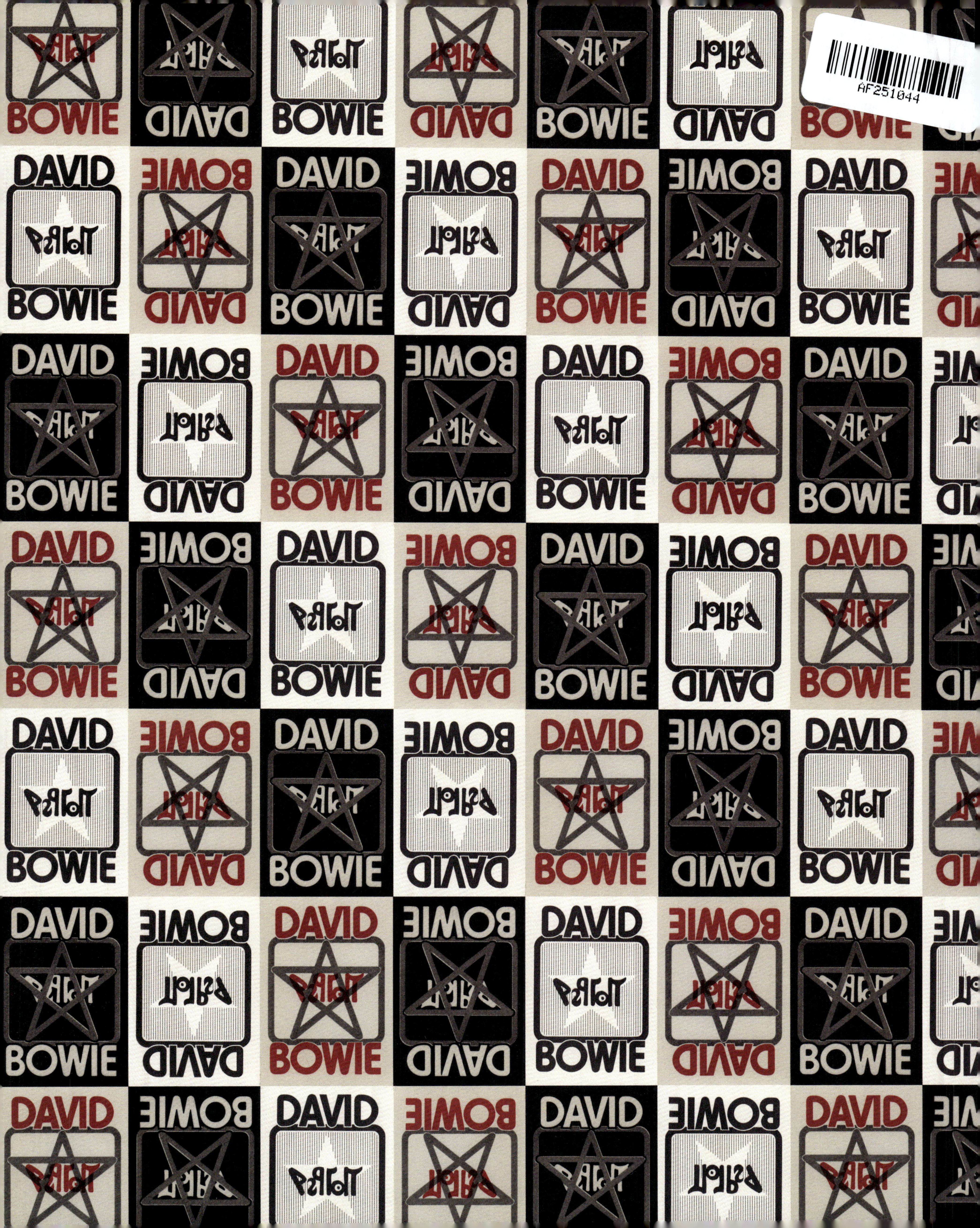

DAVID
BOWIE

BOWIE

BEHIND THE CURTAIN

ANDREW KENT

CAMERON CROWE
NEAL PRESTON

This book is dedicated, first and foremost, to David Bowie, who gave me so much. Without his guidance and encouragement as an artist I would not be the photographer I am today.

To Barbara DeWitte, David's publicist, who brought me to David and is responsible for all the good work that followed. May she rest in peace and the angels be with her. She was taken much too young.

To my parents and family. My mother, Sylvia, for her love of knowledge that rubbed off on me. My father, George, a man of great integrity who taught me countless valuable life lessons. To my siblings, Terry and Steve, and to Terry's children whom I love so much... Elizabeth and her kids Aiden, Olivia, Tommy. Taylor, and her soon-to-arrive perfect new baby.

To my close friend and business partner, Neal Preston, who helped make this all possible.

And finally, to Cameron Crowe, whom even at the age of 14 we all knew was destined for greatness.

- Andrew Kent

DAVID BOWIE : BEHIND THE CURTAIN

By Andrew Kent
Foreword by Cameron Crowe
Introduction by Neal Preston
www.bowiebehindthecurtain.com

PUBLISHED BY

Press Syndication Group
t: 646.325.3221
2850 North Pulaski Road, #9
Chicago, Illinois 60641
www.psgwire.com
warren@psgwire.com

EDITOR, PUBLISHER & DESIGNER : N. Warren Winter
TEXT EDITOR : Cara Winter

The Publisher would like to sincerely thank Cameron Crowe for granting permission to reprint quotes taken from his Rolling Stone and Playboy interviews in 1976. The quotes are reprinted on the following pages: 12, 41, 61, 78, 84-85, 114, and the back end page. The only other source for quotes used in this book is the author, Andrew Kent.

$59.95
First Edition, 2016
ISBN 978-0-9960587-5-9
Library of Congress Pre-Assigned Control Number : 2016940476
Printed in China

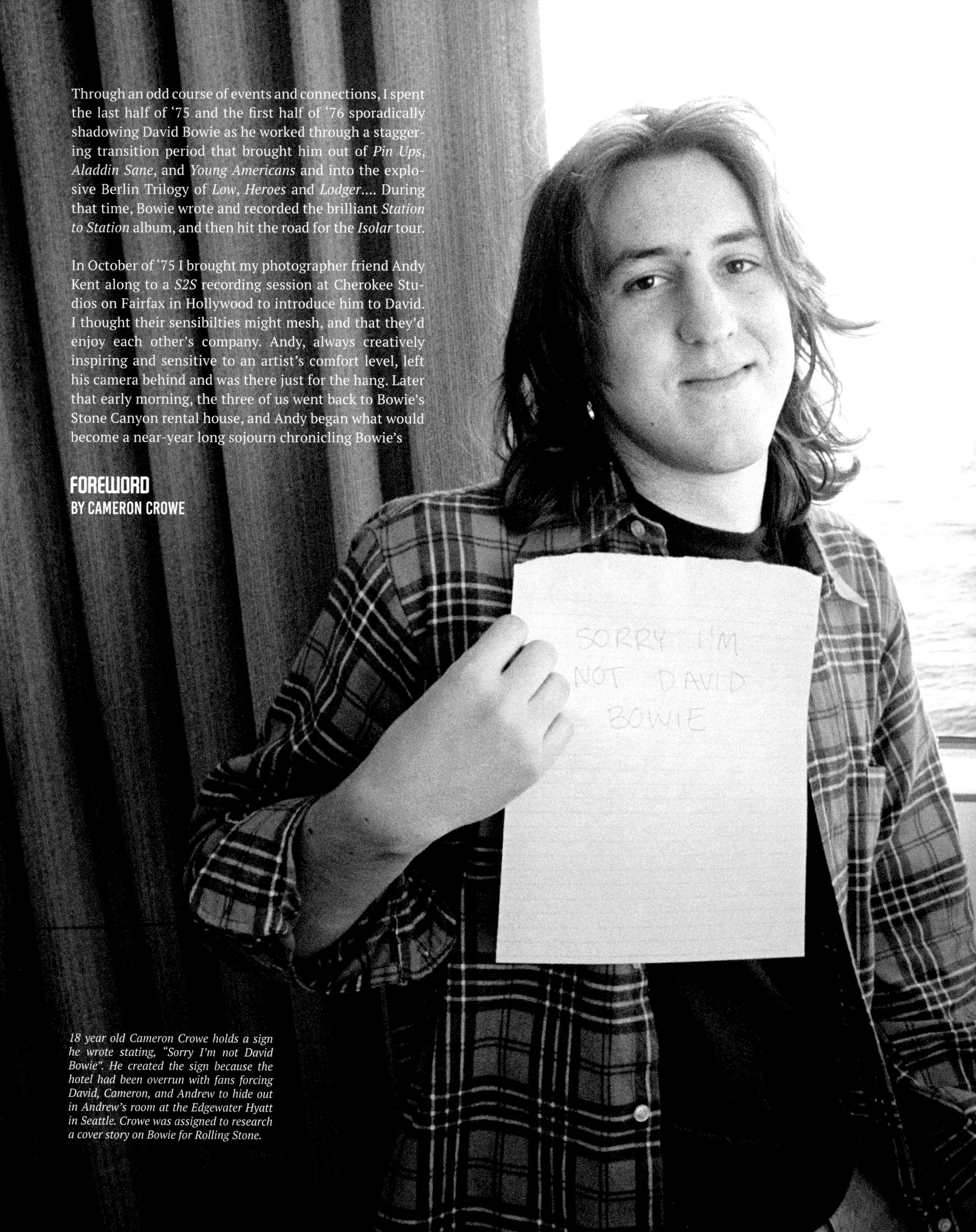

Through an odd course of events and connections, I spent the last half of '75 and the first half of '76 sporadically shadowing David Bowie as he worked through a staggering transition period that brought him out of *Pin Ups*, *Aladdin Sane*, and *Young Americans* and into the explosive Berlin Trilogy of *Low*, *Heroes* and *Lodger*.... During that time, Bowie wrote and recorded the brilliant *Station to Station* album, and then hit the road for the *Isolar* tour.

In October of '75 I brought my photographer friend Andy Kent along to a *S2S* recording session at Cherokee Studios on Fairfax in Hollywood to introduce him to David. I thought their sensibilties might mesh, and that they'd enjoy each other's company. Andy, always creatively inspiring and sensitive to an artist's comfort level, left his camera behind and was there just for the hang. Later that early morning, the three of us went back to Bowie's Stone Canyon rental house, and Andy began what would become a near-year long sojourn chronicling Bowie's

FOREWORD
BY CAMERON CROWE

18 year old Cameron Crowe holds a sign he wrote stating, "Sorry I'm not David Bowie". He created the sign because the hotel had been overrun with fans forcing David, Cameron, and Andrew to hide out in Andrew's room at the Edgewater Hyatt in Seattle. Crowe was assigned to research a cover story on Bowie for Rolling Stone.

travels - from Soul Train to Vancouver and Seattle, Portland and LA, New York to Munich, Moscow and Finland, and everywhere in-between.

Bowie the chameleon was typically ever-changing back then - his unfinished biography from the time took its name from a line in the title track to *Station to Station*, "The Return of the Thin White Duke," and David was knee-deep in that persona. Bowie was an intellectual. A conversationalist par excellence. An entertainer. Guarded, but ebullient and gregarious. It was uncharted territory for Andy and myself. We'd never met - much less covered - an artist quite like David Bowie.

Andy followed Bowie across the globe - shared boat and train rides, hung out in hotels and backstage dressing rooms, and he captured the images and emotions of all his moods and poses. The showman. The actor. The friend. The generous mentor to Iggy Pop. The artist. The myth. The Thin White Duke. The huckster. The musician. The quicksilver legend. The philosopher. And most important... the man himself. Even if - *especially* if? - the man himself, as he later claimed, didn't even know who he was at the time.

Bowie's personas throughout the years (Alladin Sane, TWD, Ziggy, etc...) made it difficult to break down the barriers, strip away the characters, and bring out something real. Something true. Something iconic and unforgettable. Few photographers ever had the access afforded to - nay, bestowed upon - Andy Kent, and he made the most of that unprecedented proximity.

Bowie was a larger than life figure, and Andy's pictures showcase all that was great about the performer, but they also open a historic window into the soul of... David Jones. Exhaustion and effort, insecurity, joy... these pictures tell the story of Bowie with the very sensitivity that Andy showed him that first time they met. "Get to know me first, then we'll see if we can work together," Andy seemed to be saying that night. Thankfully, they did.

Unguarded and naked, even when fully clothed, the images in this book capture a time that Bowie himself would call "the most difficult time of my life," but Andy Kent's photos bring a humanity, a warmth and a beating heart that can only come from one highly skilled artist rightfully earning the trust of another. Artist creating art, and art creating artist.

Bowie was taken from us all too soon at the beginning of this year, days after the release of yet another highly imaginative and haunting record, *Blackstar*. He was a champion of all things creative, and he truly had ridiculously good taste... in art, fashion, women, music, friends... and collaborators. Over the years he would work with giants and unknowns in every walk of creative life - and we're blessed to have this document of the year that Andy spent traveling the globe with David Jones.

"I can't give everything," Bowie sang in the clearly autobiographical song from his final album, but to look at the images of Andy Kent, one can only take notice that in Andy's time of close personal access, Bowie most certainly, spectacularly... did exactly that.

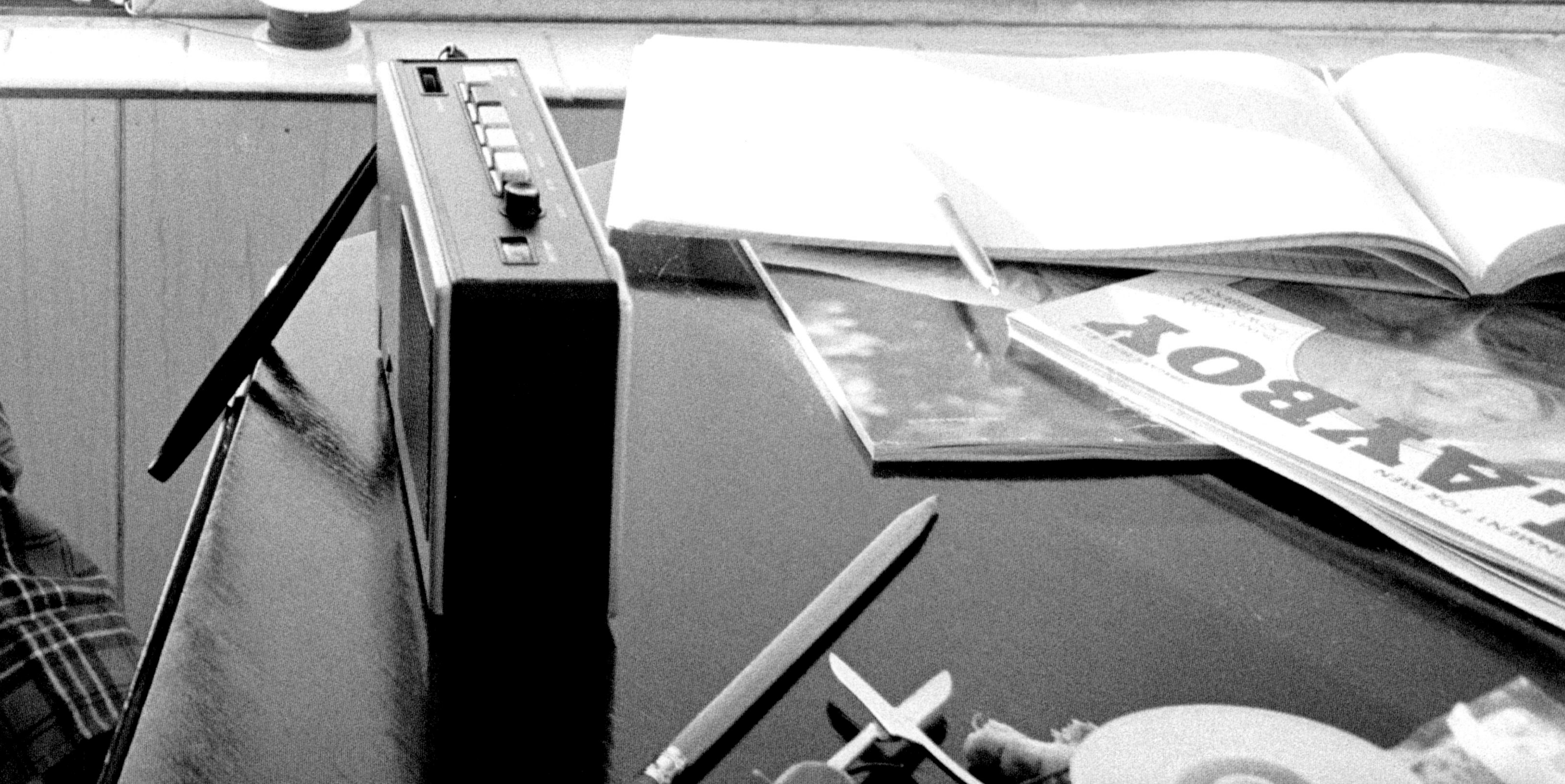

INTRODUCTION
BY NEAL PRESTON

1971 seems like a lifetime ago.

A year after graduating high school
in New York City I made one of those
heavy fork-in-the-road life-changing
decisions and moved to Los Angeles. Andy
Kent was one of the first people I met when
I landed in LA. He'd been a staff photographer
for the legendary underground newspaper the
LA Free Press, and to me that was beyond im-
pressive. Sure, I had been knocking around all the
rock venues in New York City with cameras in hand,
but Andy was the real deal - a true photojournalist. We
had a lot in common beyond photography, so it didn't
take long before we became close friends and eventually
business partners. We were a team, and a very good one at
that.

Over the next several years rarely a day would pass without one
of us (and many times both of us) being booked for some kind
of photo assignment, usually a rock concert or some other music
business-related job. Not every shoot was stimulating or glamorous.
On any given day you could find one of us at Atlantic Records, A&M,
or Elektra Records, and later that night we'd show up at the Forum, the
Universal Amphitheatre, or one of a dozen other rock venues. We ran
thousands, if not tens of thousands of rolls of film through our Nikons.
This was normal life for us. We were paying our dues, working in the trenches.

From the first day a photographer picks up a camera, he or she has a "dream
assignment"… the one job meant for you and only you. If you hone your craft and
practice a solid work ethic, sooner or later - and always when you least expect it -
the dream assignment will land in your lap. You don't find it, it finds you. You've just
got to be ready for it when it happens.

The dream assignment came for Andy the day he had been offered the job to go out on the
road with David Bowie, with whom he'd bonded in LA. Even though we were both used to
working with big-time rock bands, there was a definite gleam in Andy's eye that said this one
was different. He attacked the gig with a vengence.

When I first saw the pictures Andy brought back from the tour I was speechless. They were stun-
ning, and beyond iconic. I feel they are as important as any set of photographs of any musician who
has ever lived. Andy shot exquisite, highly intimate, surreal portraits that are more alive now than the
day they were made.

Given David's penchant for role-playing, and that he seemingly lived his entire life as one extended exer-
cise in performance art, Andy achieved something quite remarkable: he somehow managed to penetrate the
veneer of a rock superstar known for being the ultimate chameleon. It takes a true artist to accomplish that.
Andy's photographs of David will not only stand the test of time; they have become even more fascinating with
David's passing earlier this year. They are significant works of art that are as important to the history of pop cul-
ture as any photos every made of any musician.

As a photographer you can't dream of anything better than that.

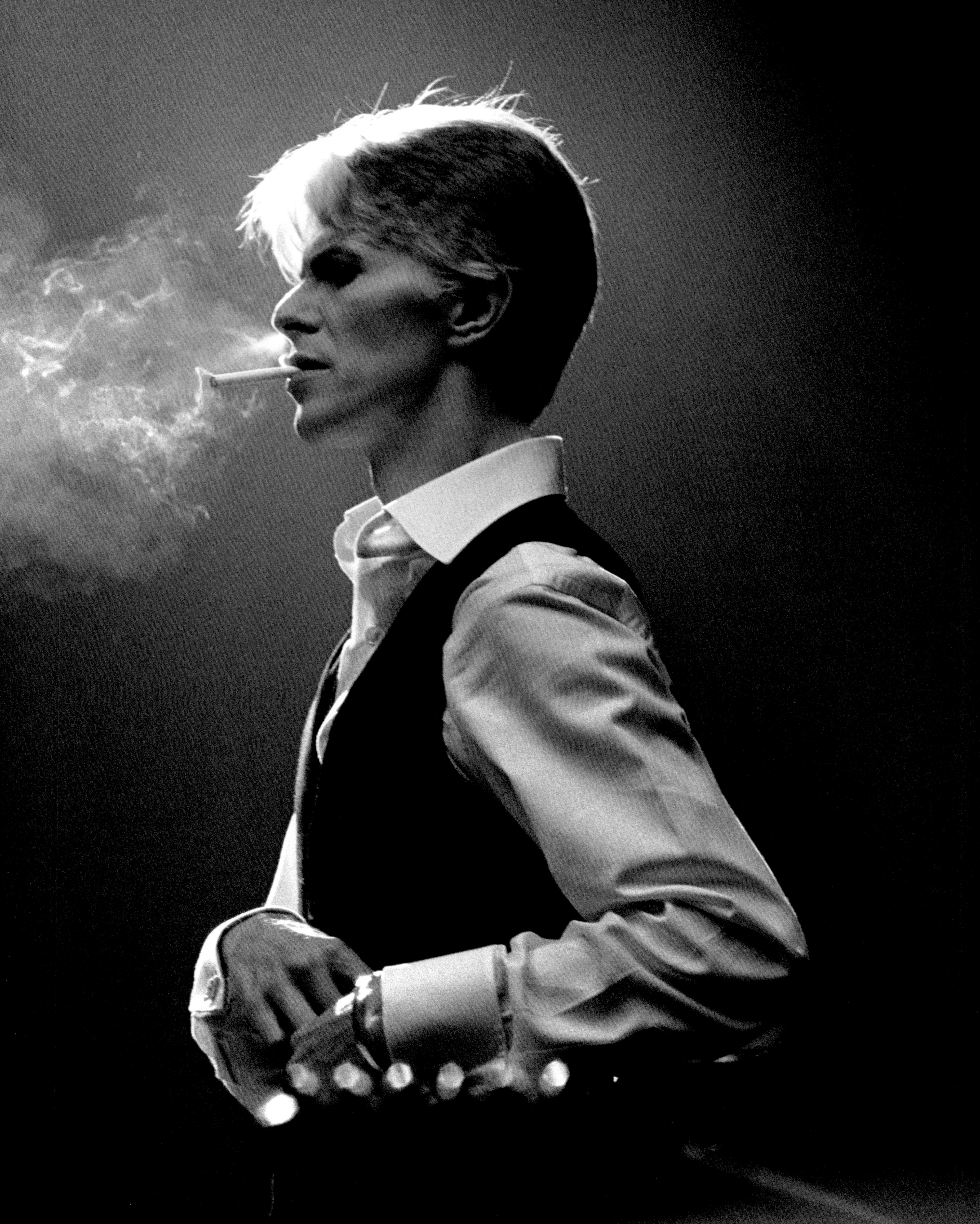

 With Ziggy fading fast in the rear view mirror and the Duke rising like a fashionable pharaoh, the only thing certain was the future would be thoroughly entertaining and tantilizingly unpredictable.

Sitting in room 207 of the Beverly Wilshire Hotel, after having been up all night, Bowie says to Ron Woods, "I've never been so happy, I've got that good old 'I'm gonna change the world' thing back again. I had that once. I was a strong idealist once, then when I saw all my efforts being mistranslated, I turned into an avid pessimist. A manic depressive. Now, I feel strong mentally again. You could probably hear from Young Americans that I'm on an upper. It's the first record I've actually liked since Hunky Dory.

And then, in one of his tantilizingly unpredictable swings, Bowie says, "Rock & roll has been really bringing me down lately. It's in great danger of becoming an immobile, sterile fascist that constantly spews its propaganda on every arm of the media. It rules a level of thought and clarity of intelligence that you'll never raise above. You don't have a fucking chance to hear Beethoven on any radio station anymore. You've got to listen to the O'Jays. I mean, disco music is great. I used disco to get my first Number One single "Fame" but it's an escapist's way out. It's musical soma. Rock & roll too - it will occupy and destroy you that way. It lets in lower elements and shadows that I don't think are necessary. Rock has always been the devil's music. You can't convince me that it isn't."

As his new album, Station to Station was charting due to the success of the single, "Golden Years" Bowie broke his 2nd widely publicized promise to retire from music and touring. On February 2nd, 1976, Bowie launched, as only he could, into an ambitious 64 show world tour, called Isolar, that would take him and his entourage through 12 countries over 4 months.

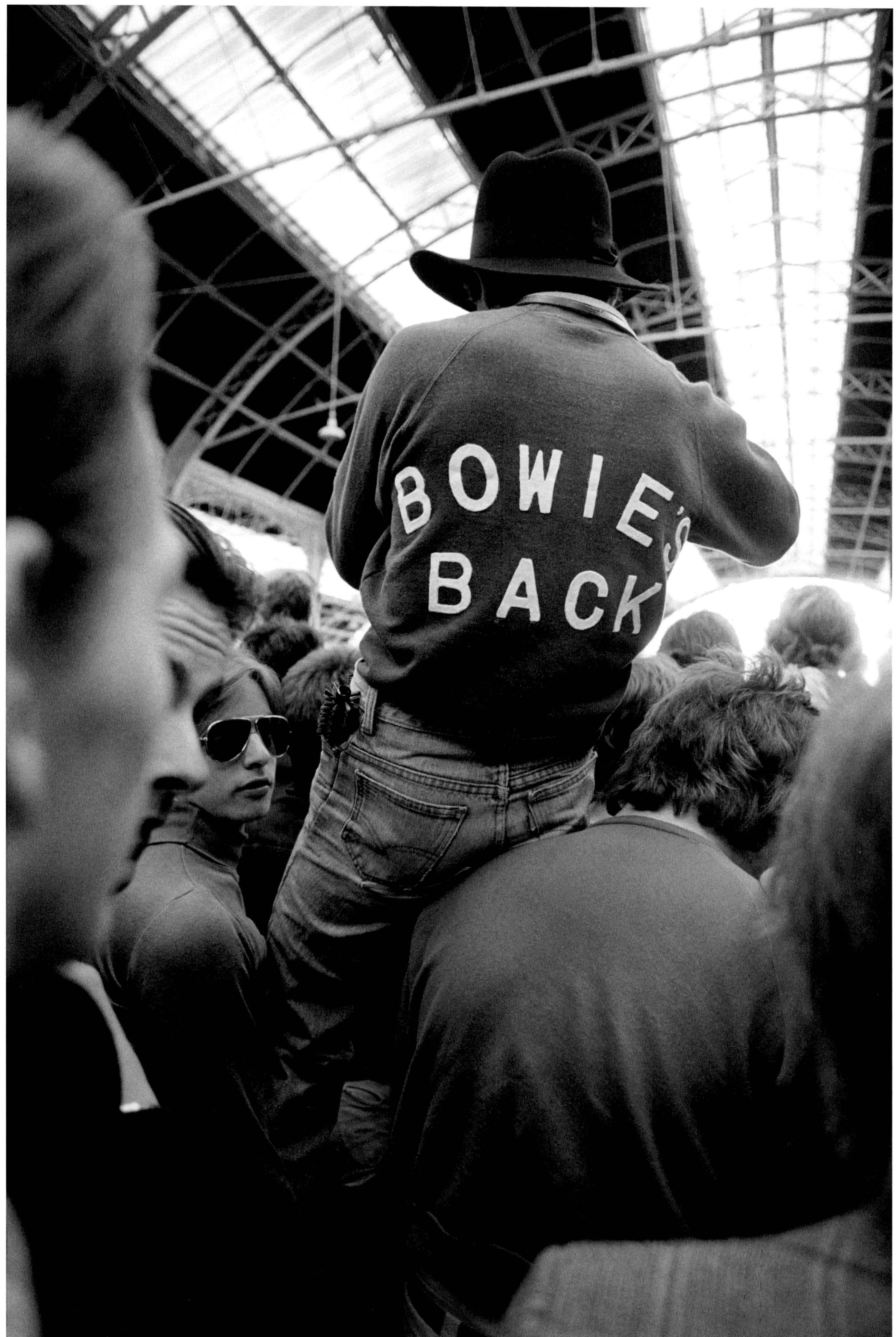
BOWIE'S
BACK

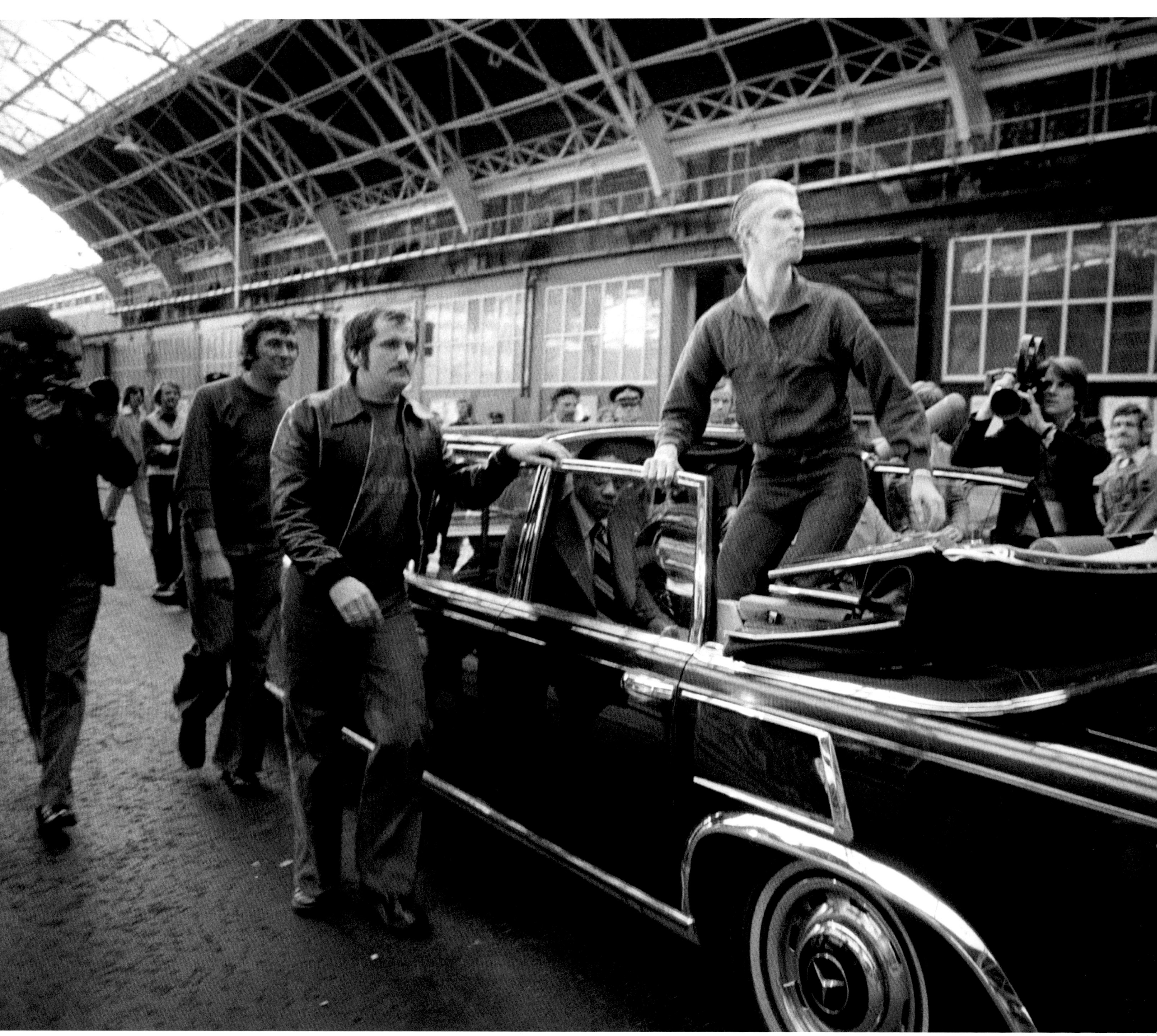

(Previous page, above, and right)
In 1976, David returned to London from Paris by train arriving into Victoria Station. The local icon was welcomed by throngs of fans hoping to catch a glimpse or get their records signed.

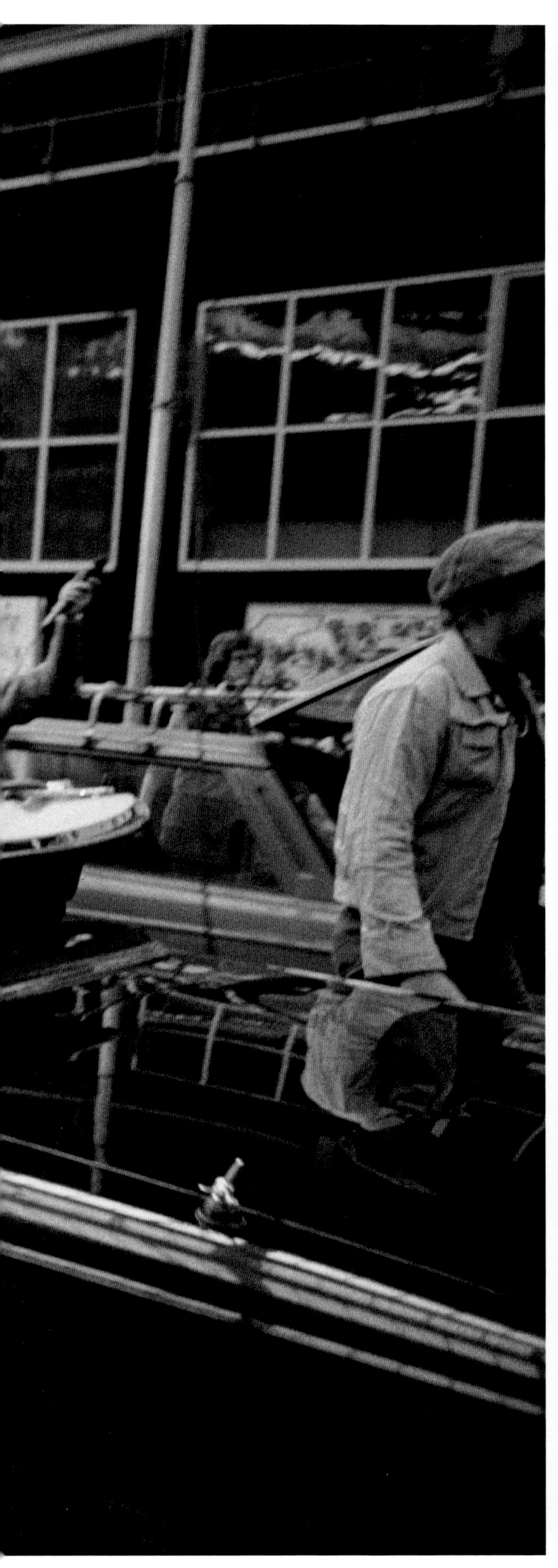

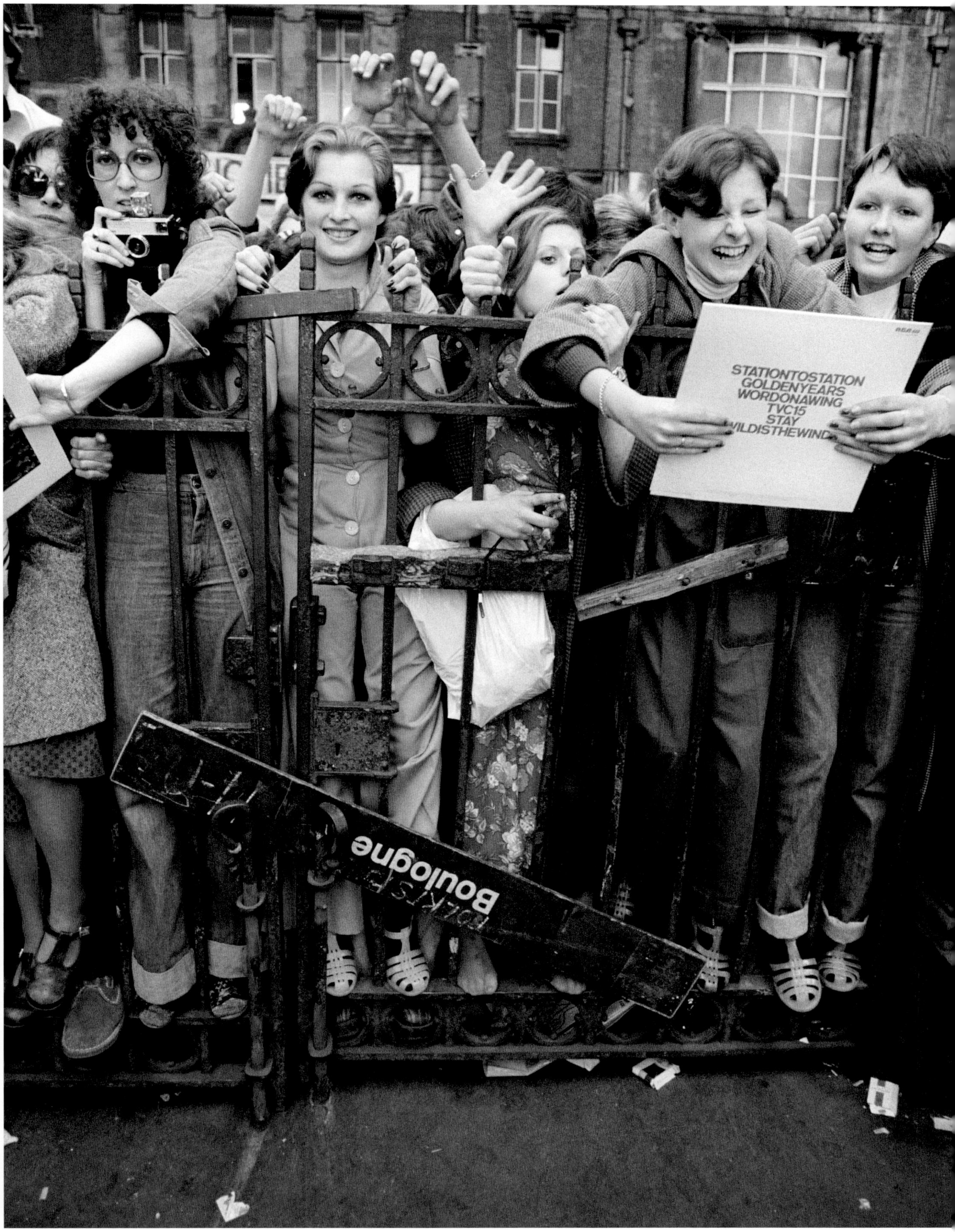

STATIONTOSTATION
GOLDENYEARS
WORDONAWING
TVC15
STAY
WILDISTHEWIND

Boulogne

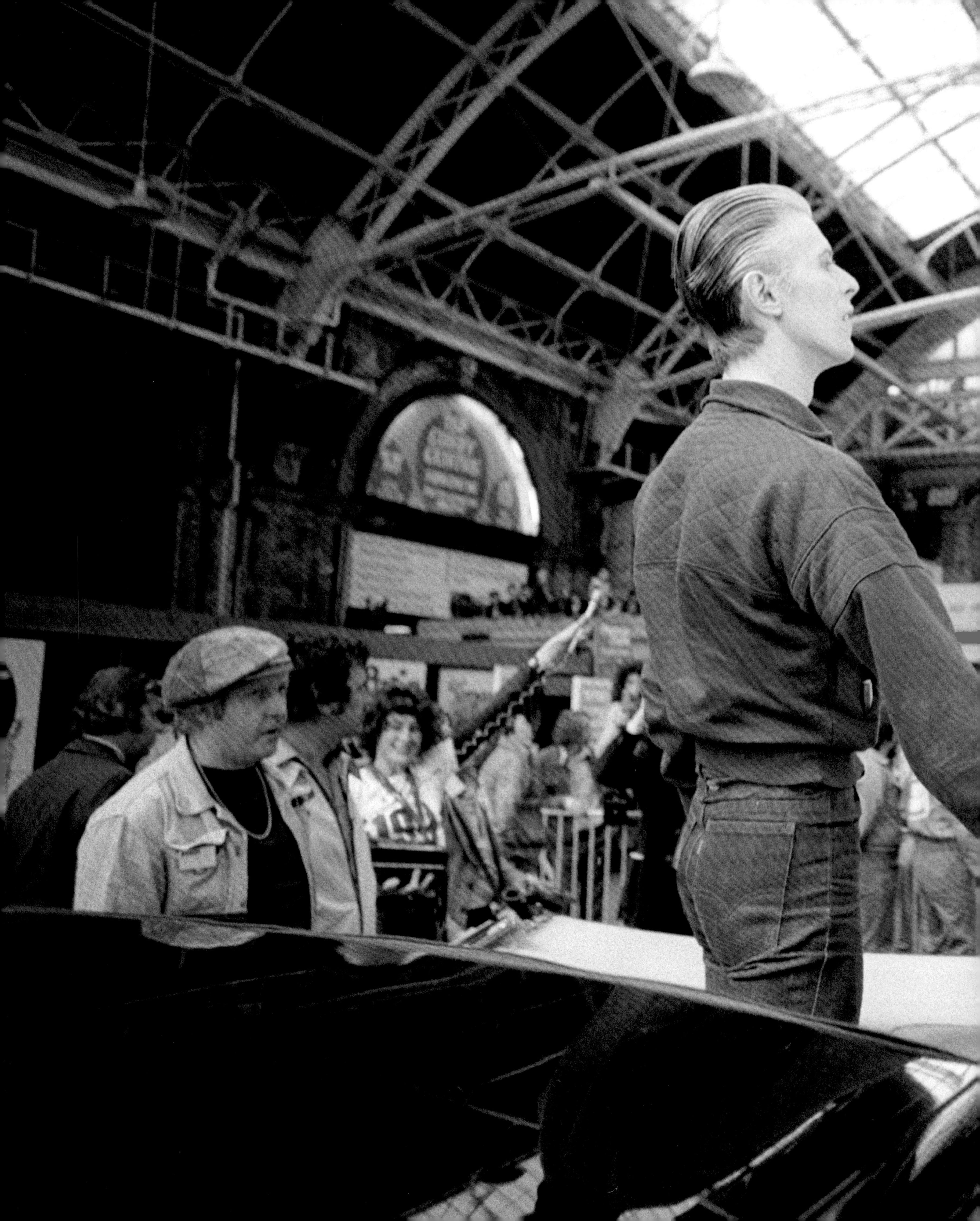

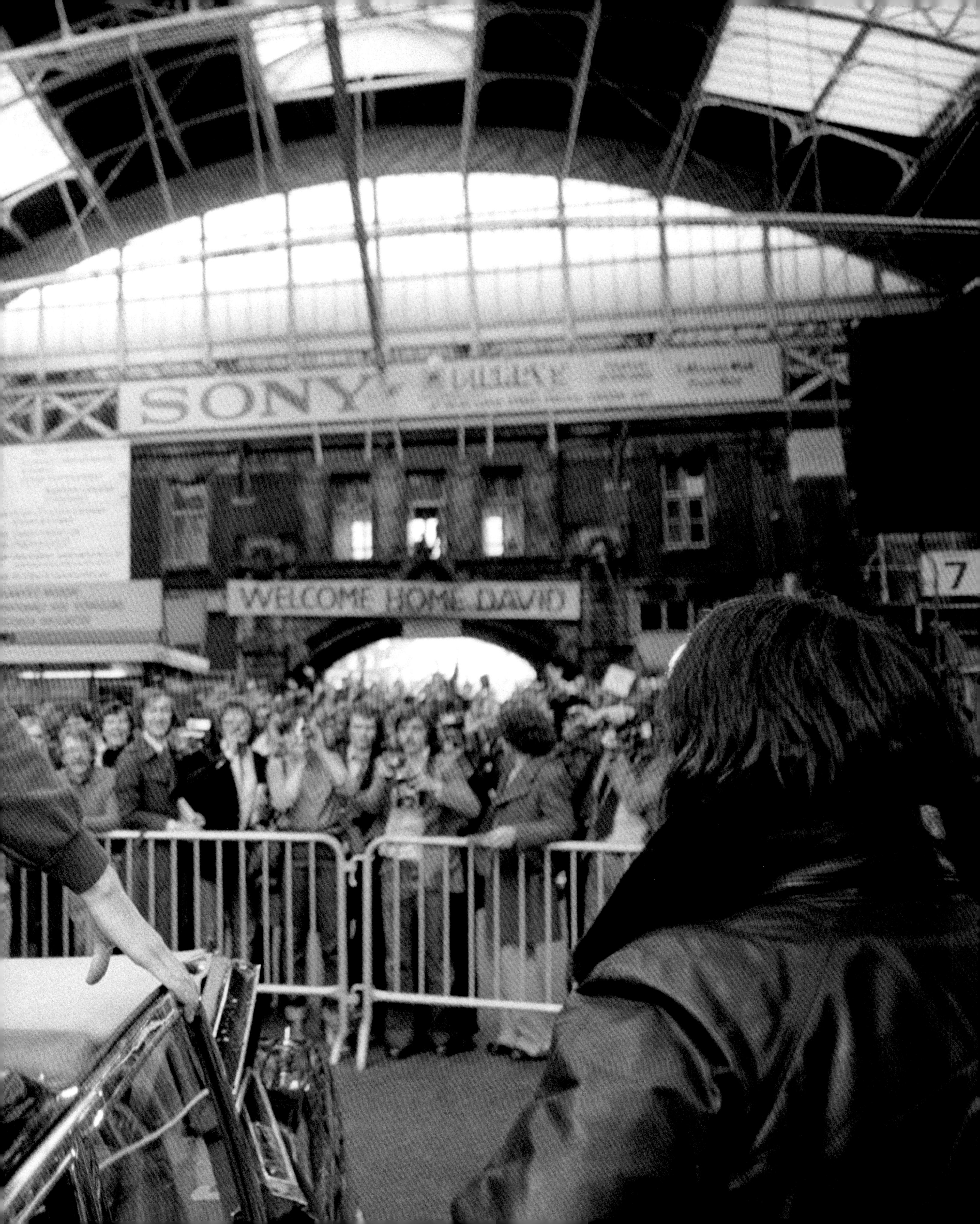
SONY
WELCOME HOME DAVID
7

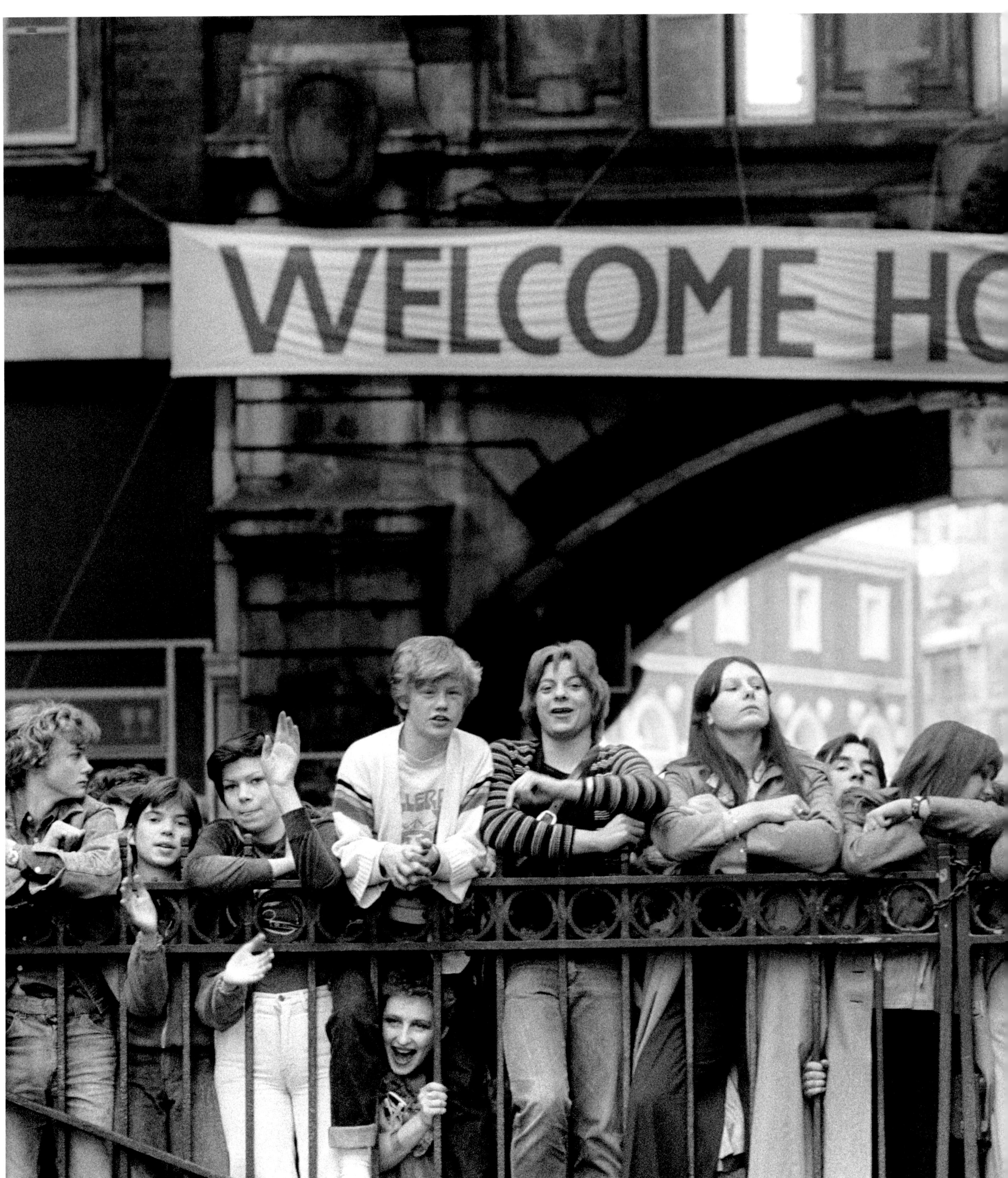

WELCOME HO

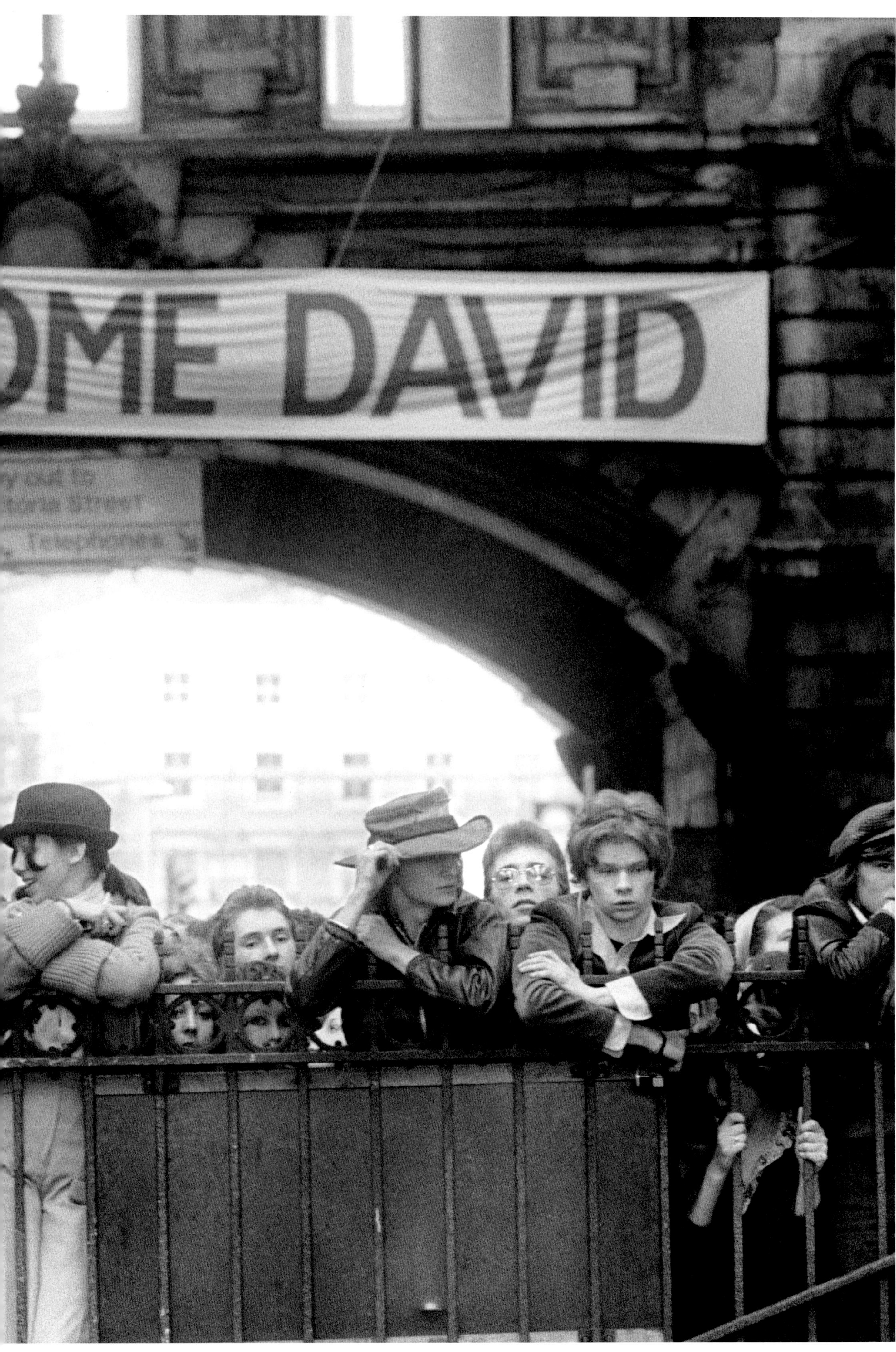

Hundreds of dedicated fans waited for hours anticipating Bowie's arrival into Victorial Station in London.

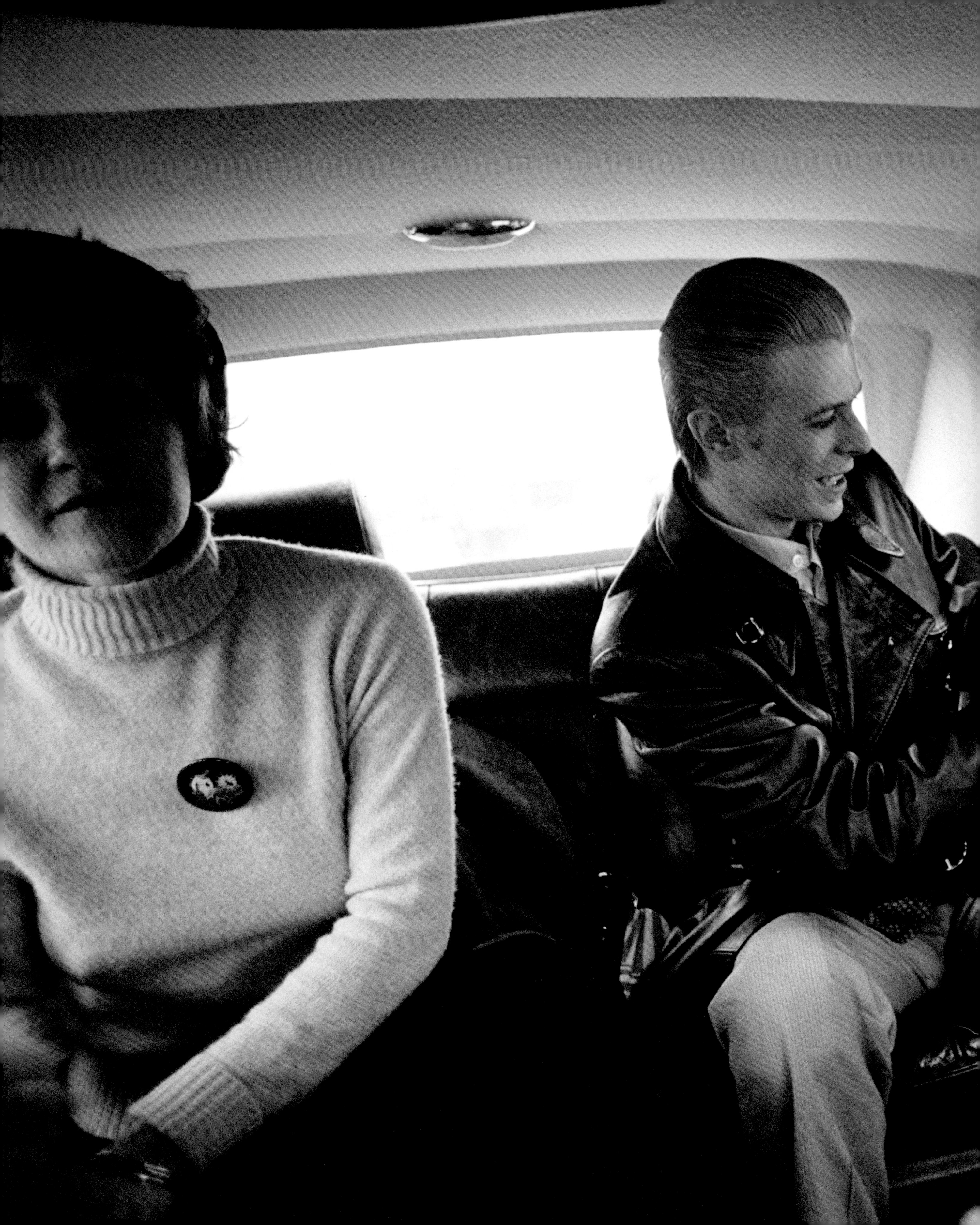

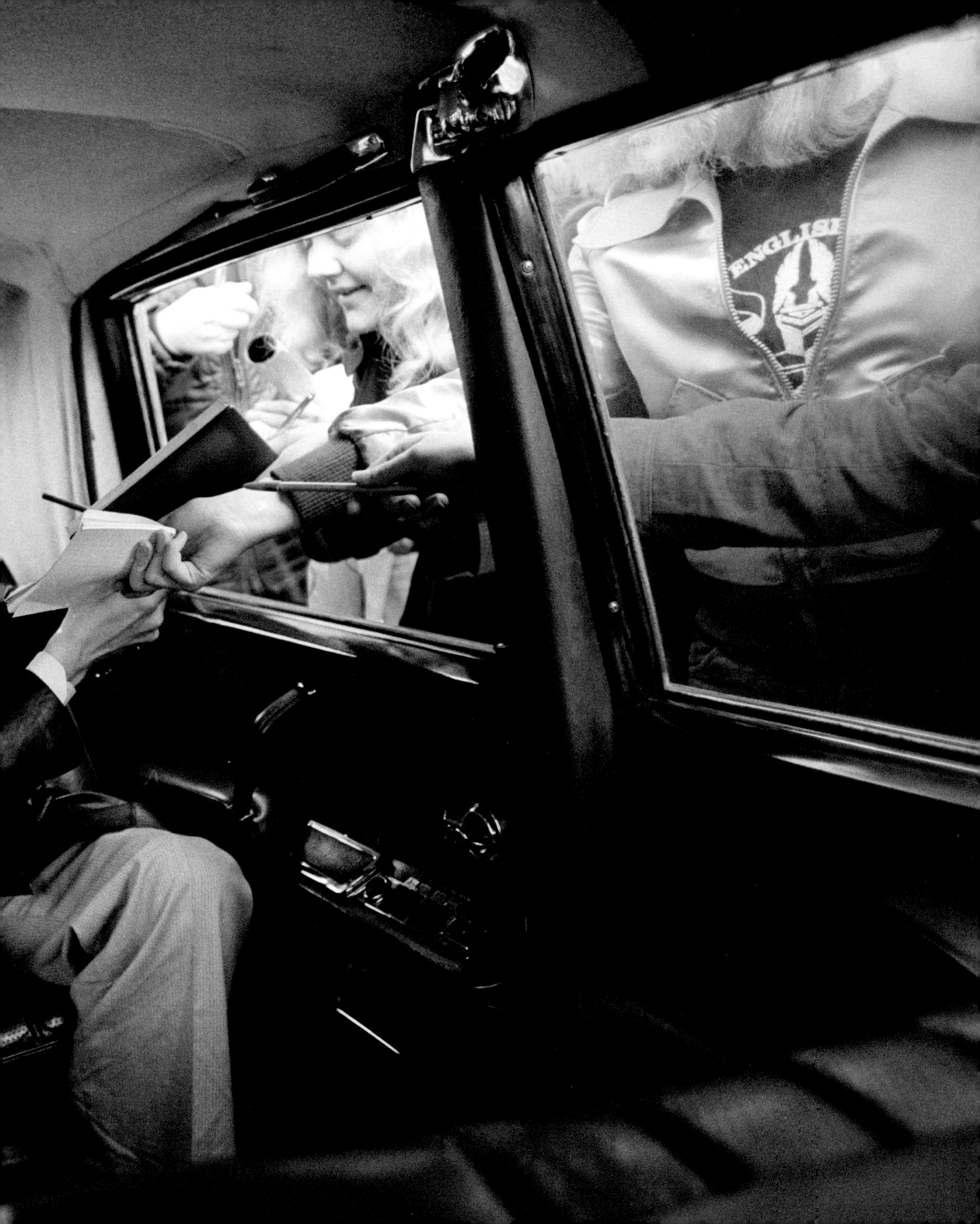
ENGLISH

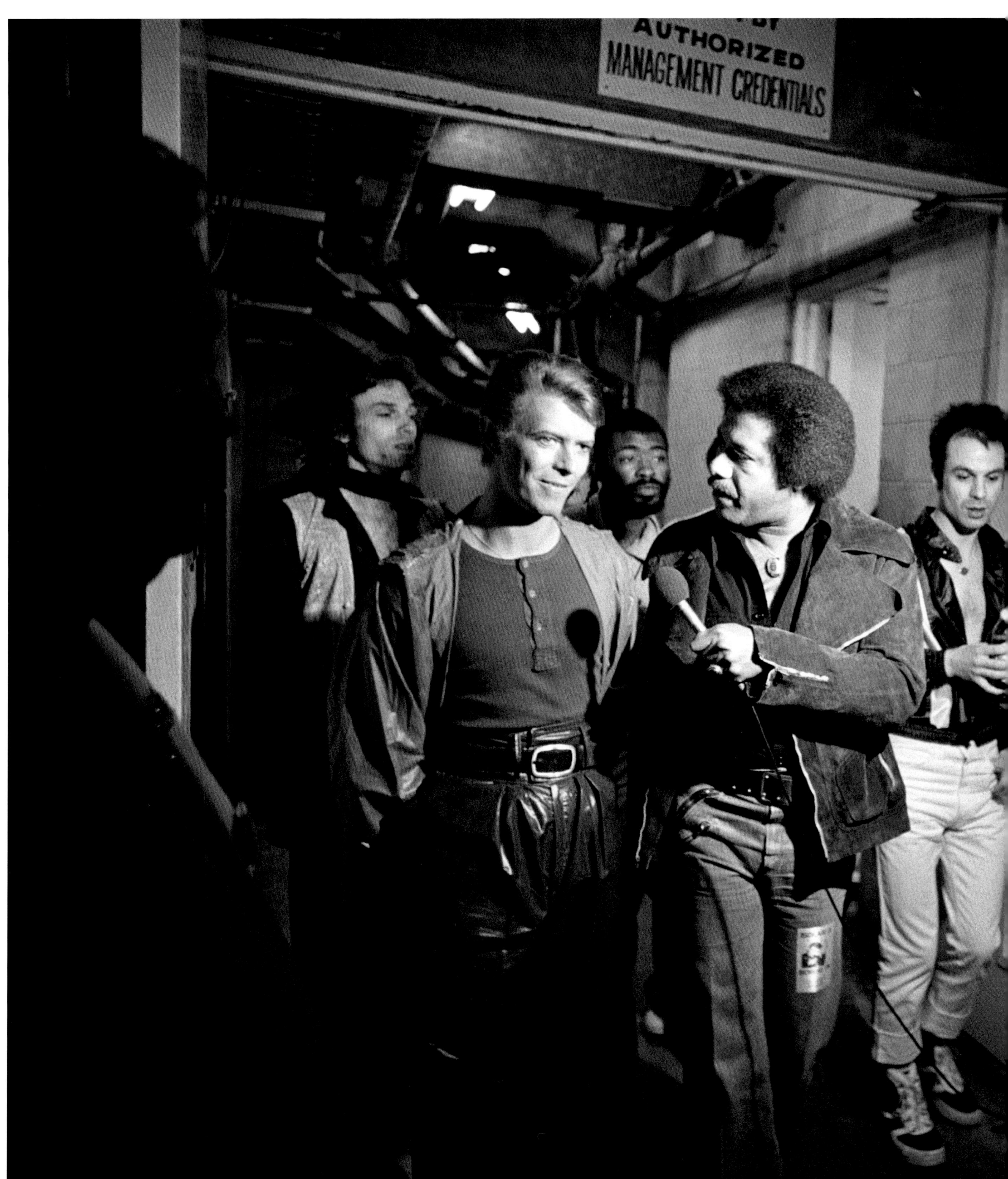
AUTHORIZED
MANAGEMENT CREDENTIALS

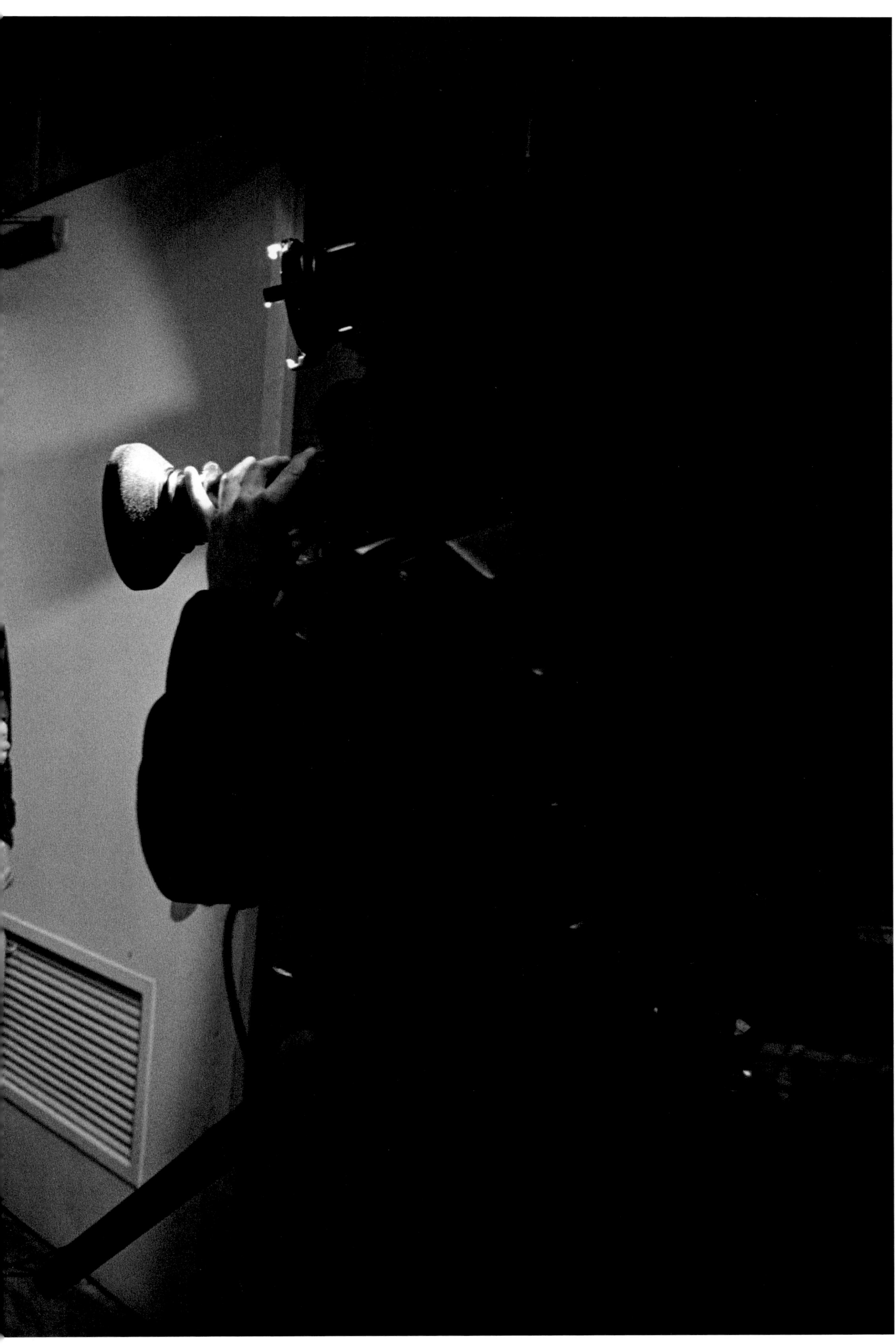

David is interviewed on-the-fly by a television station as he makes his way towards the stage at the Los Angeles Forum.

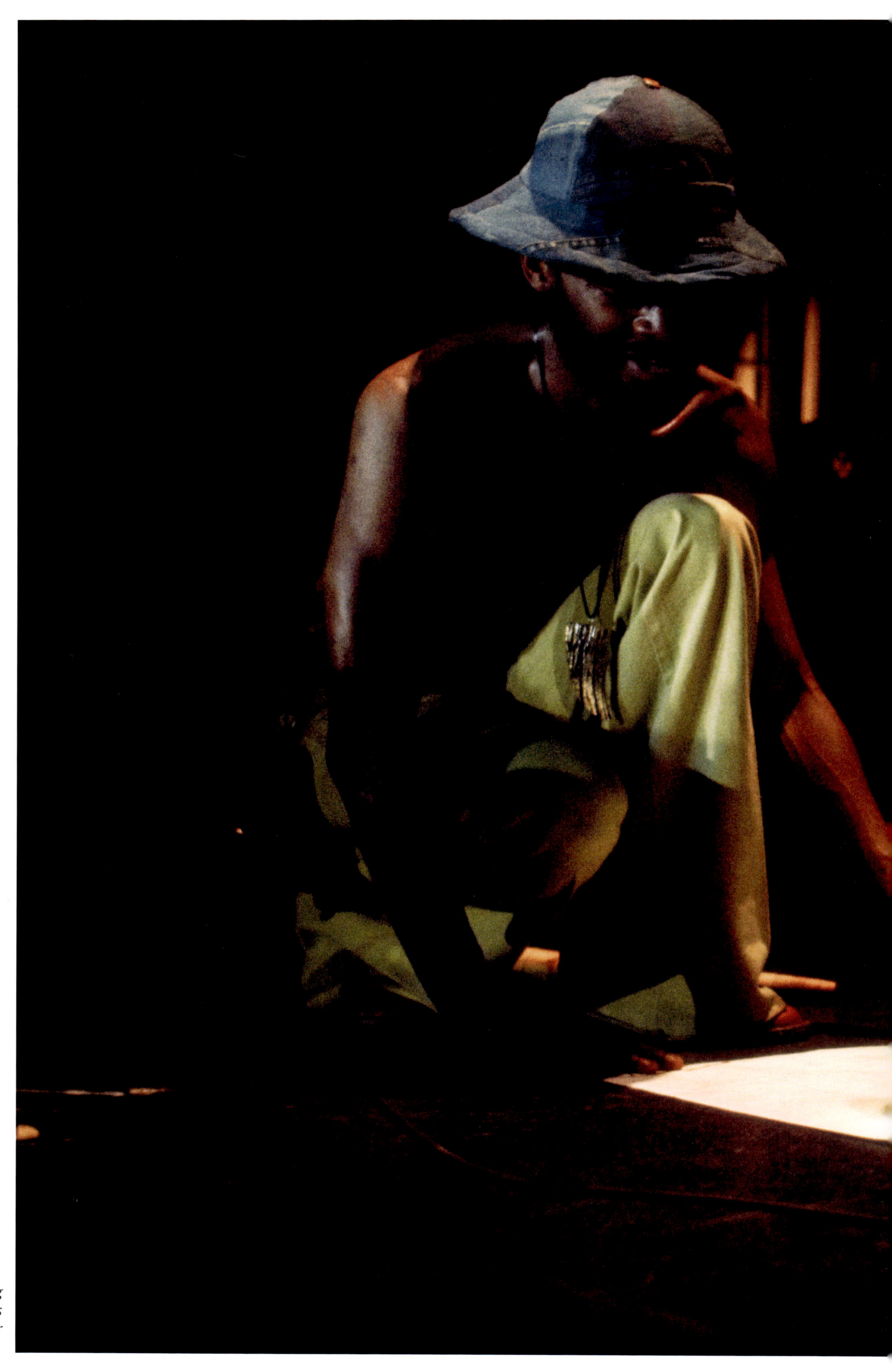

David, with drummer Dennis Davis looking on, decided to name his band "Raw Meat" as he scrolls the name across a section of poster board prior to a show in Berlin.

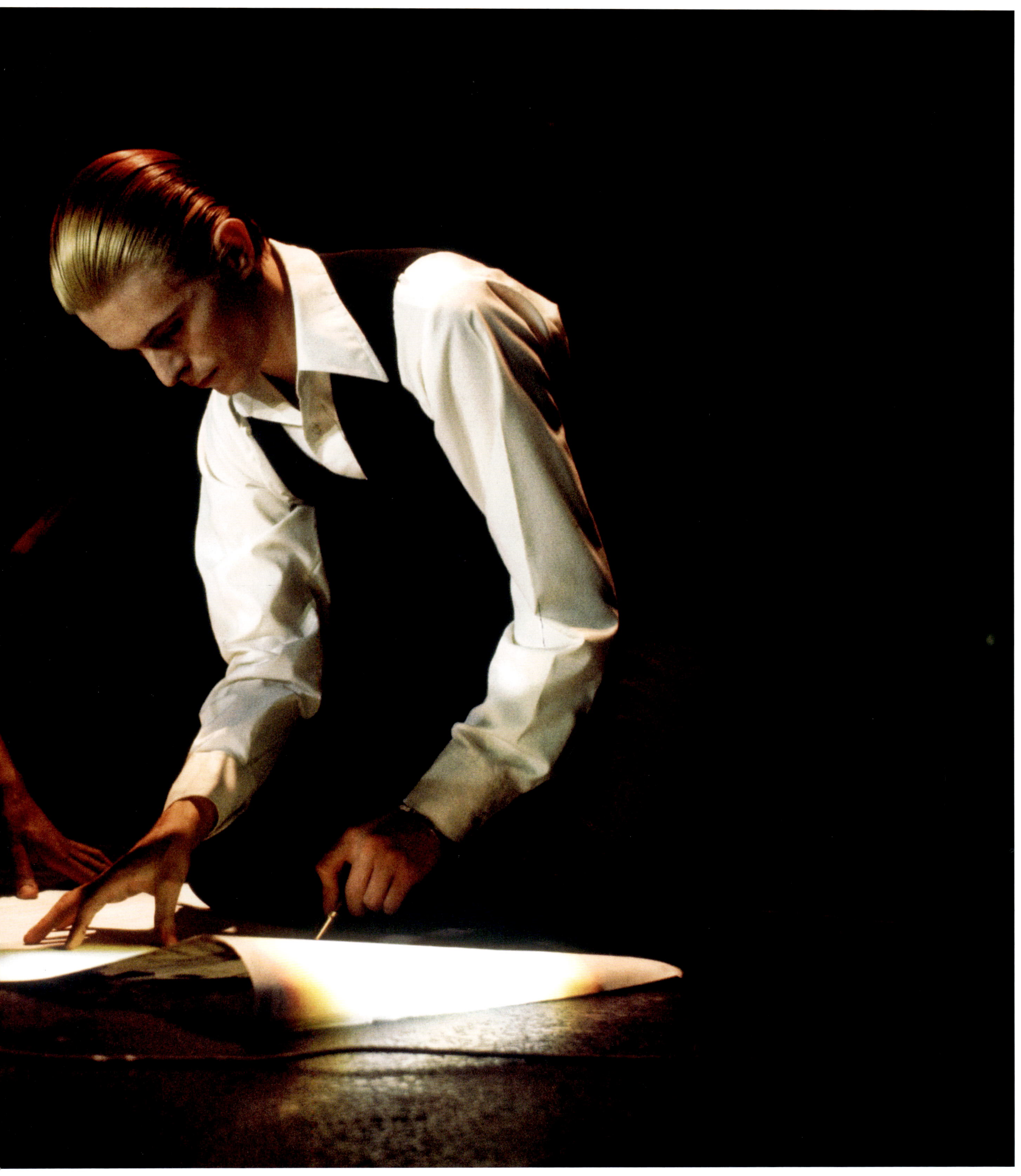

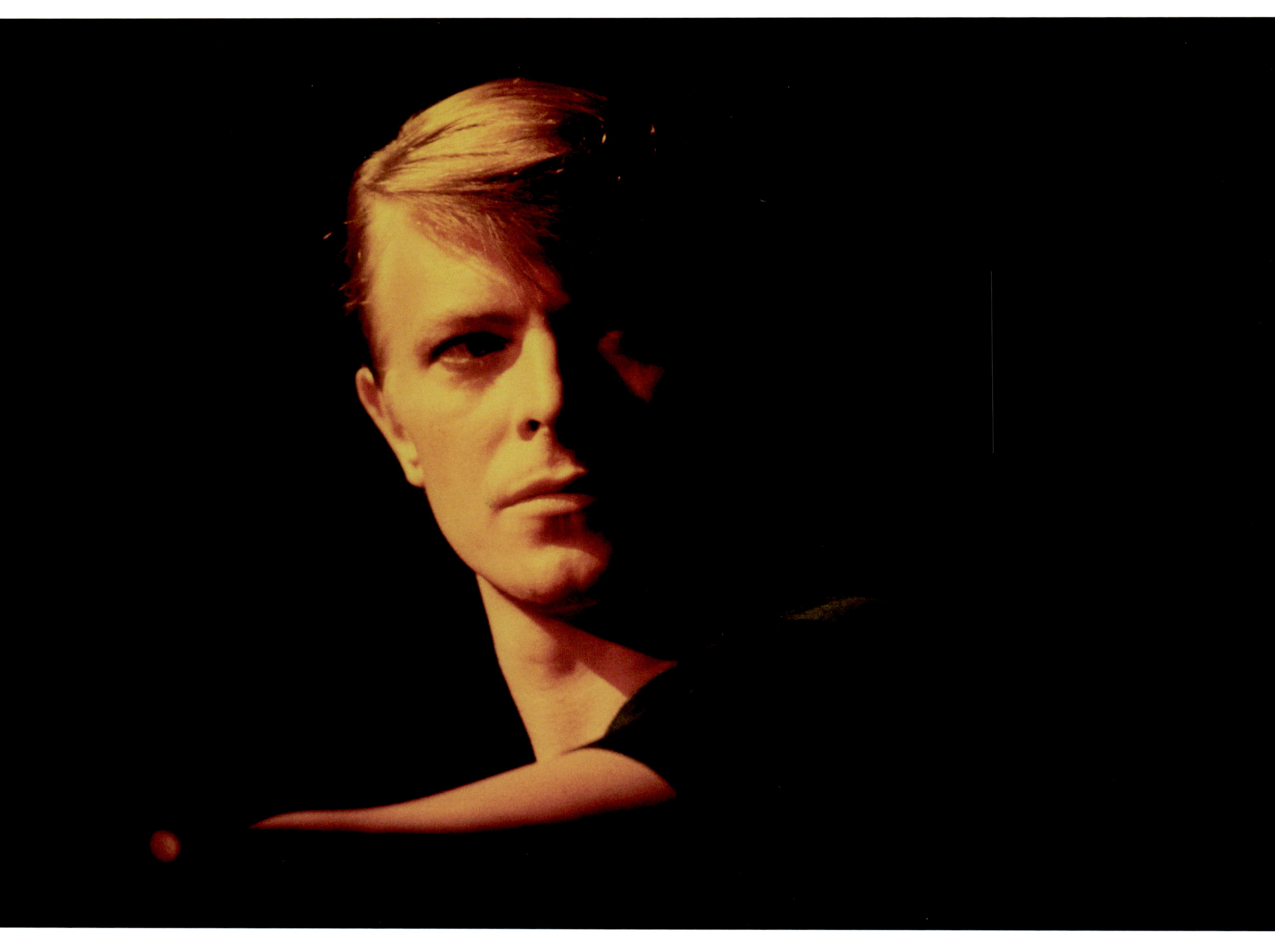

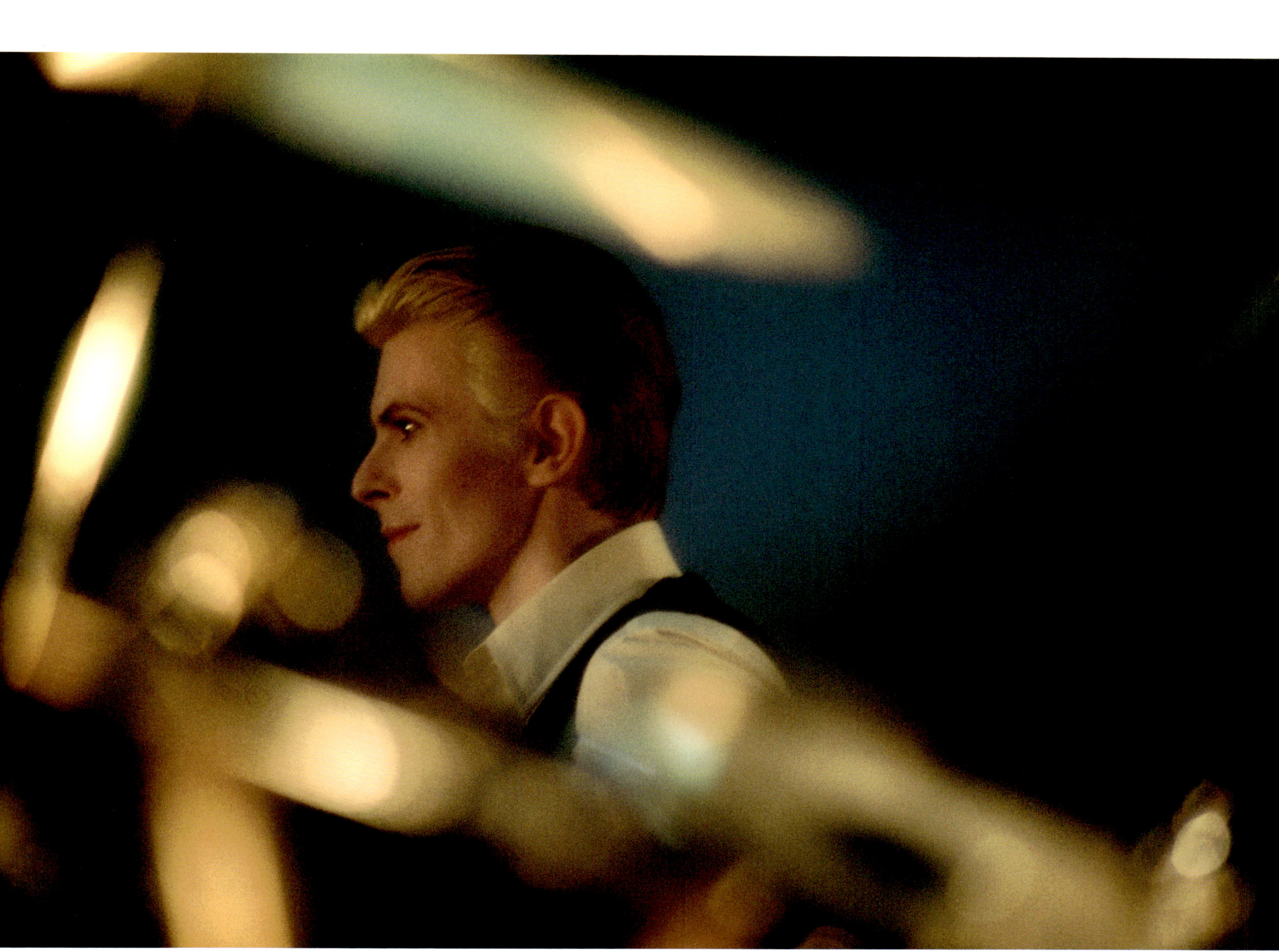

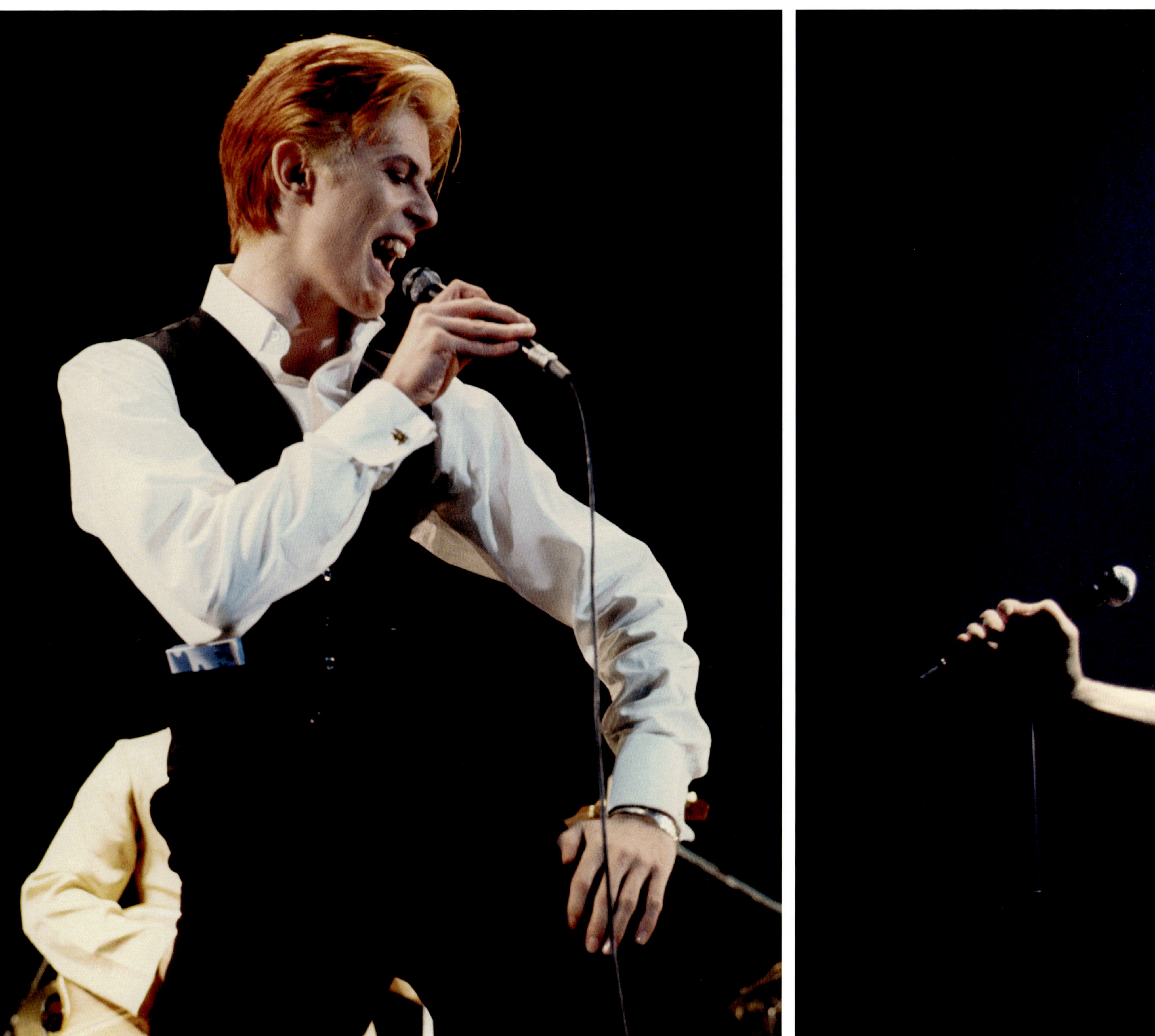

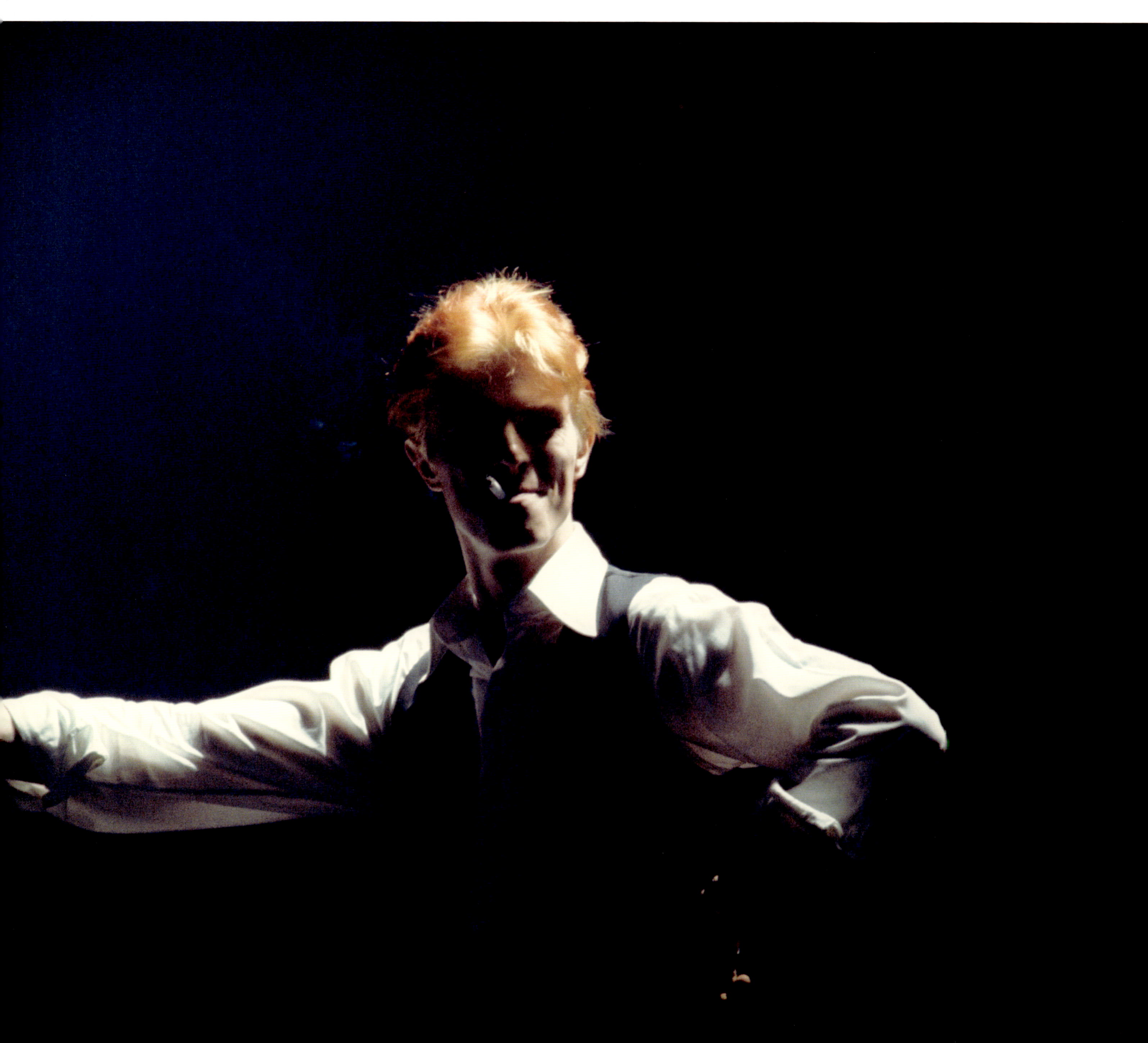

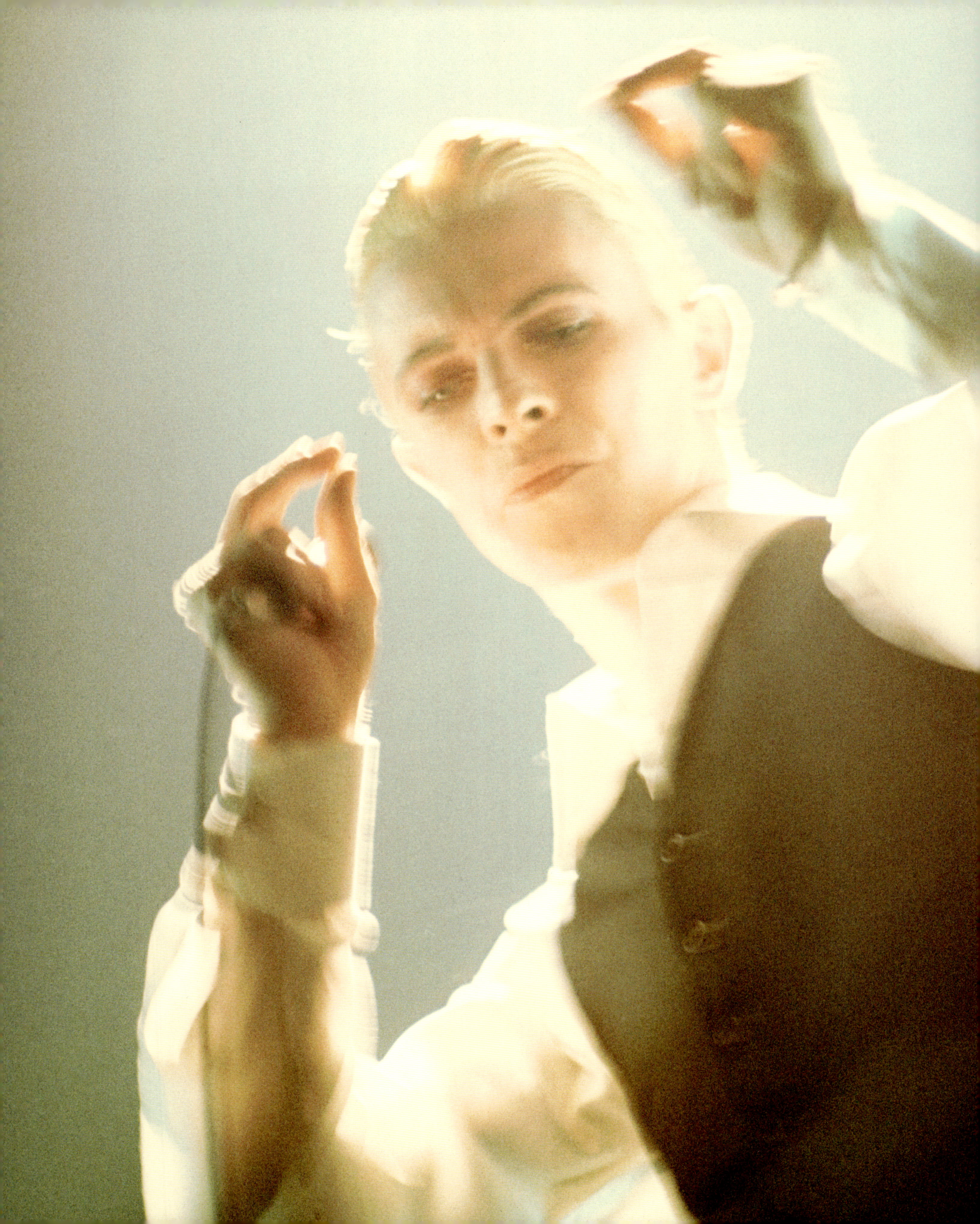

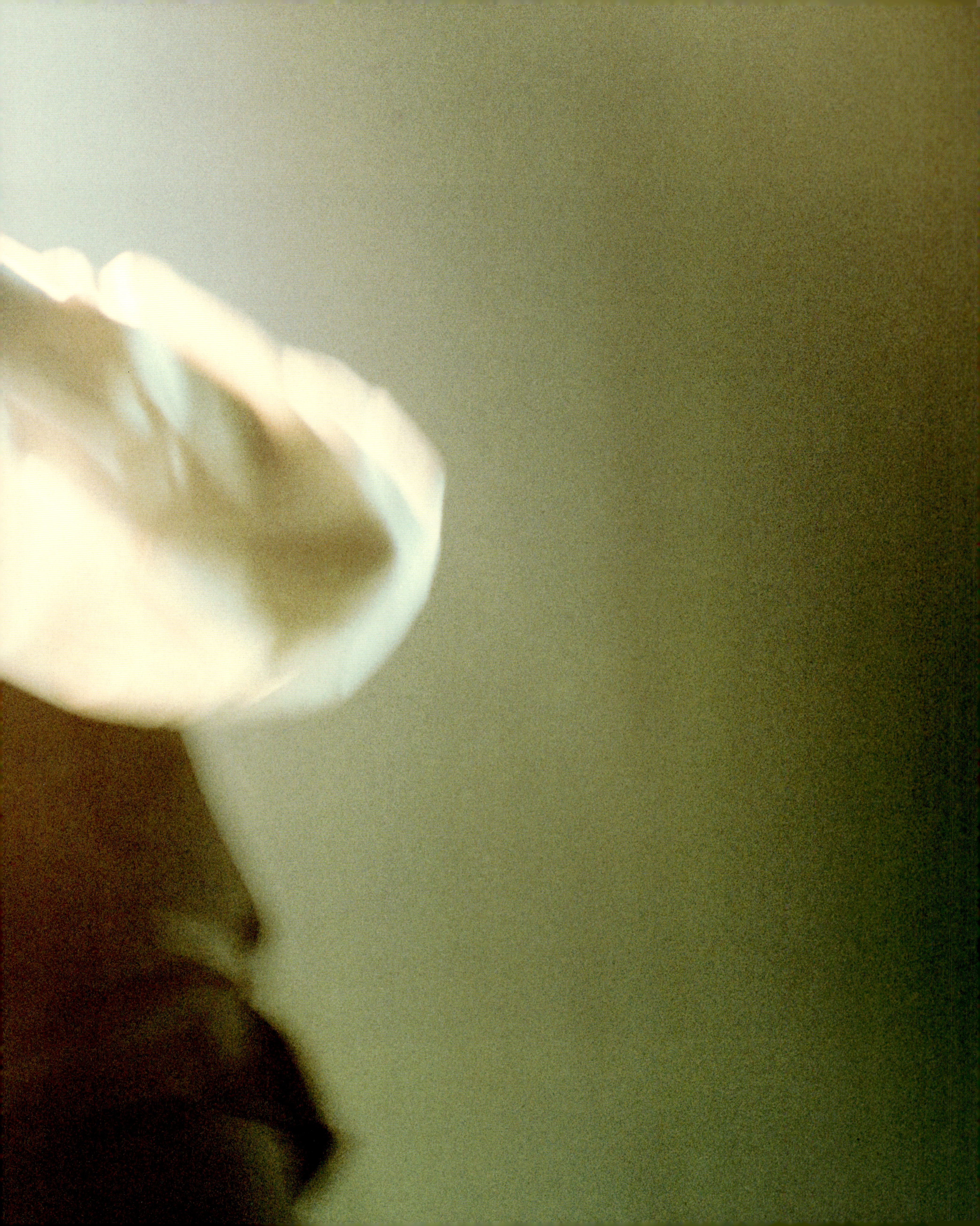

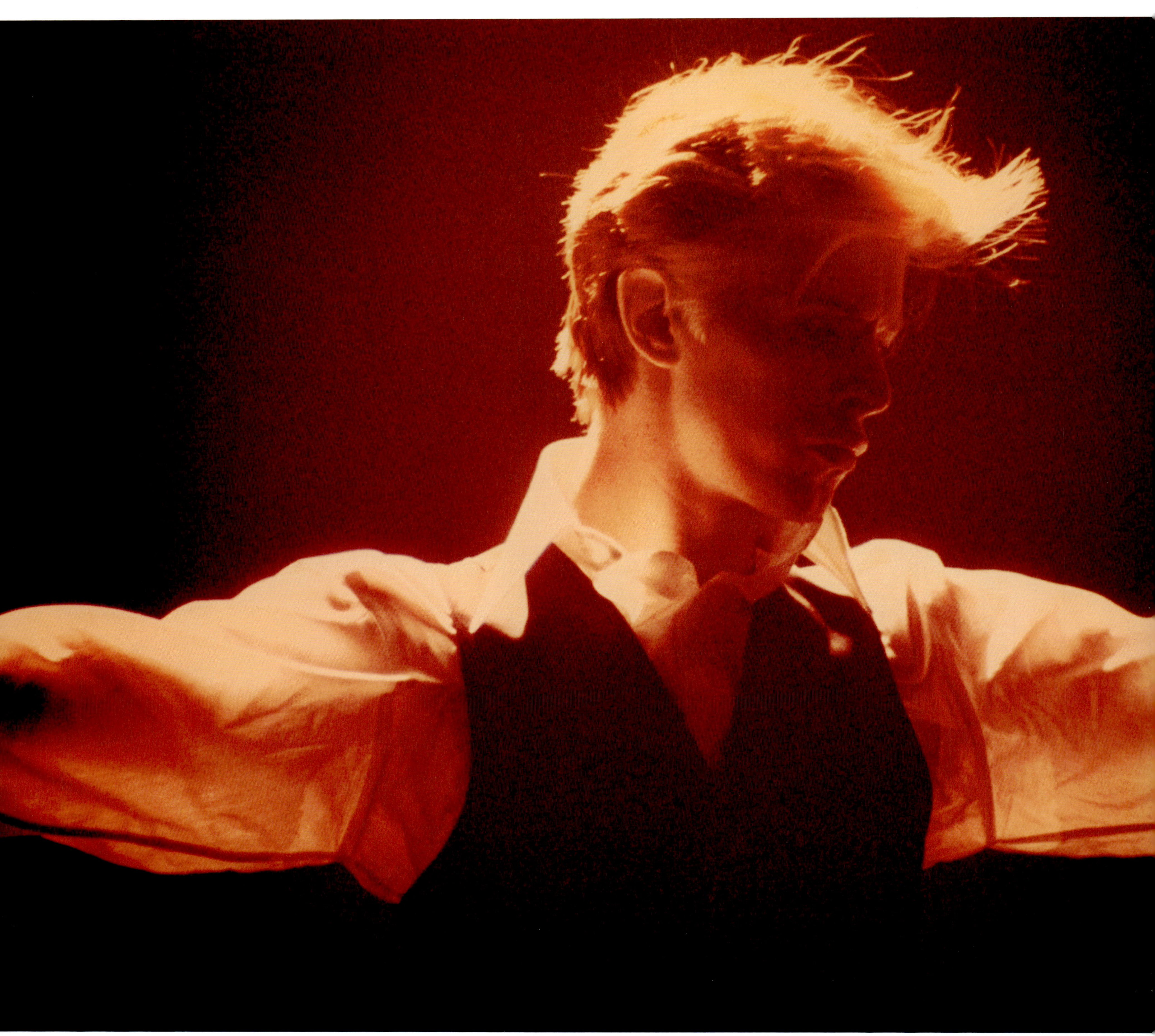

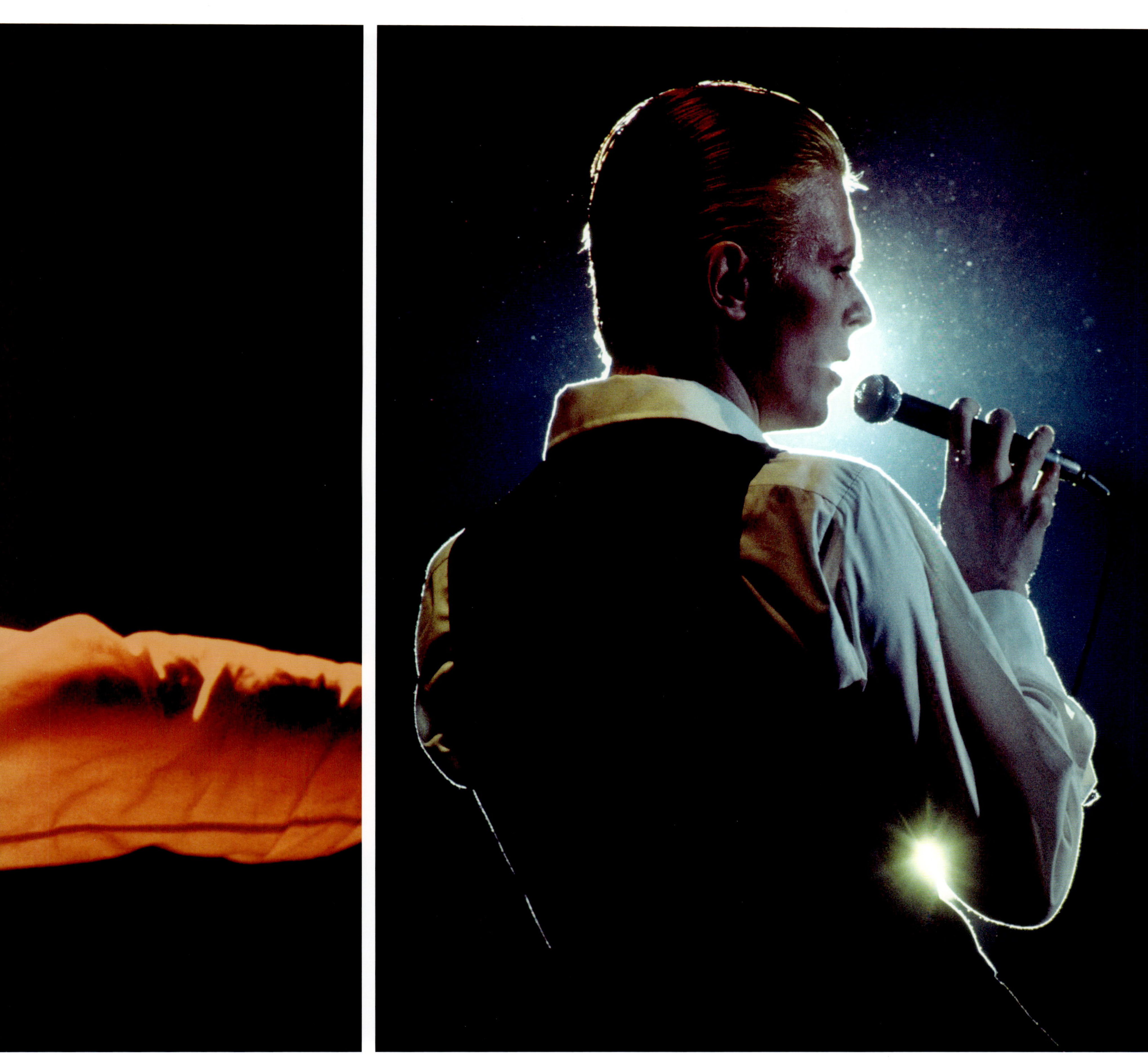

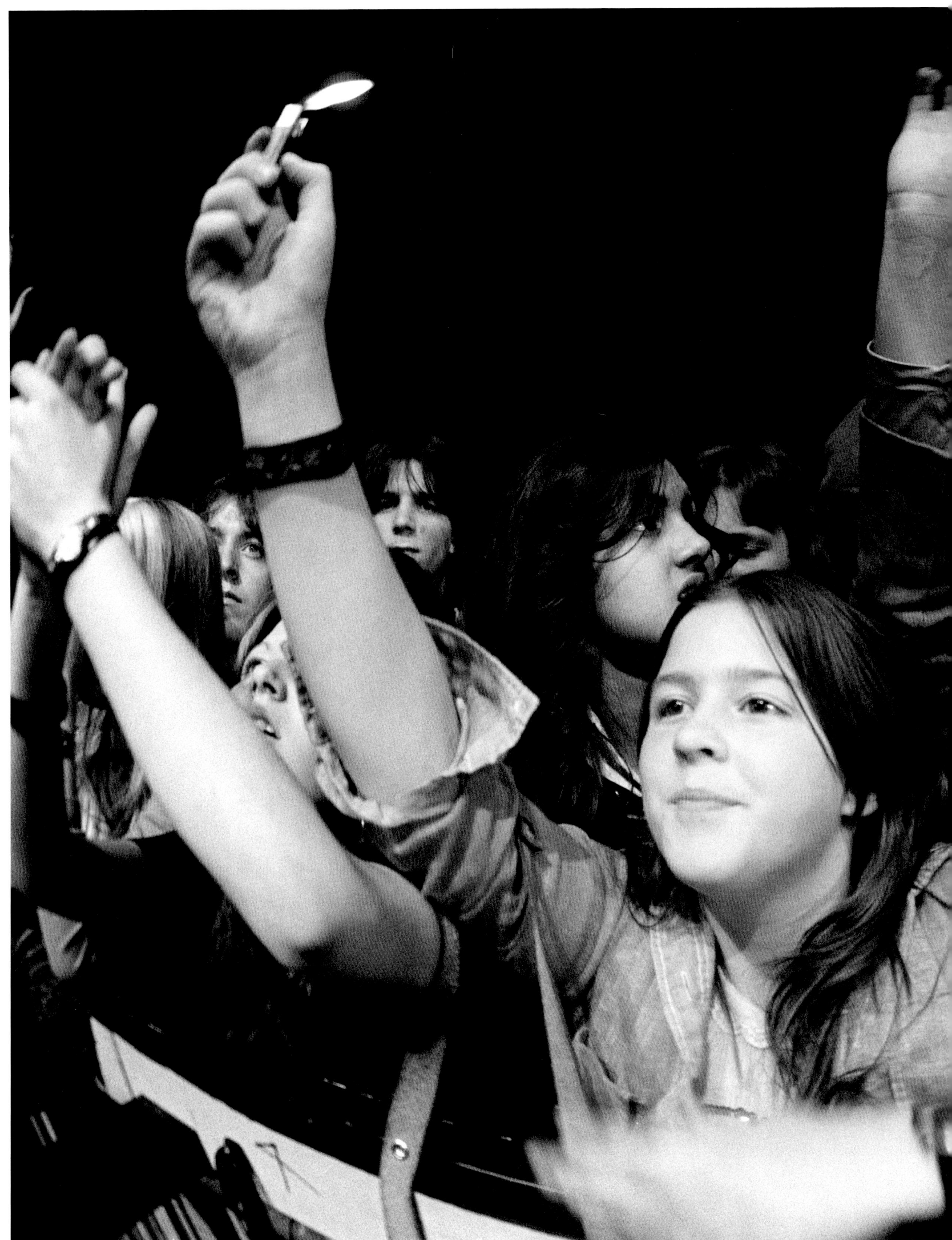

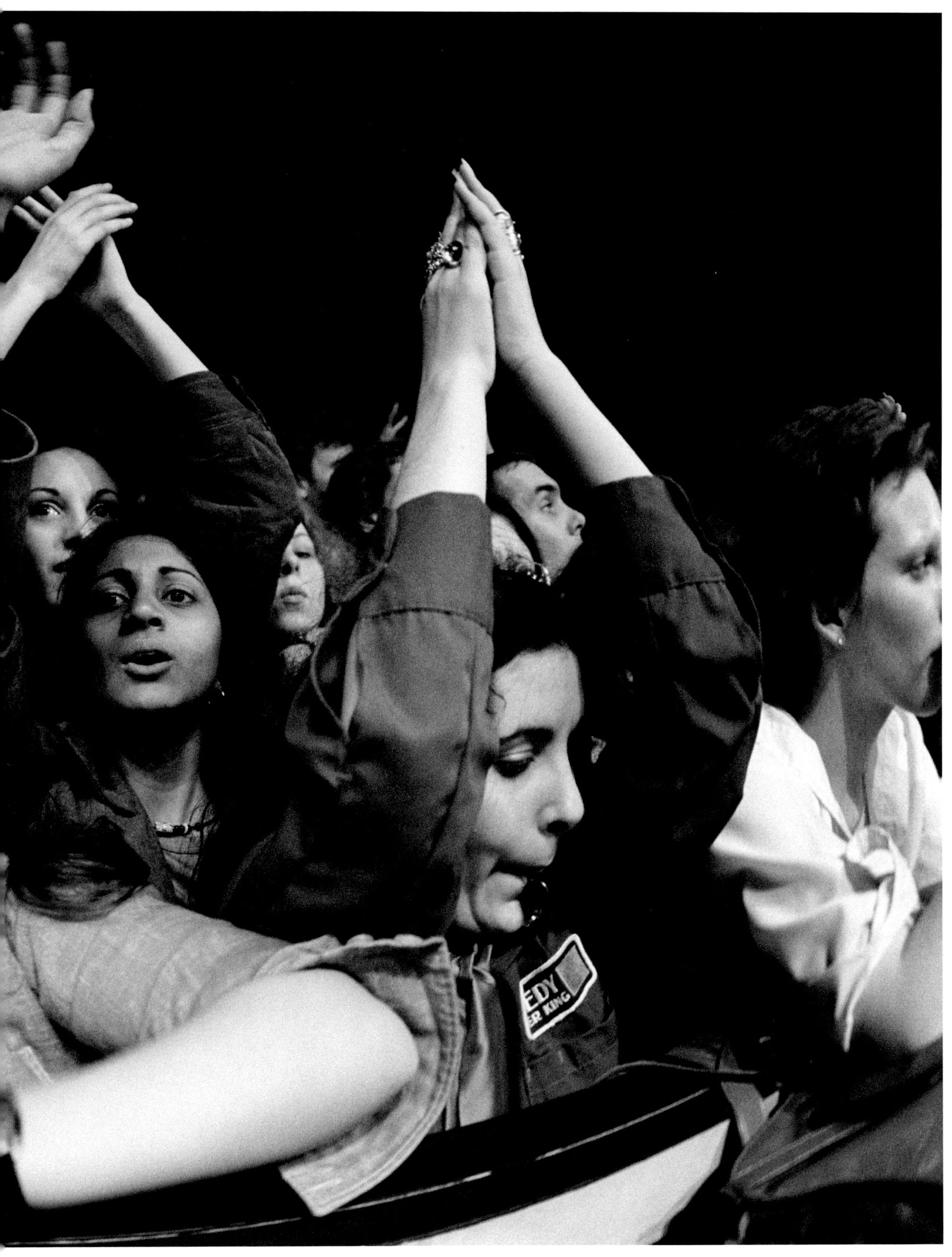

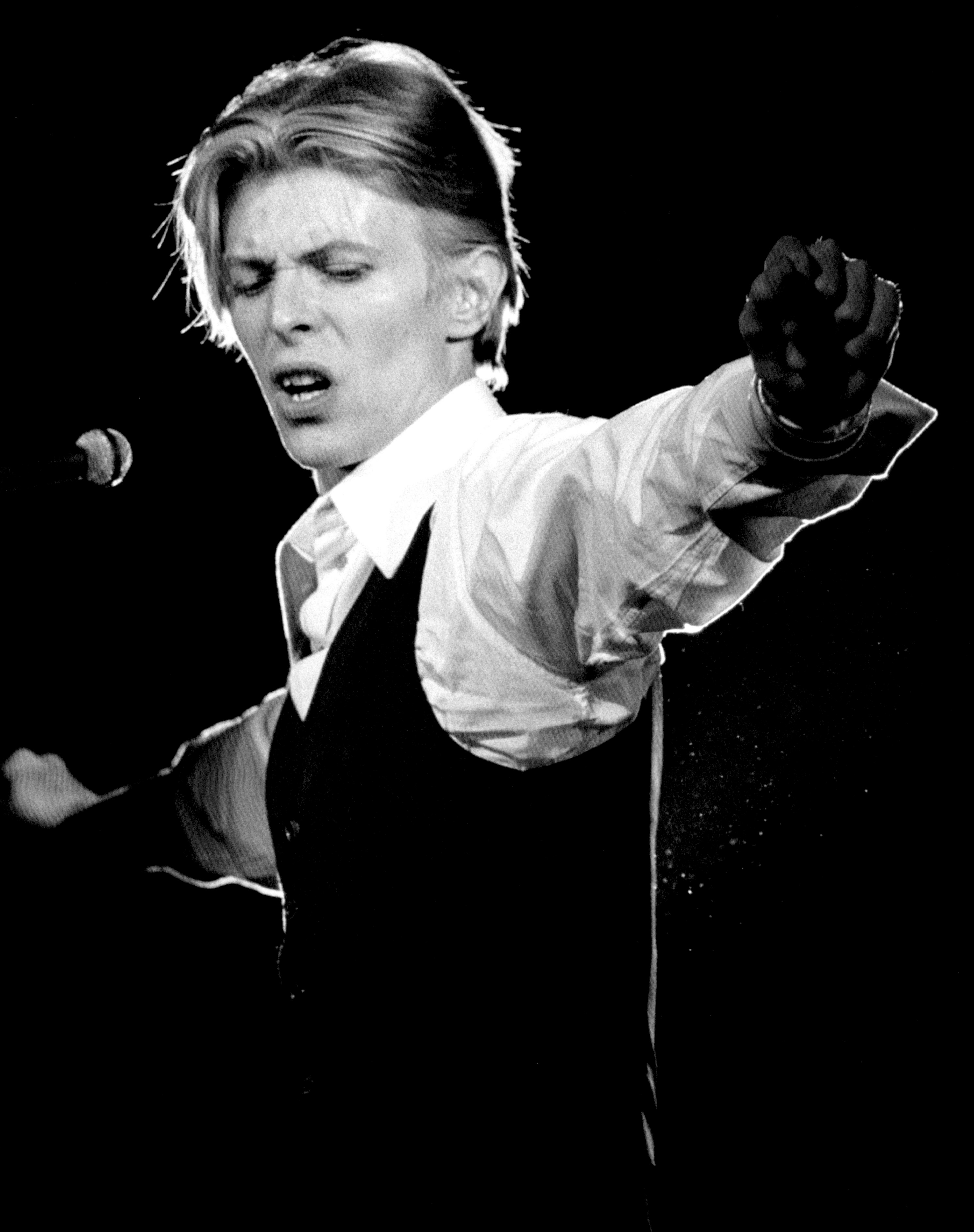

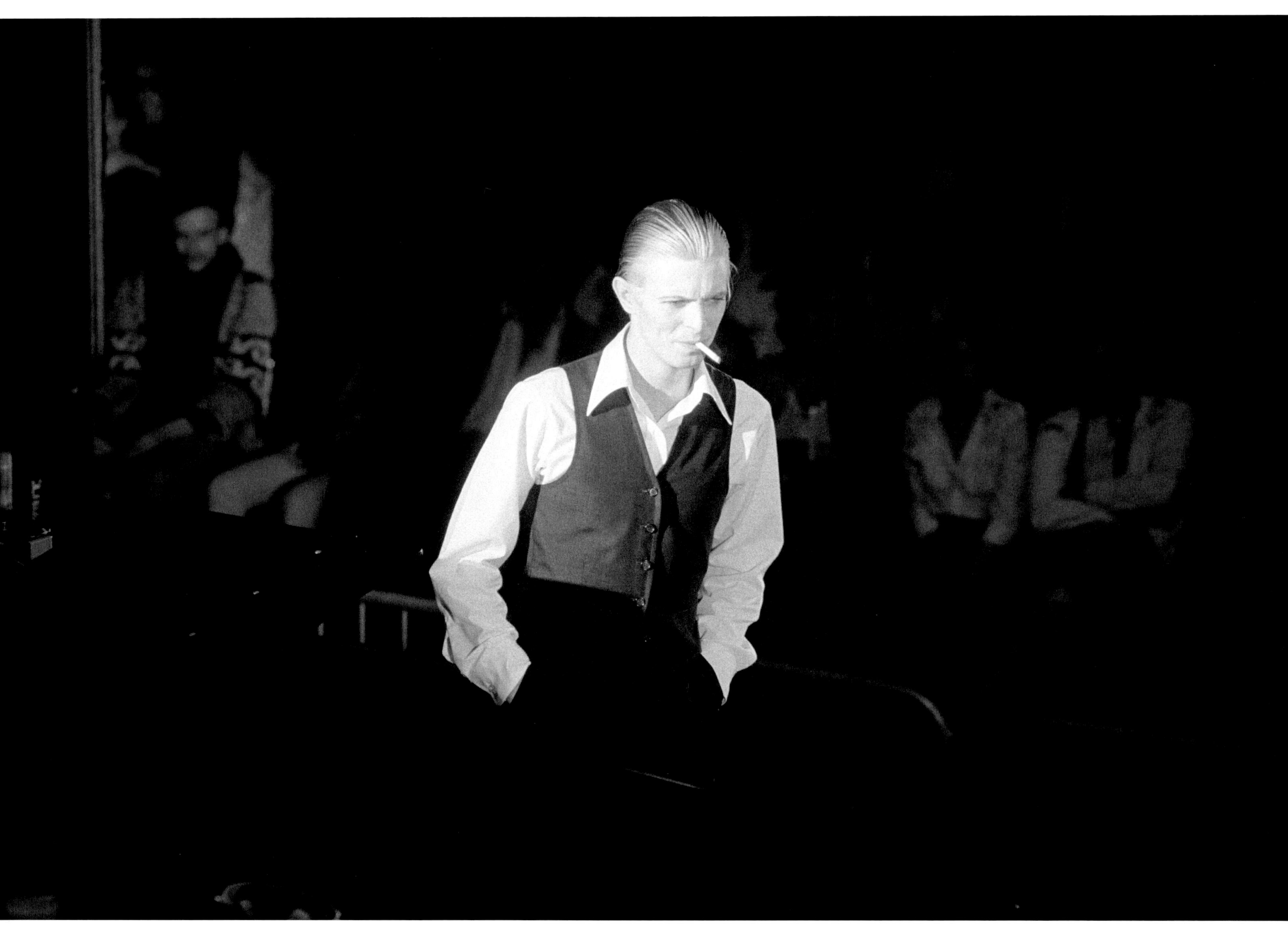

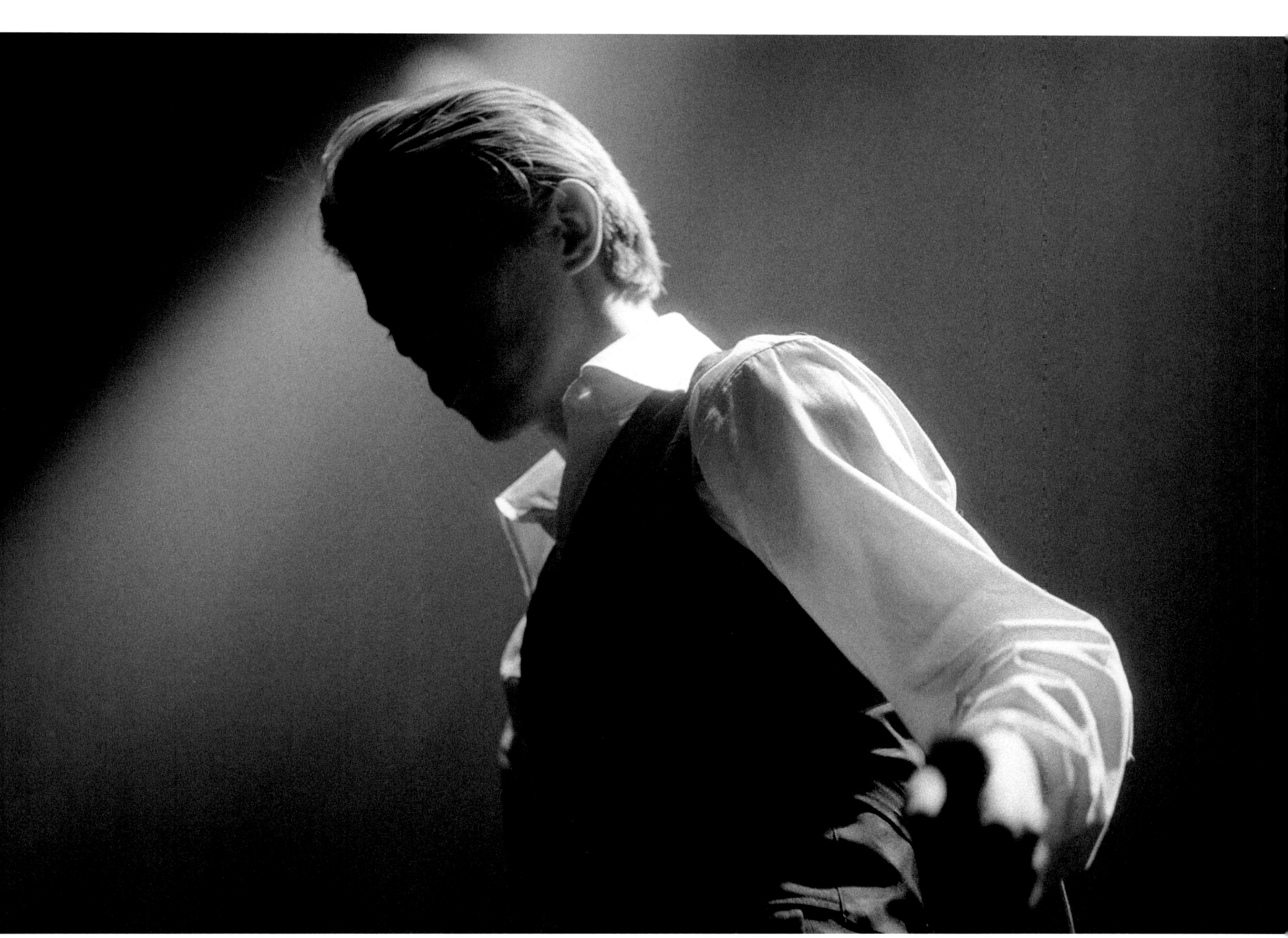

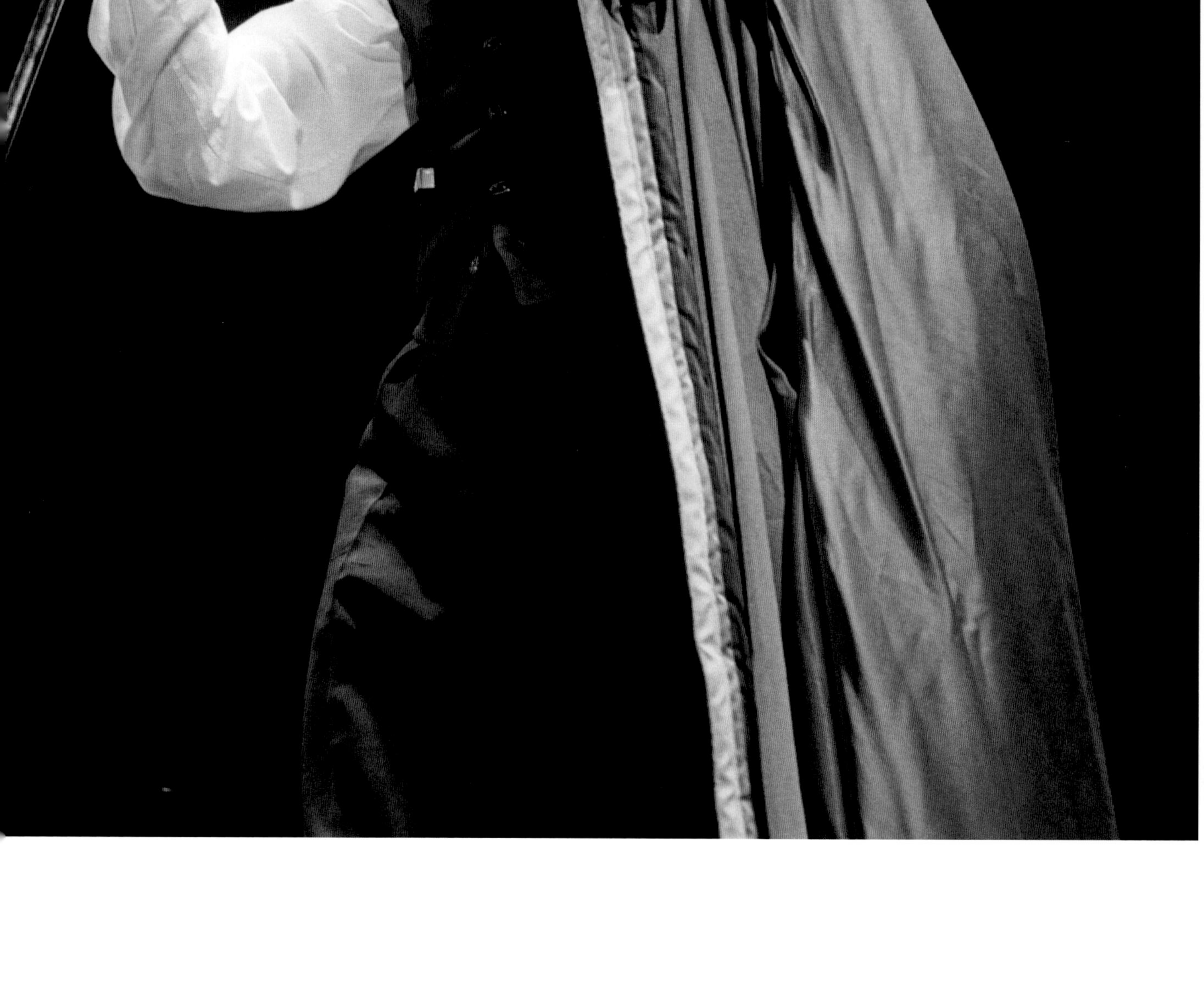

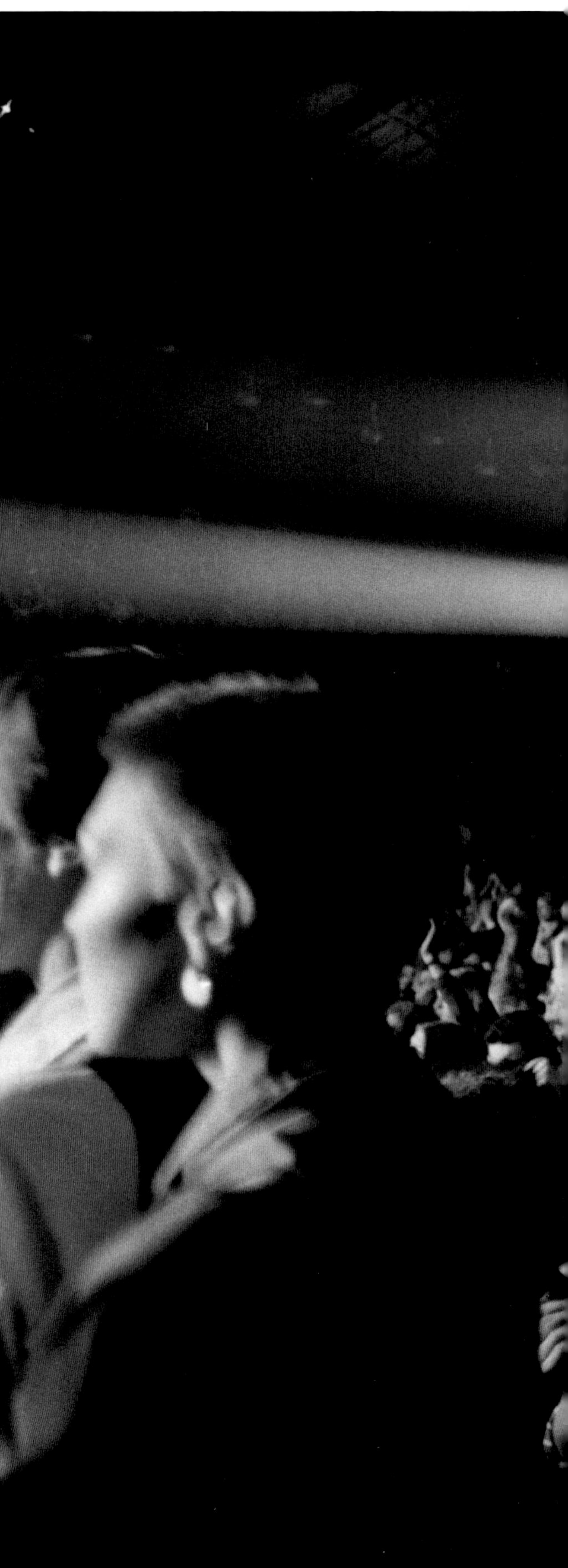

"FAME WAS AN INCREDIBLE BLUFF THAT WORKED. VERY FLATTERING. I'LL DO ANYTHING UNTIL I FAIL AND WHEN I SUCCEED, I QUIT TOO." – DB

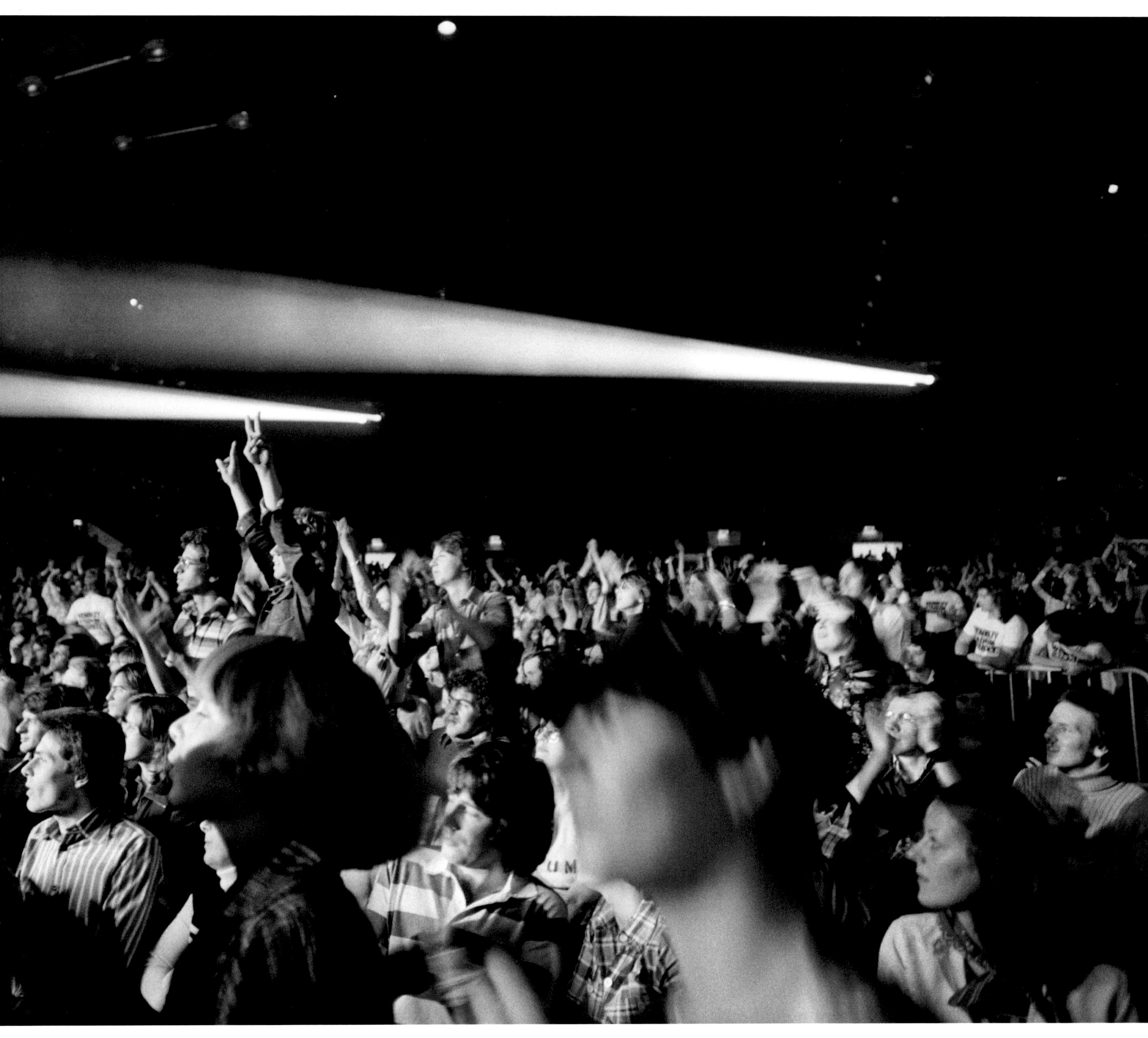

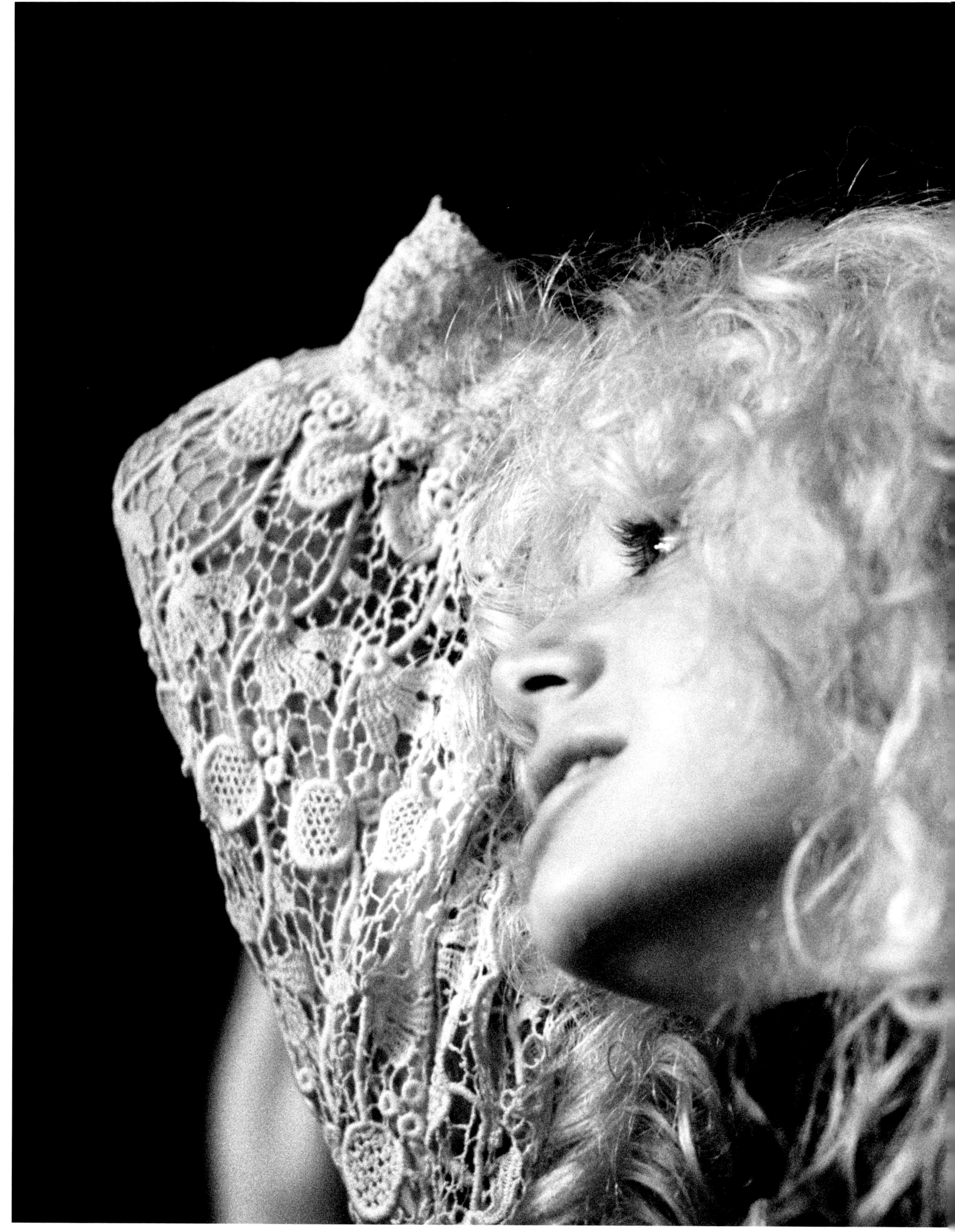

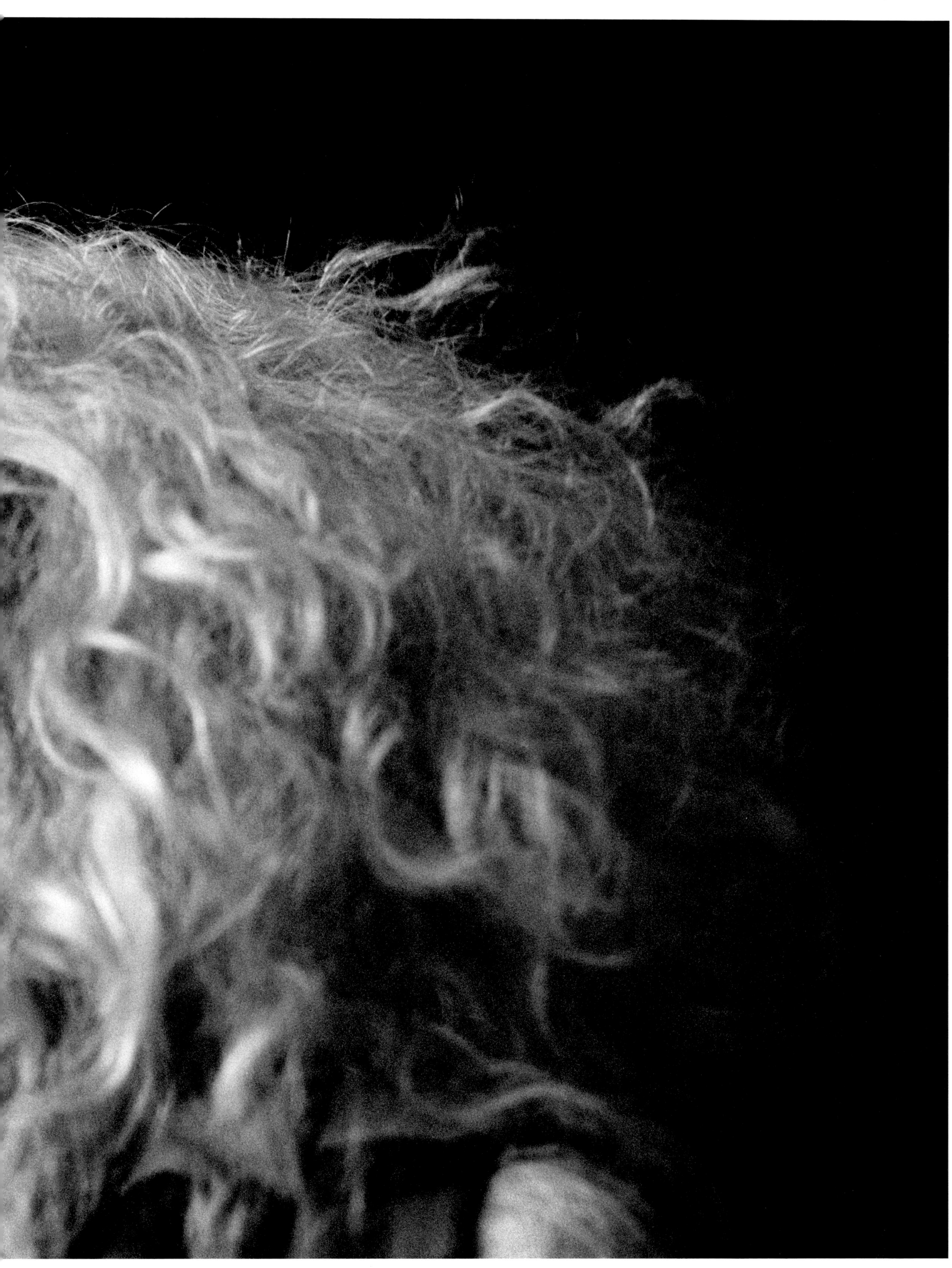

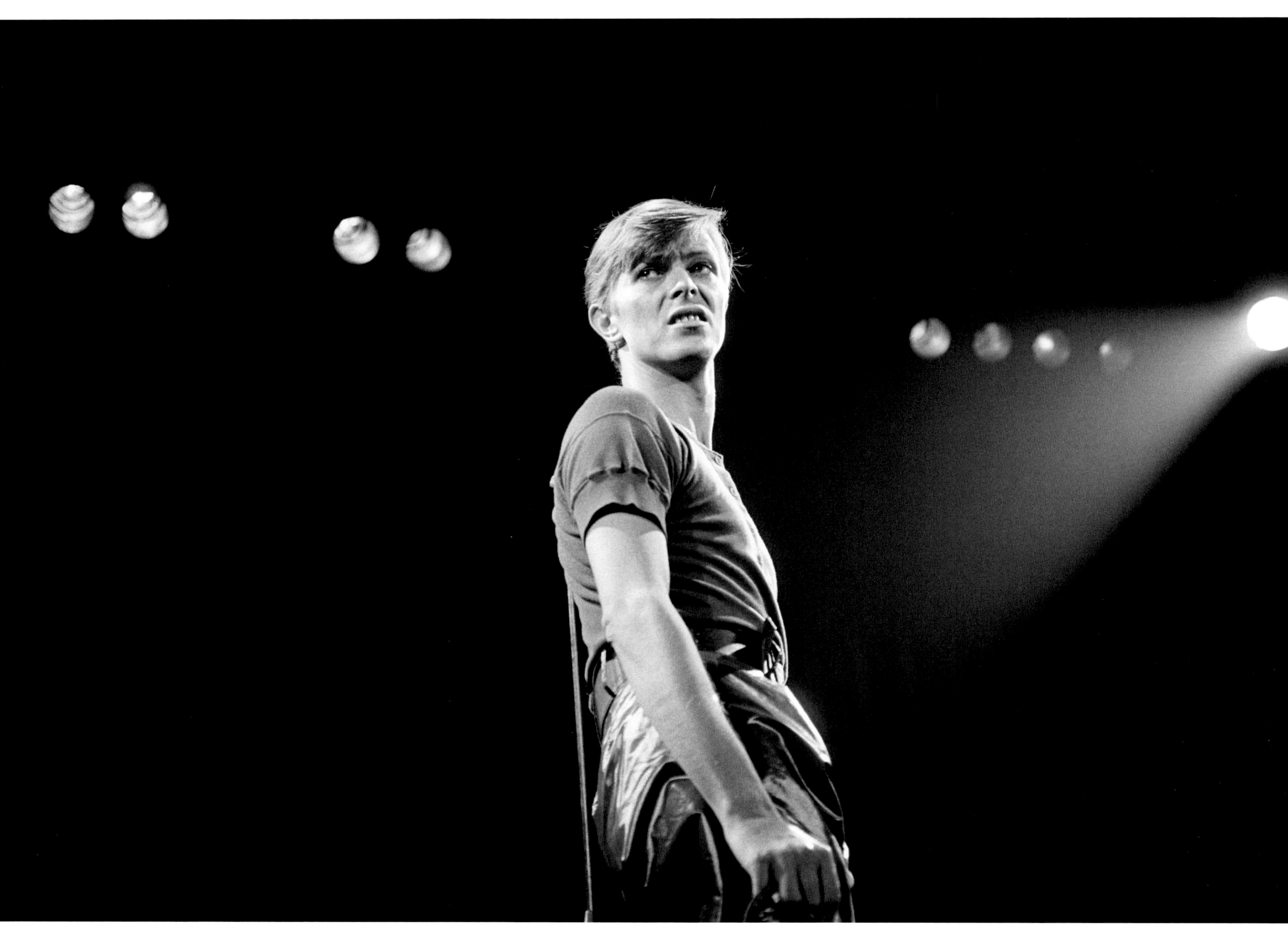

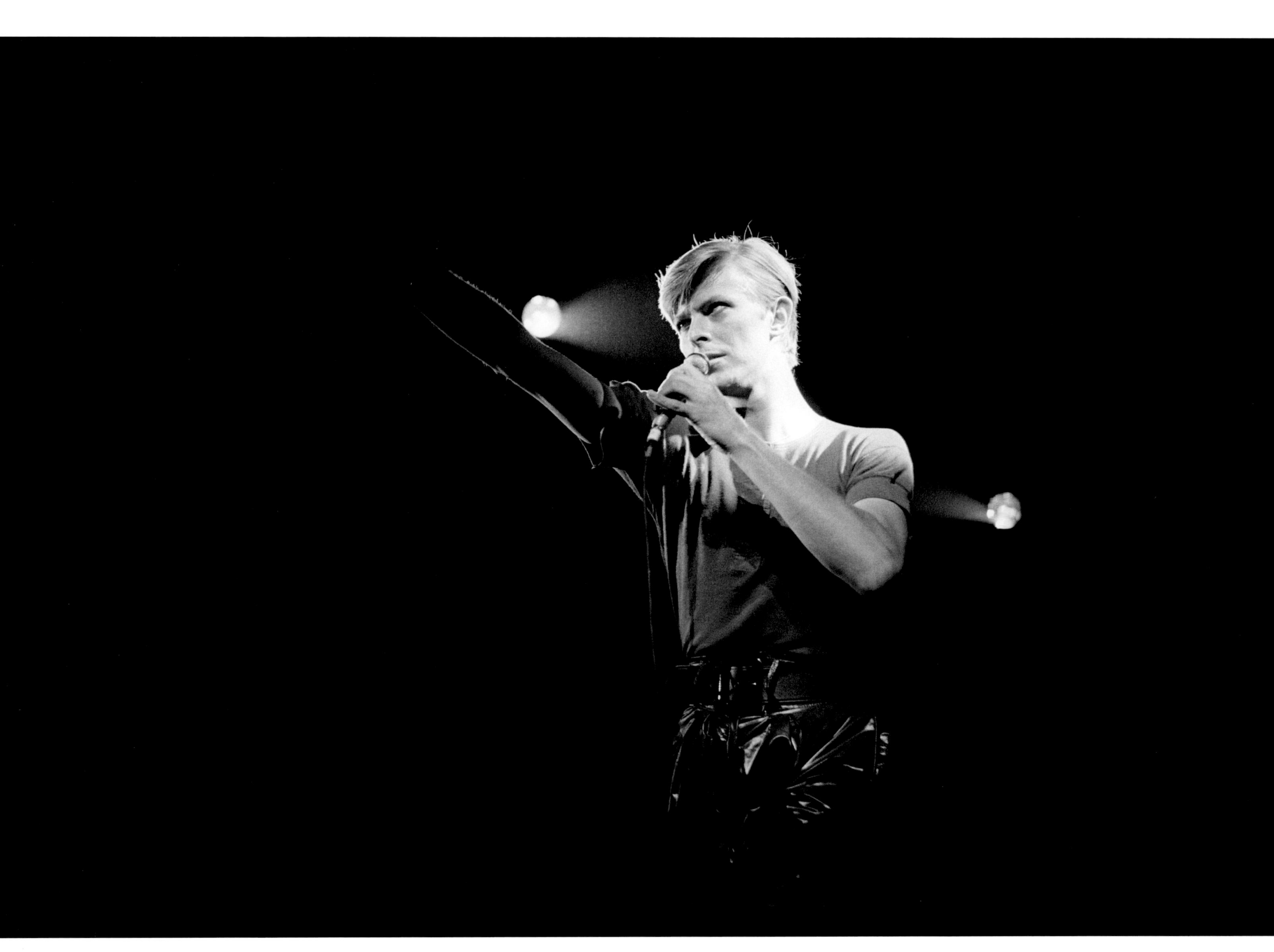

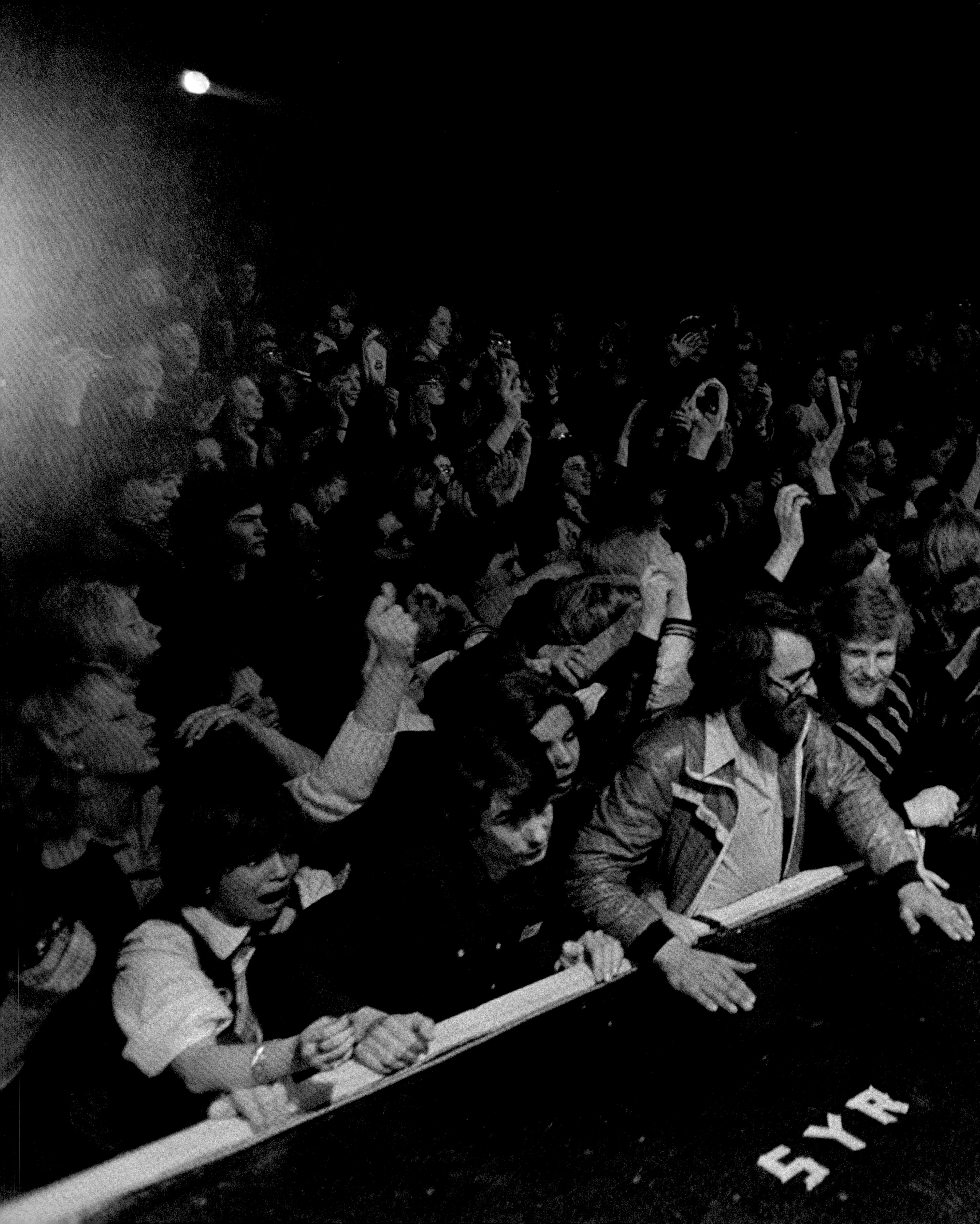

SYR

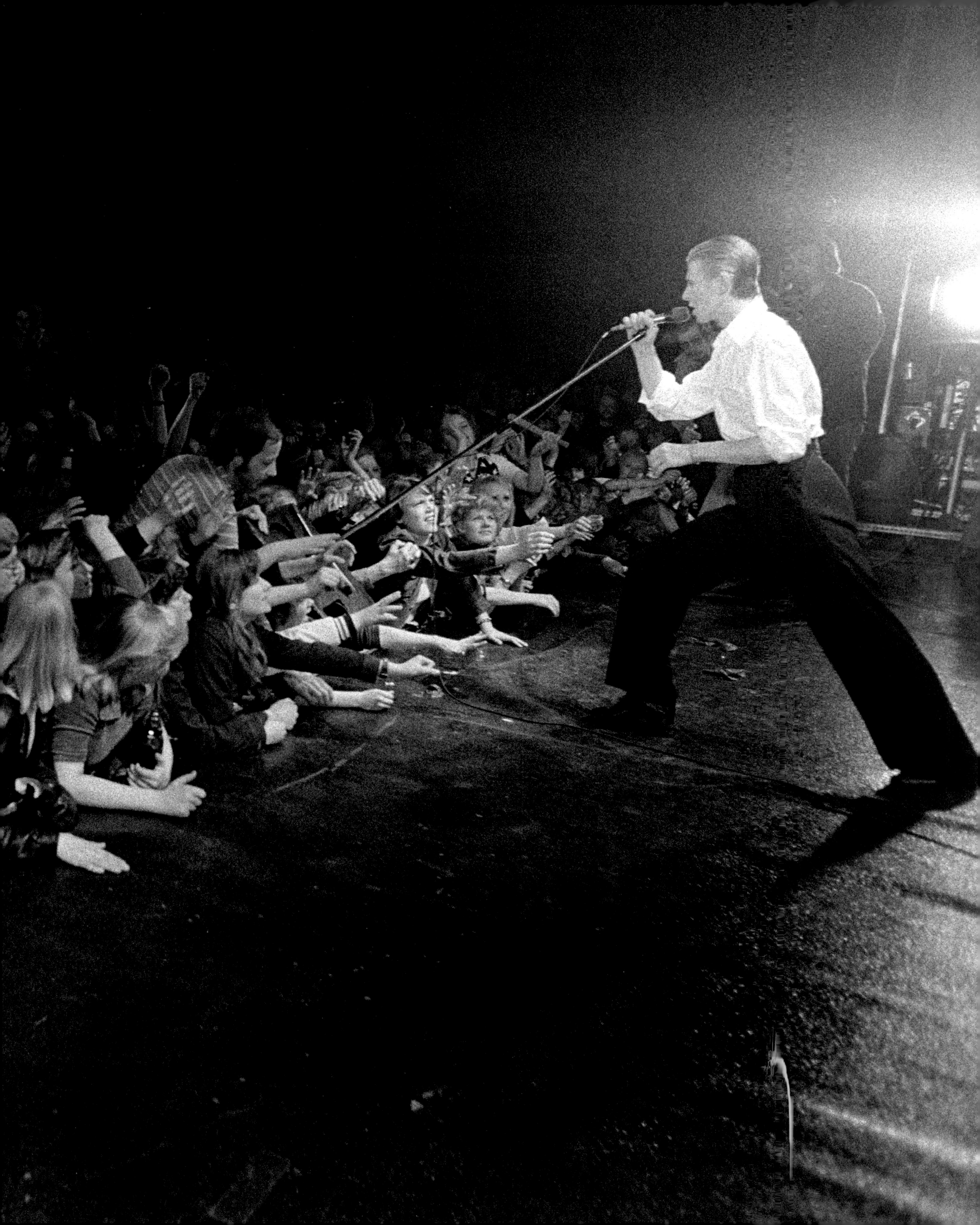

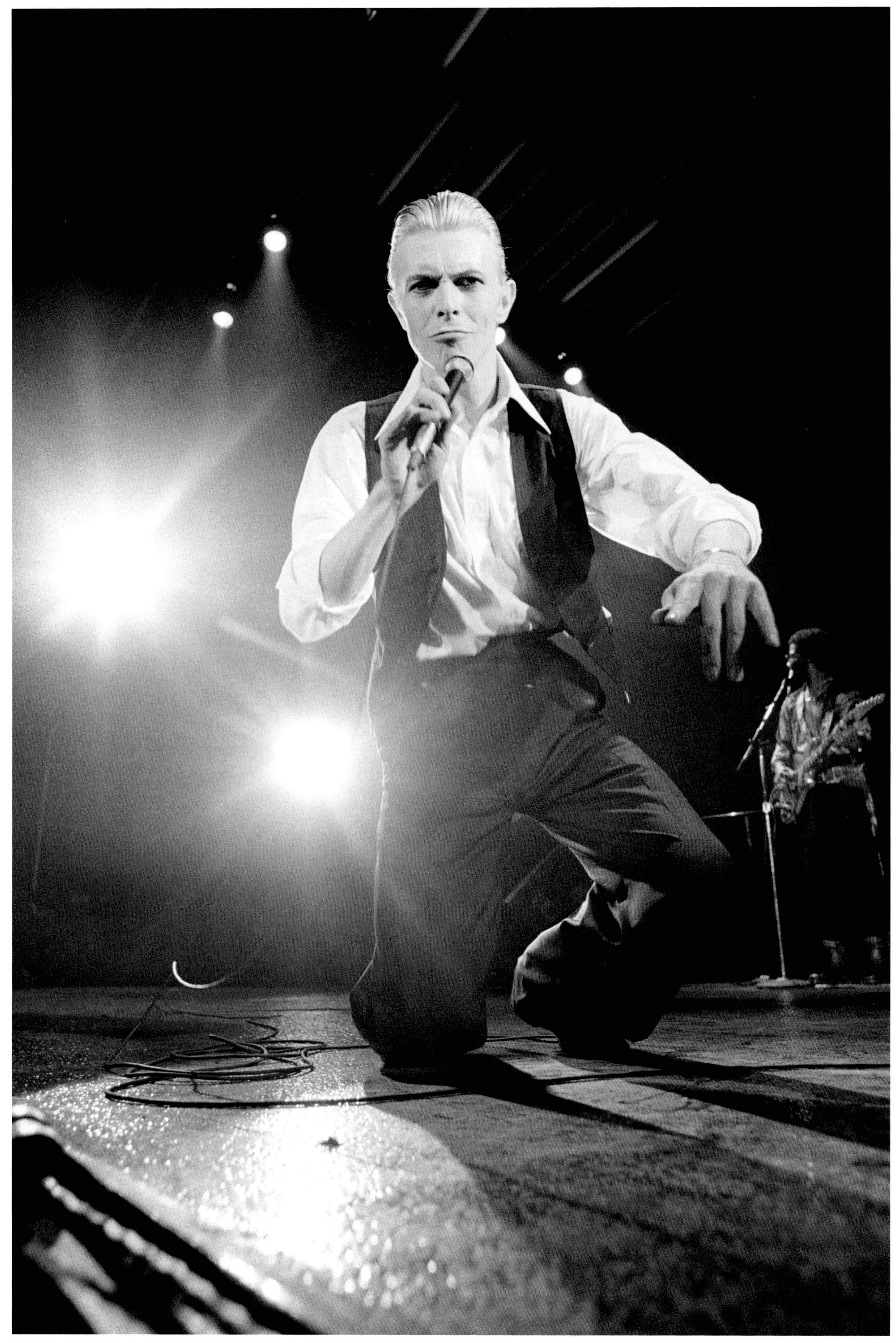

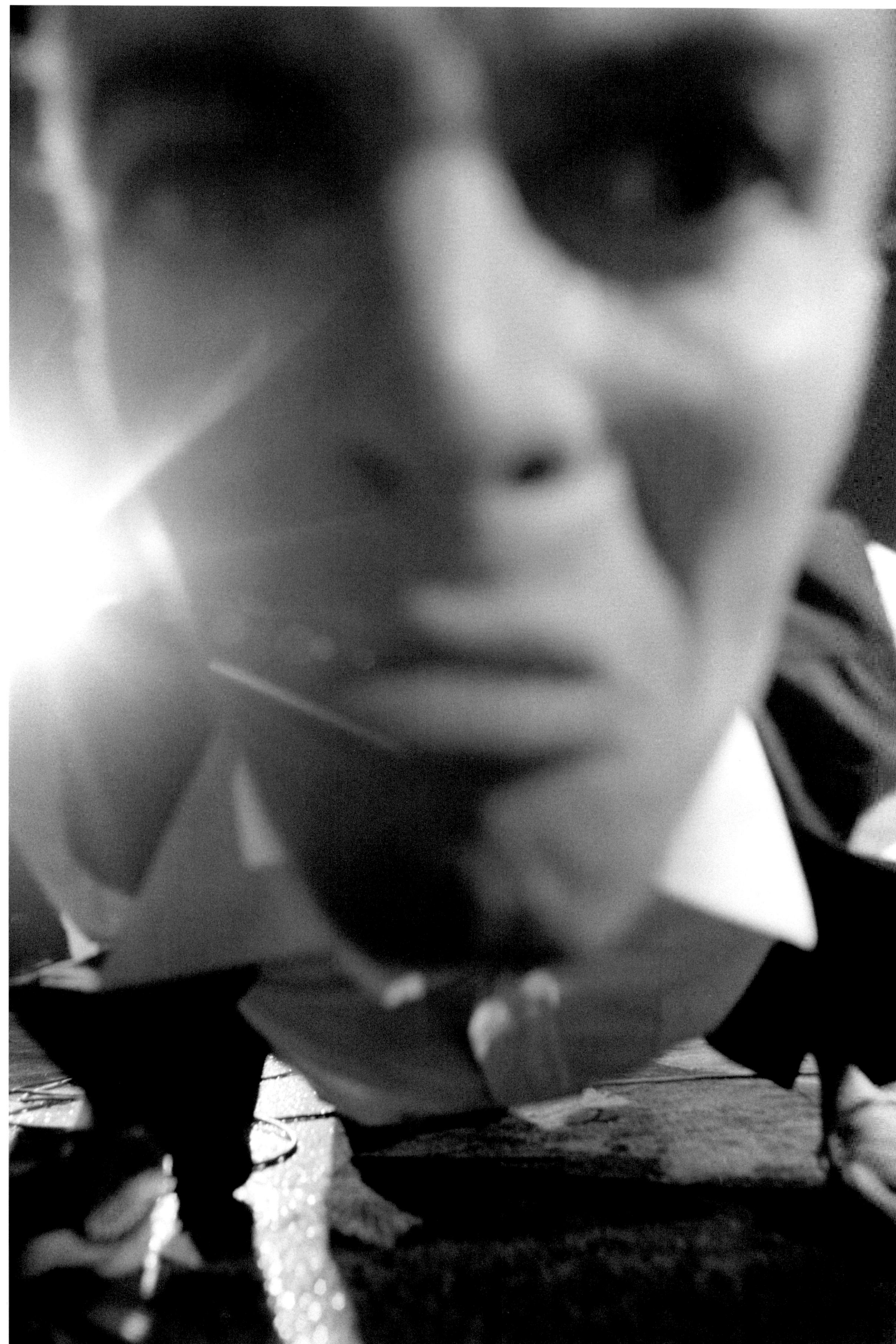

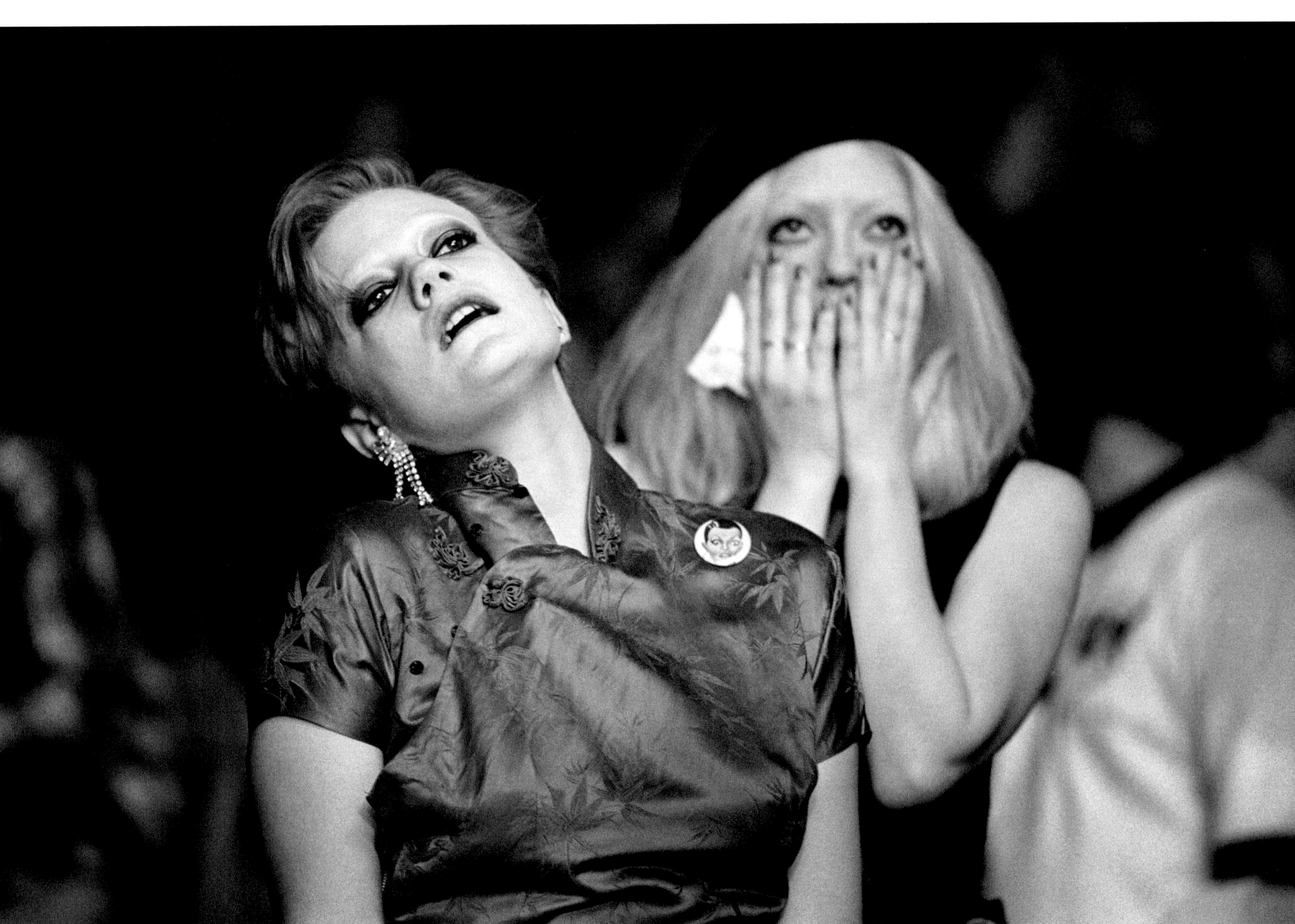

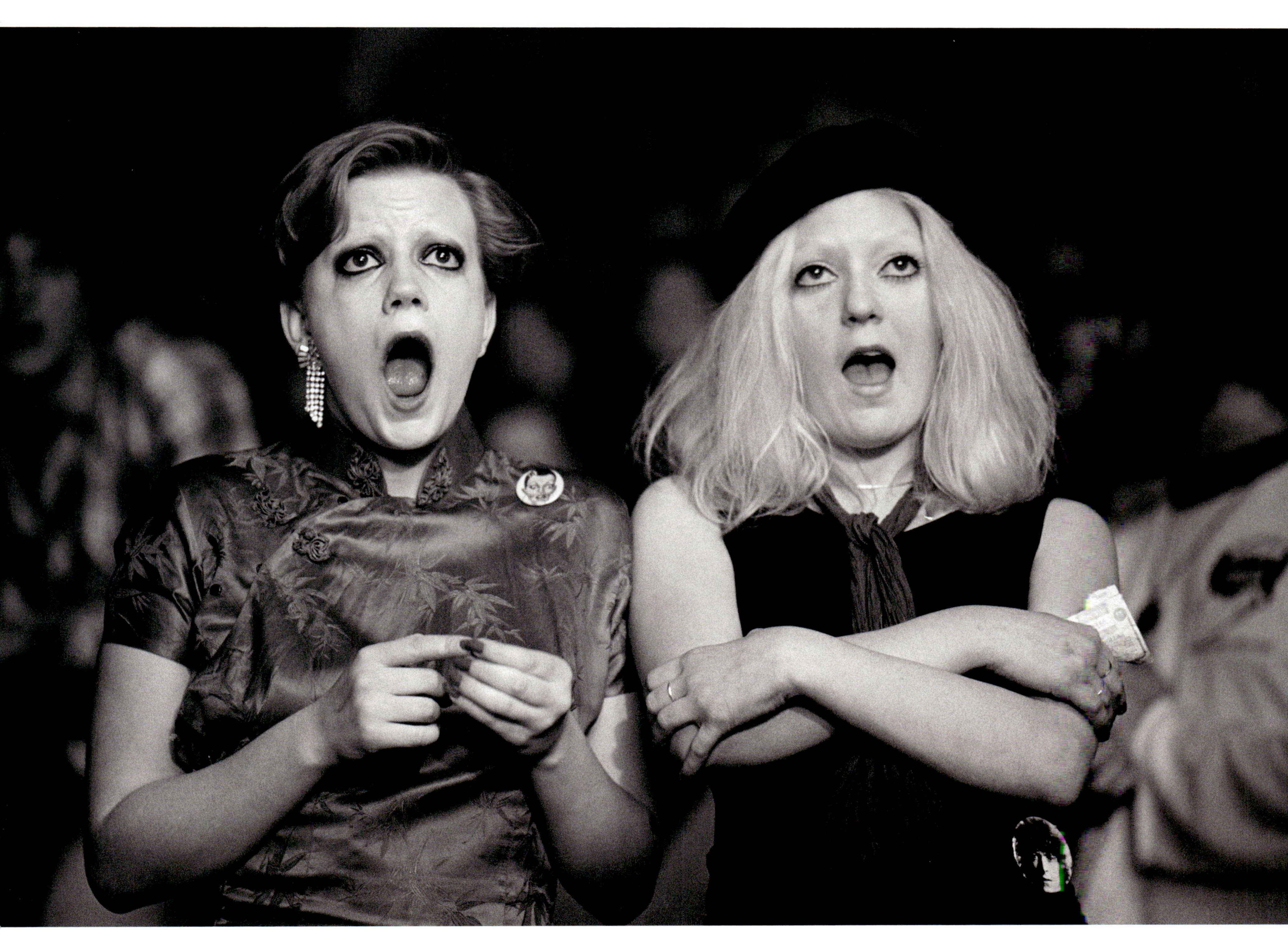

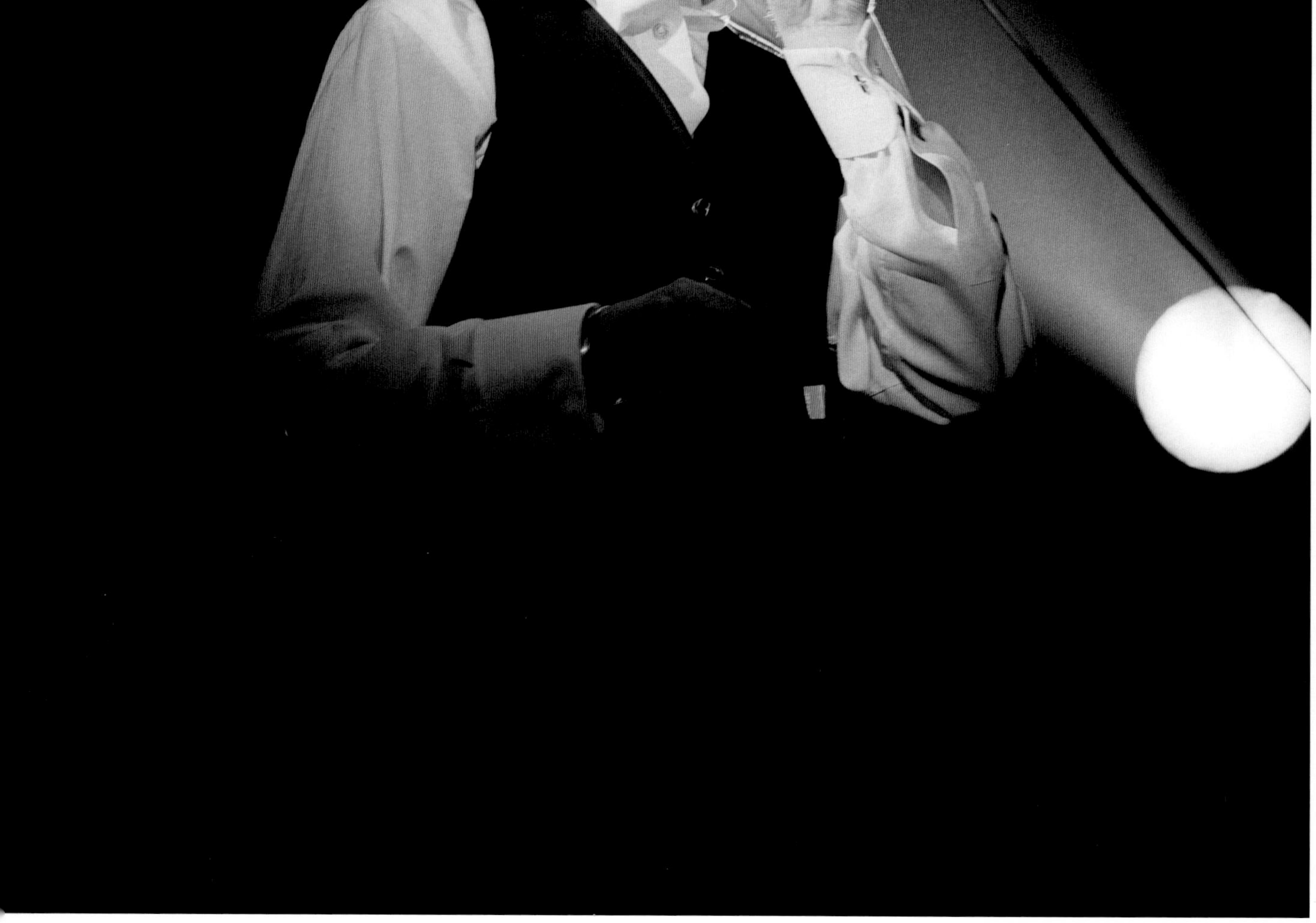

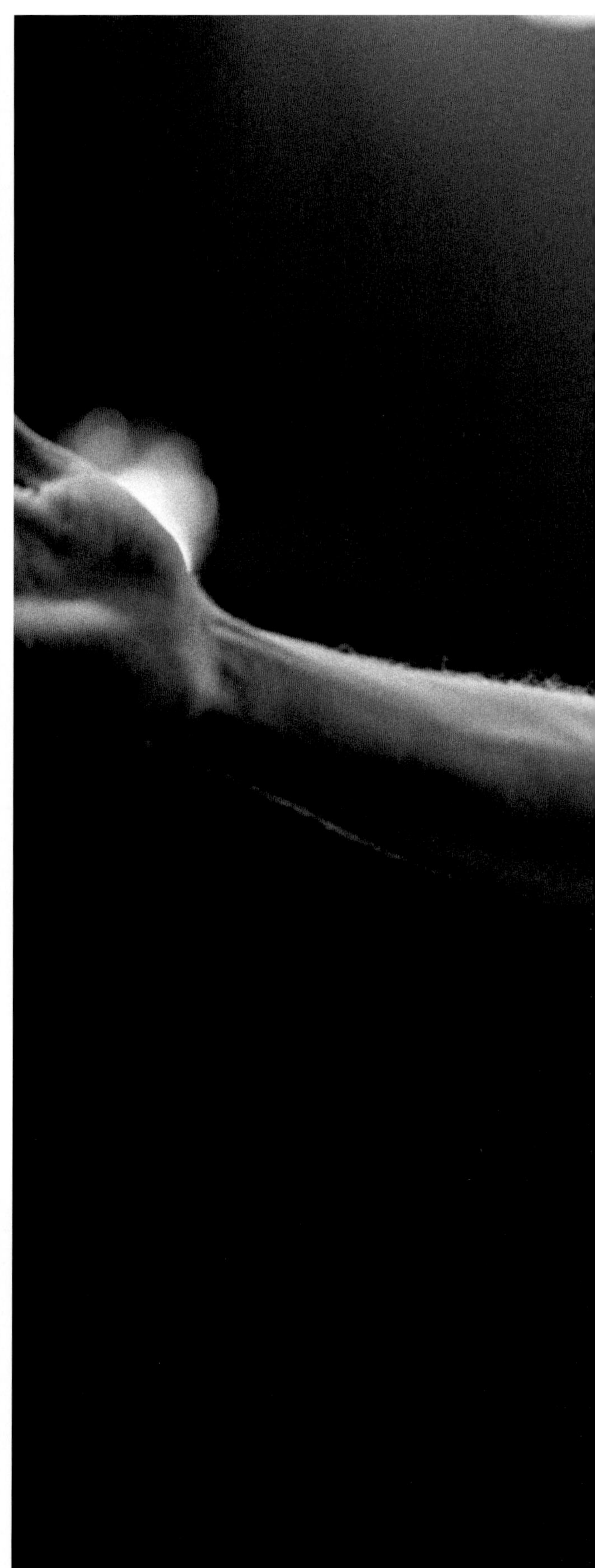

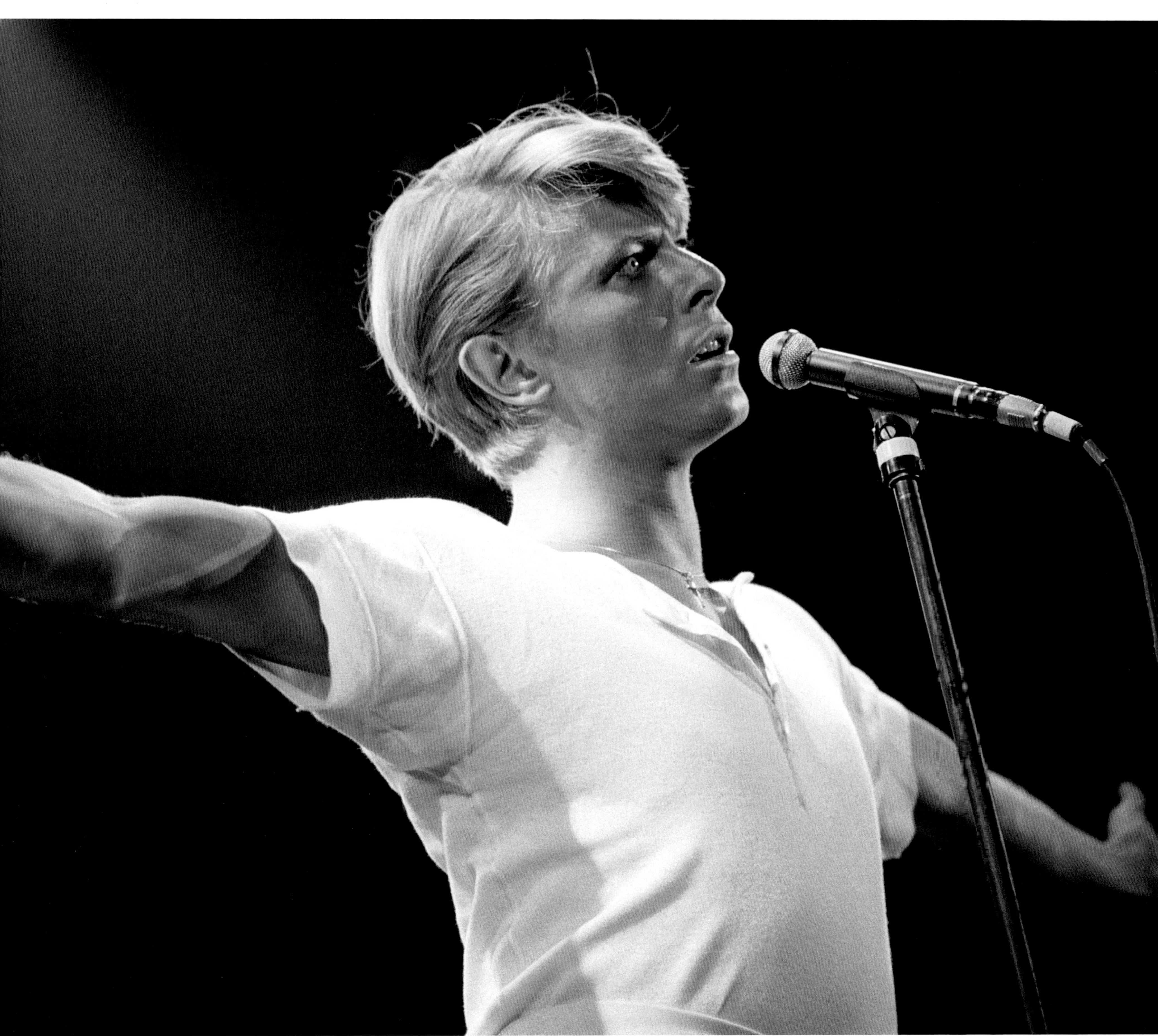

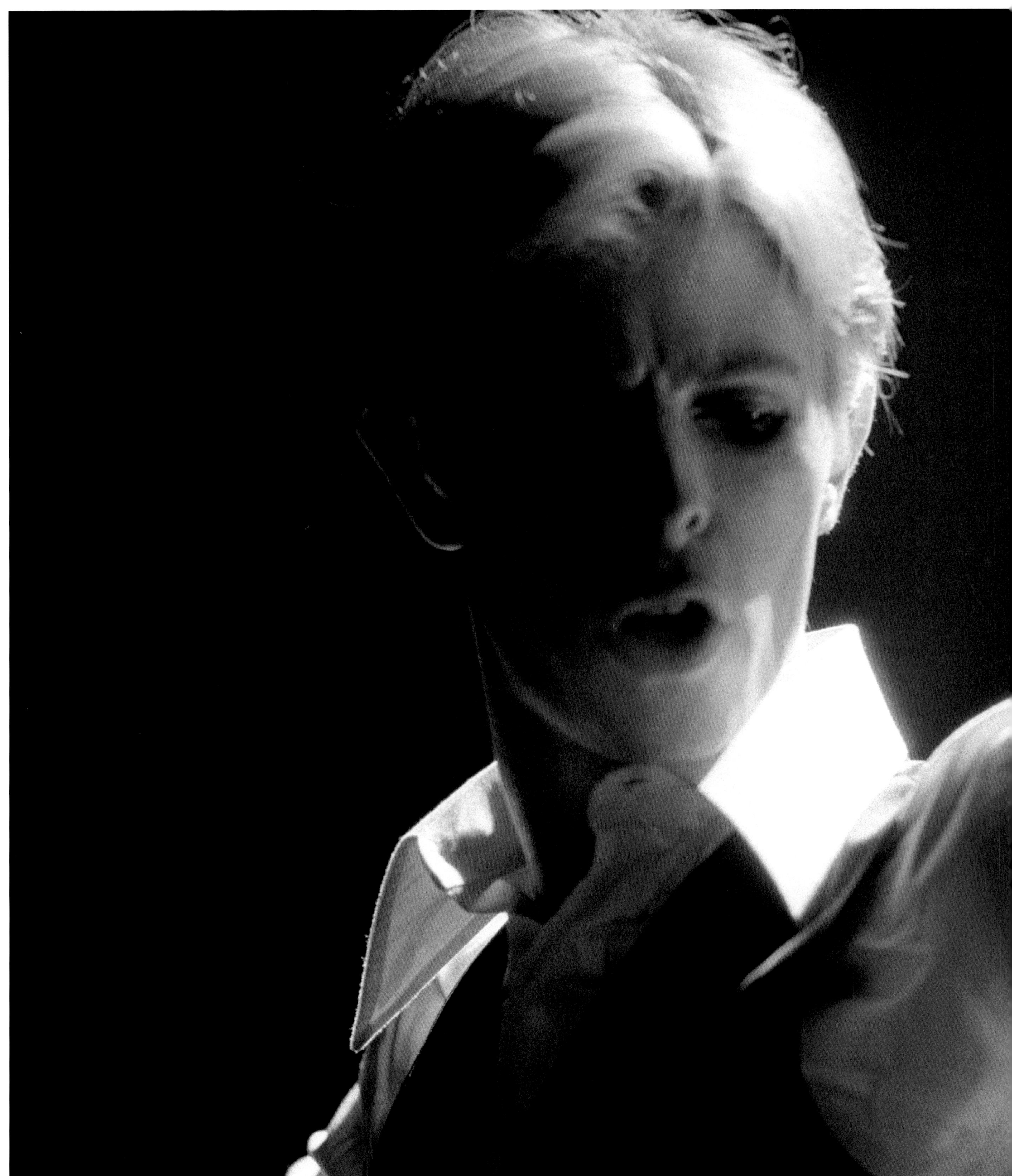

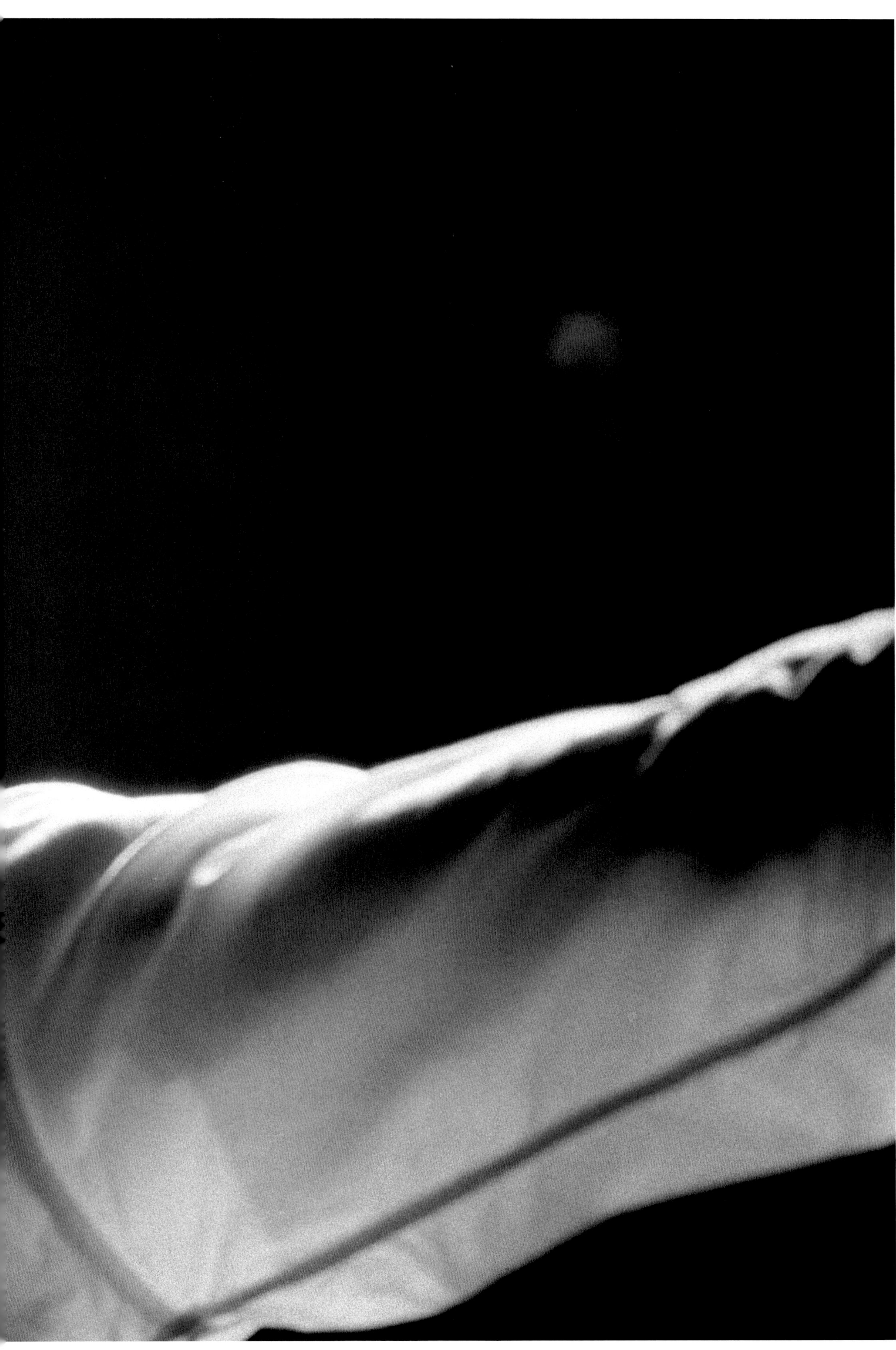

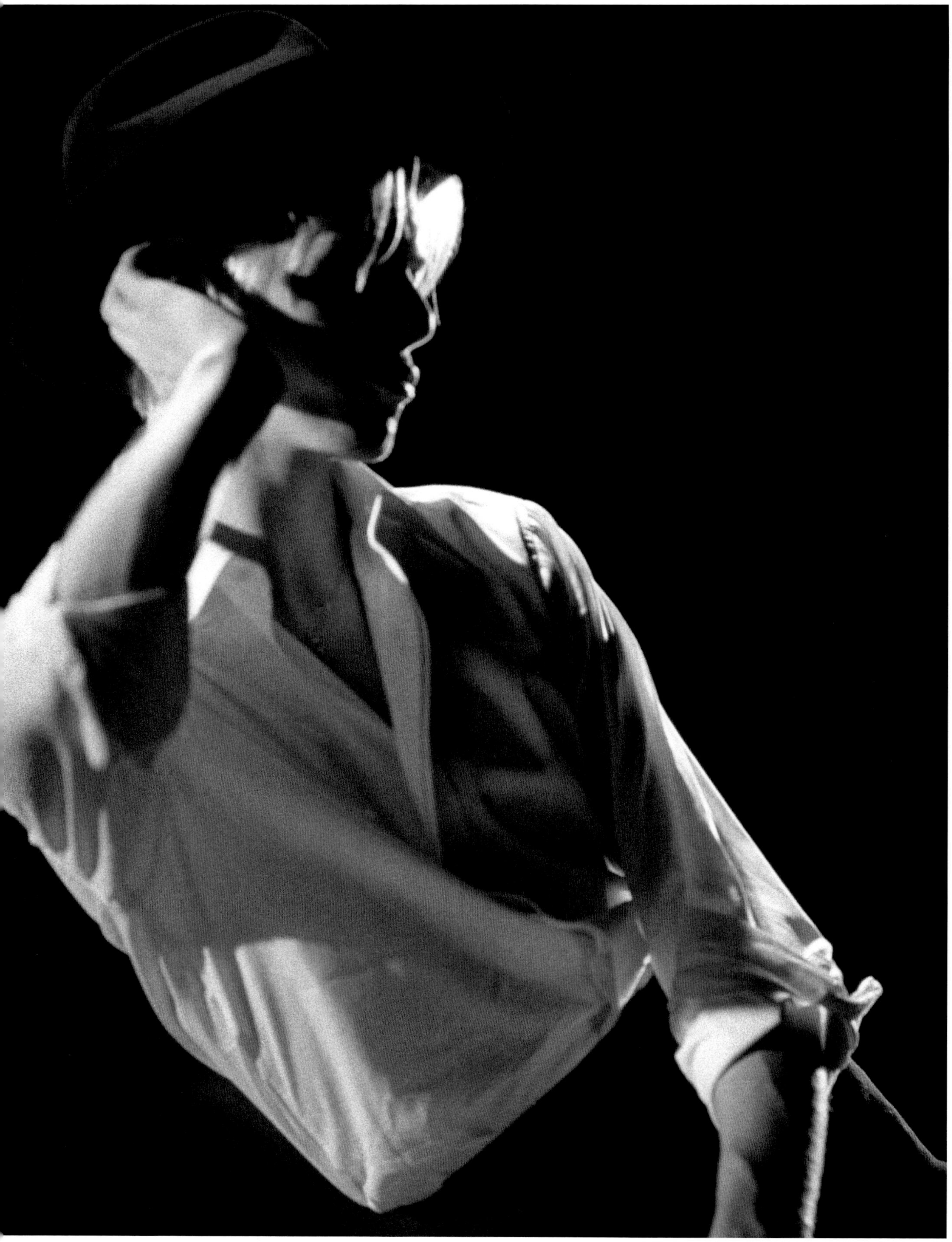

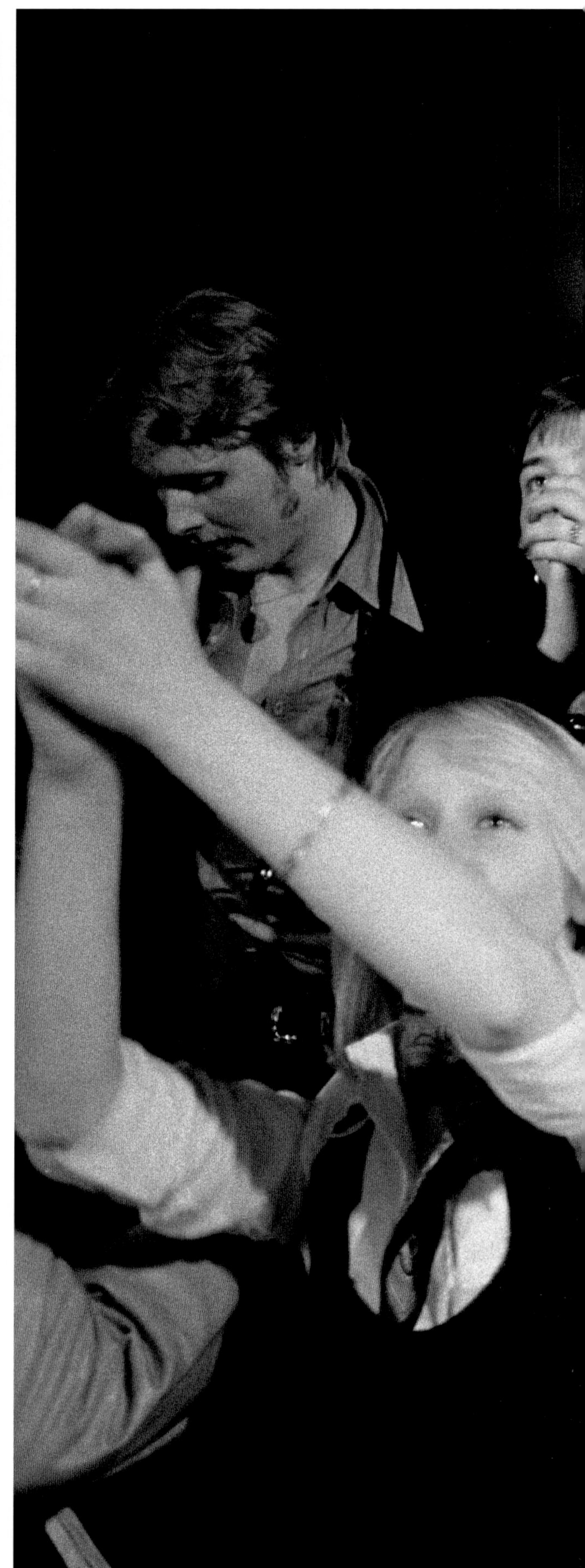

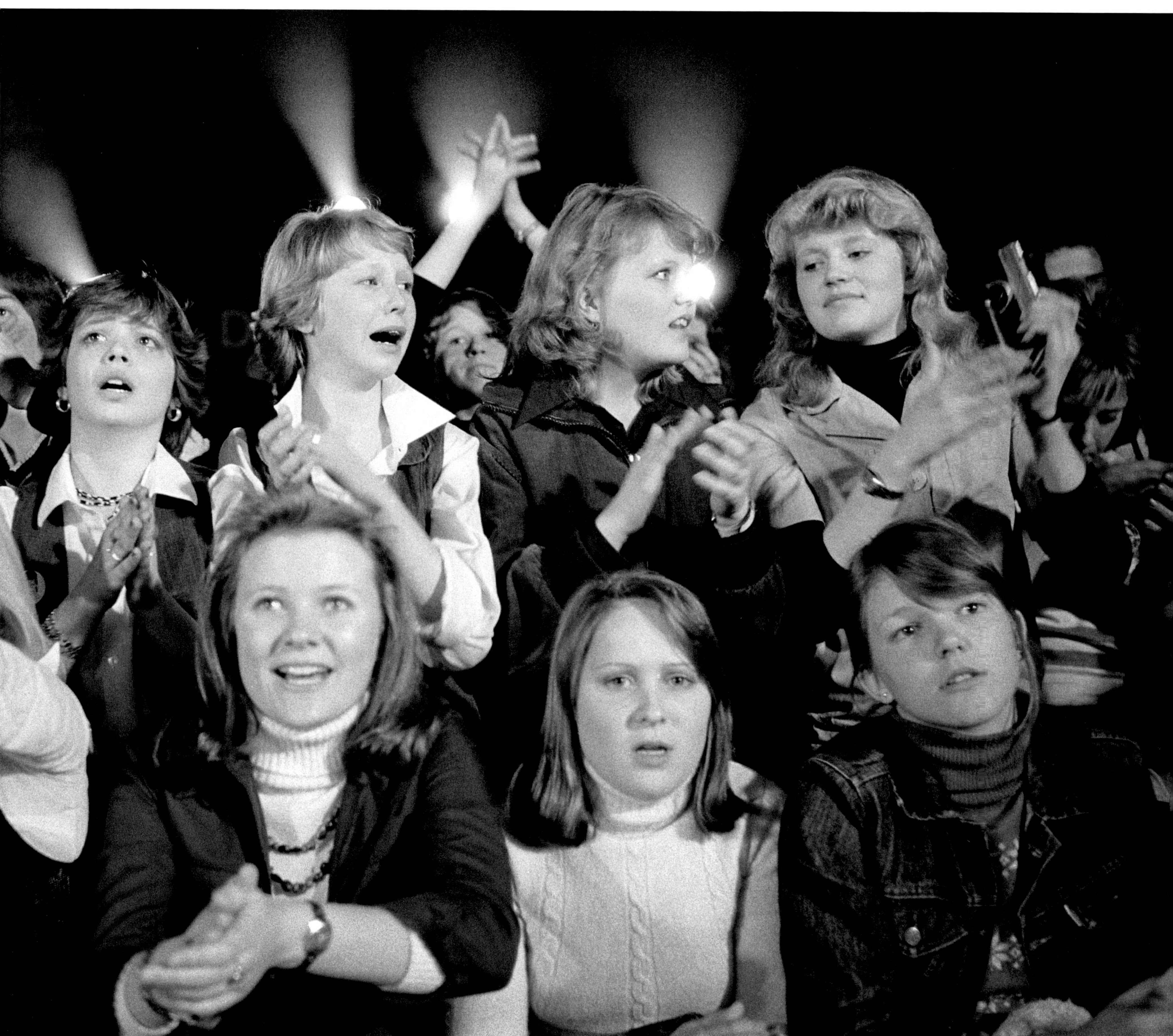

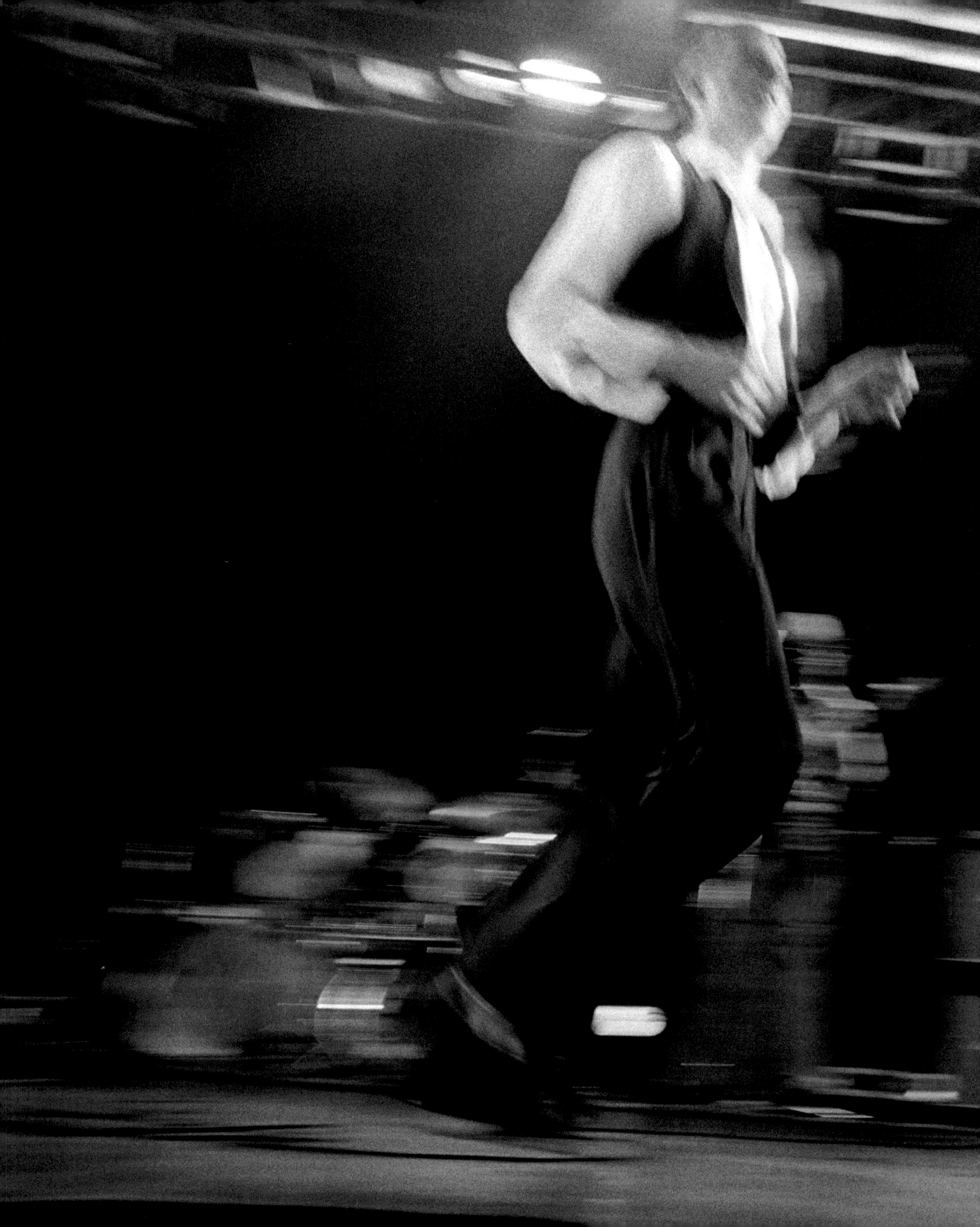

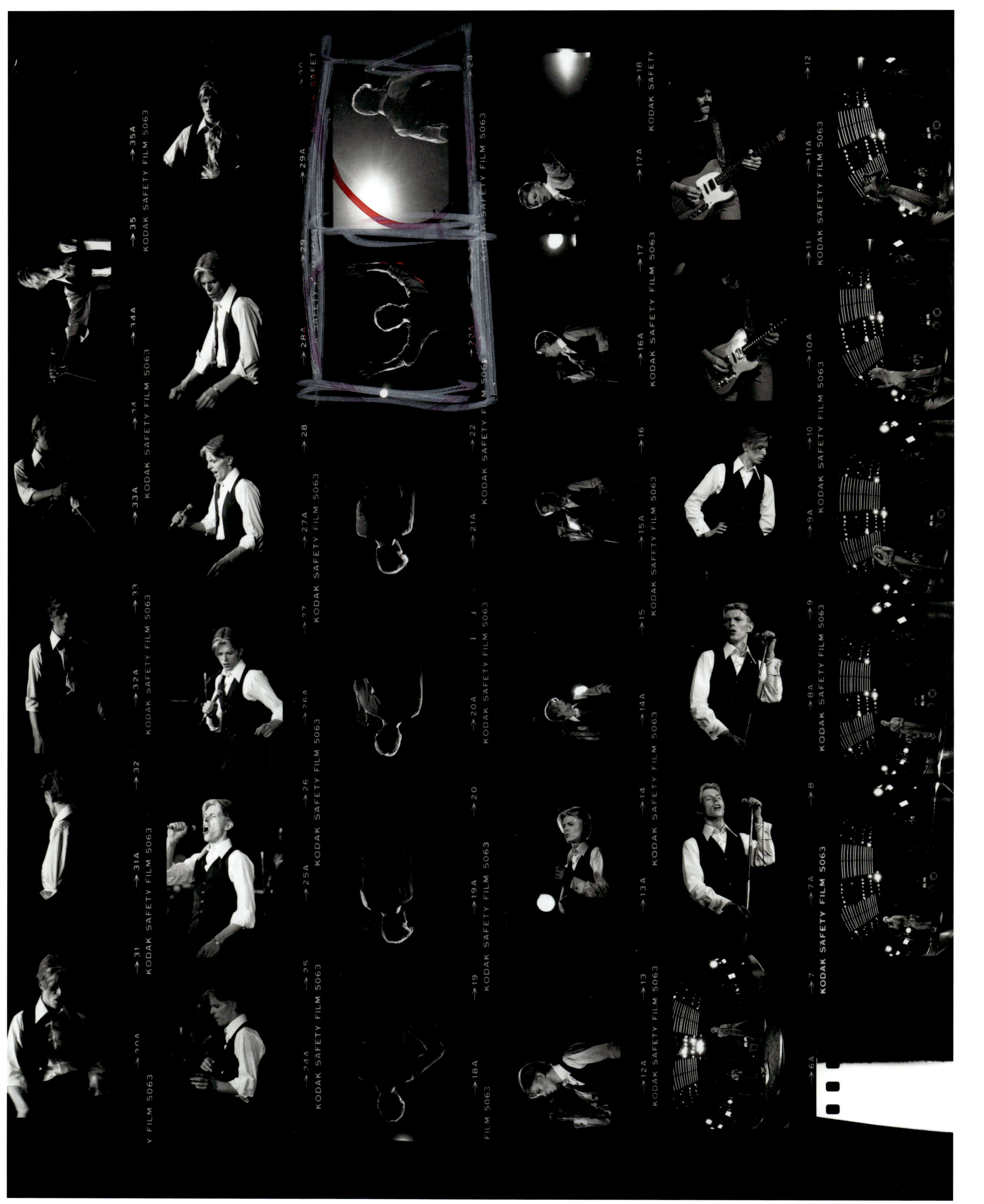

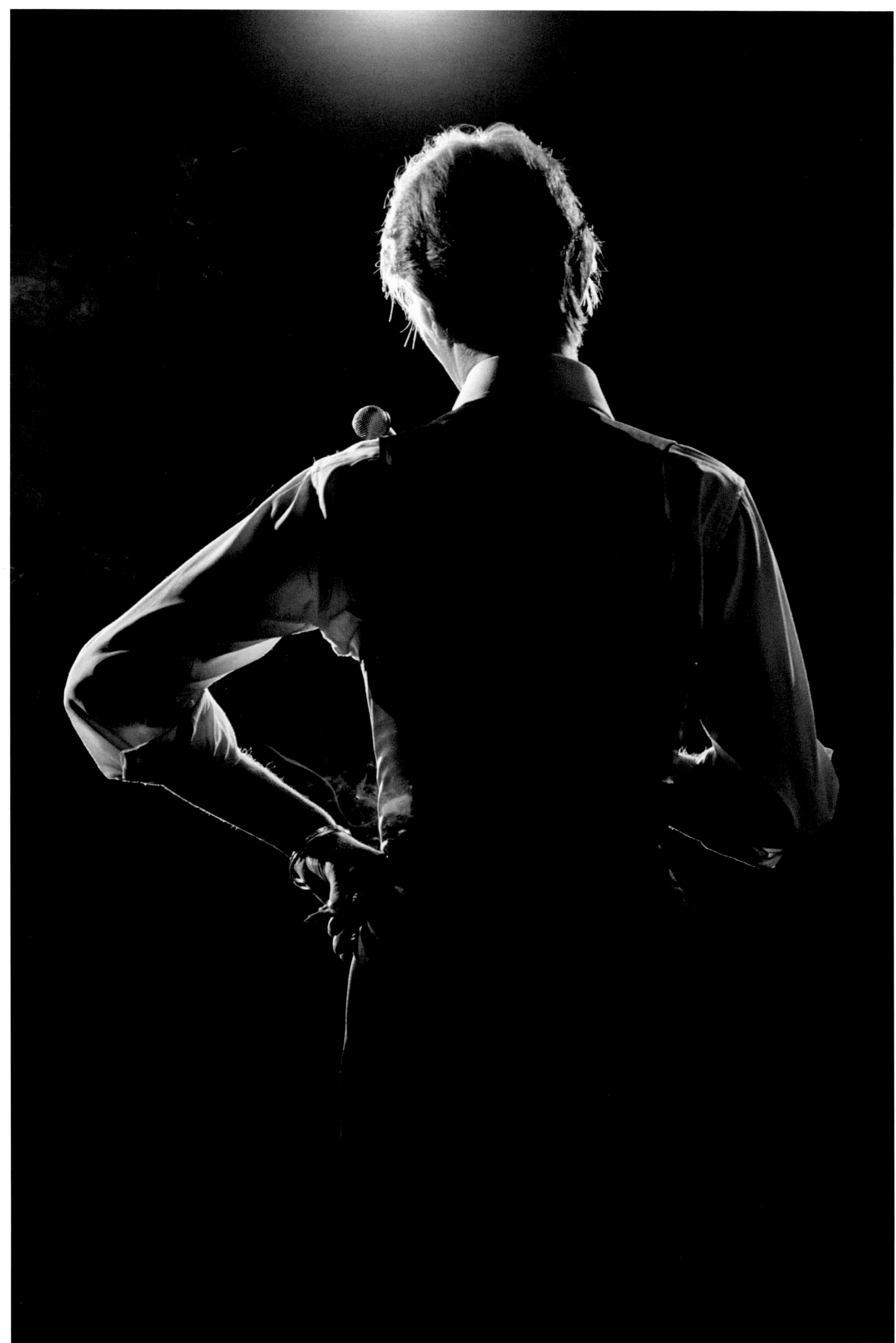

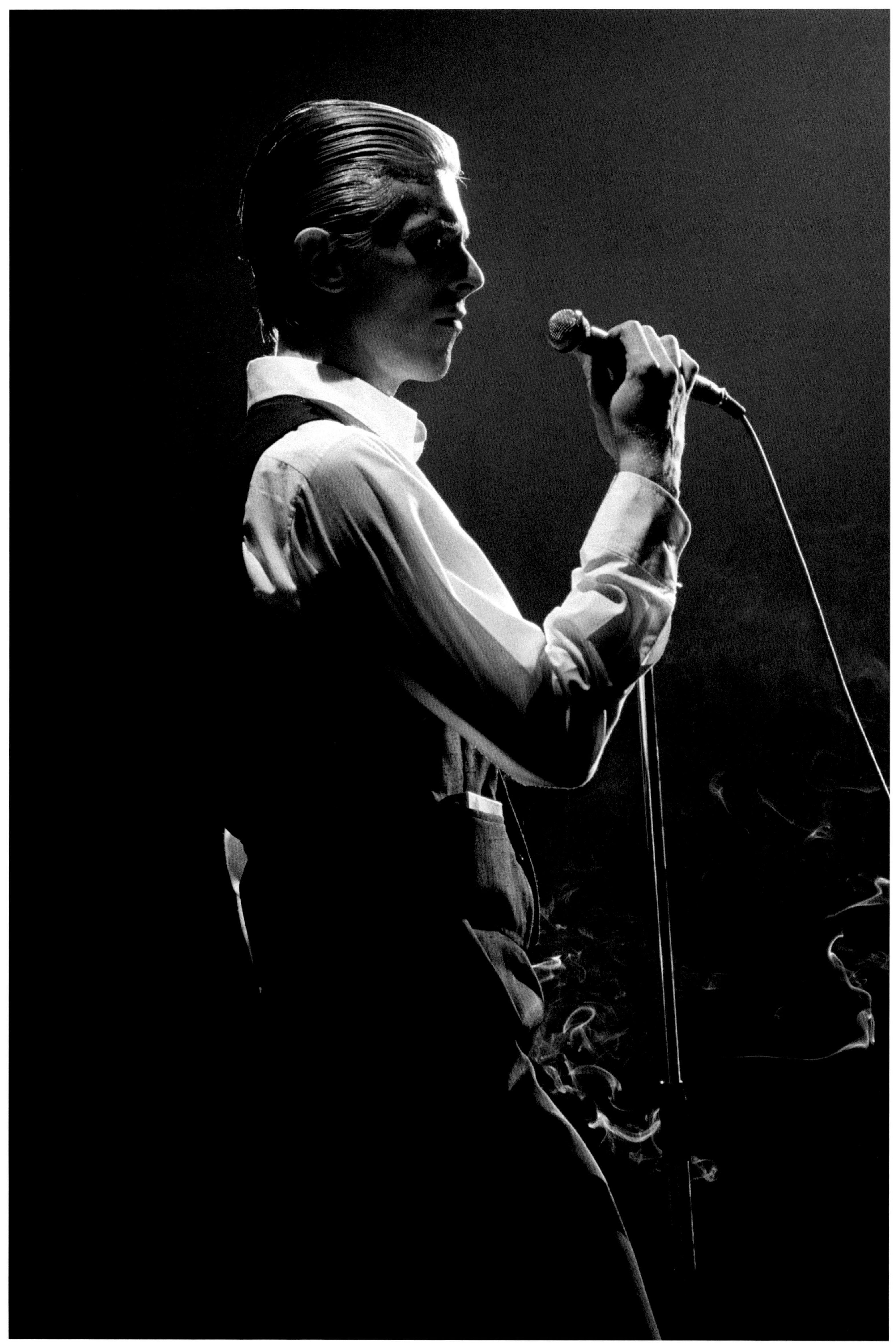

"(JAMES) DEAN WAS PROBABLY VERY MUCH LIKE ME. ELIZABETH TAYLOR TOLD ME THAT ONCE. DEAN WAS CALCULATING. HE WASN'T CARELESS. HE WAS NOT THE REBEL HE PORTRAYED SO SUCCESSFULLY. HE DIDN'T WANT TO DIE. BUT HE DID BELIEVE IN THE PREMISE OF TAKING YOUSELF TO EXTREMES. JUST TO ADD A DEEPER CUT TO ONE'S PERSONALITY." -DB

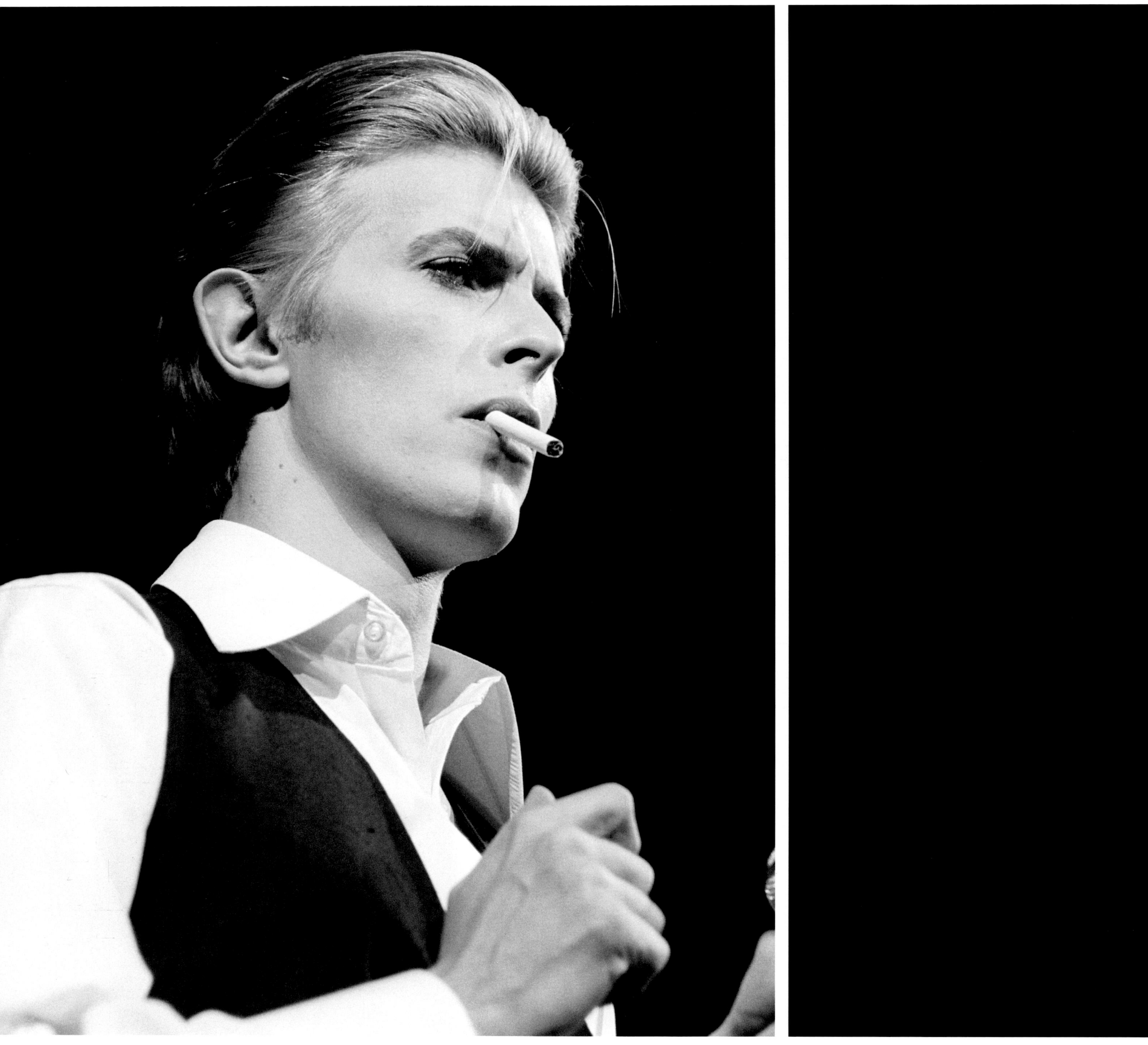

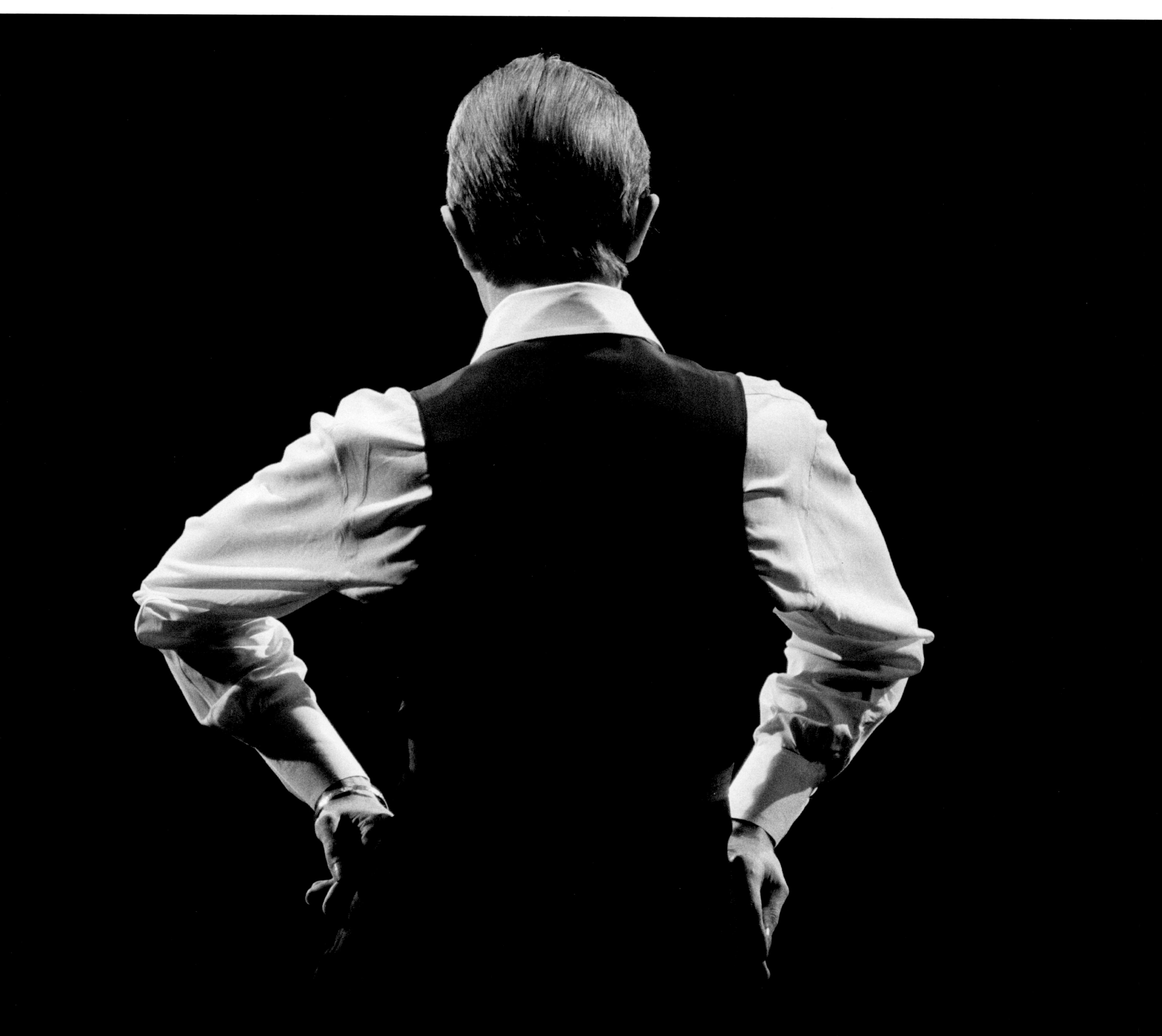

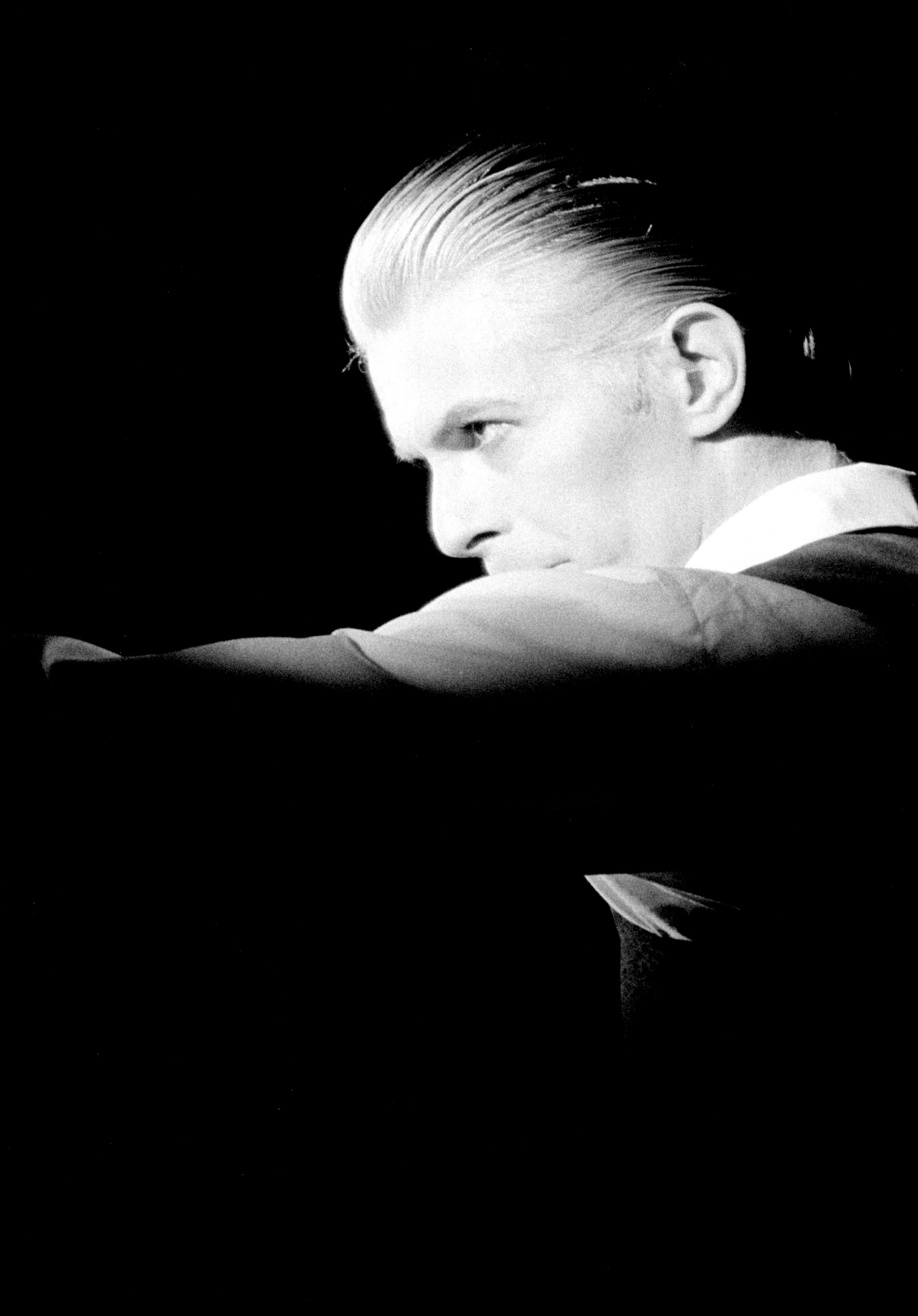

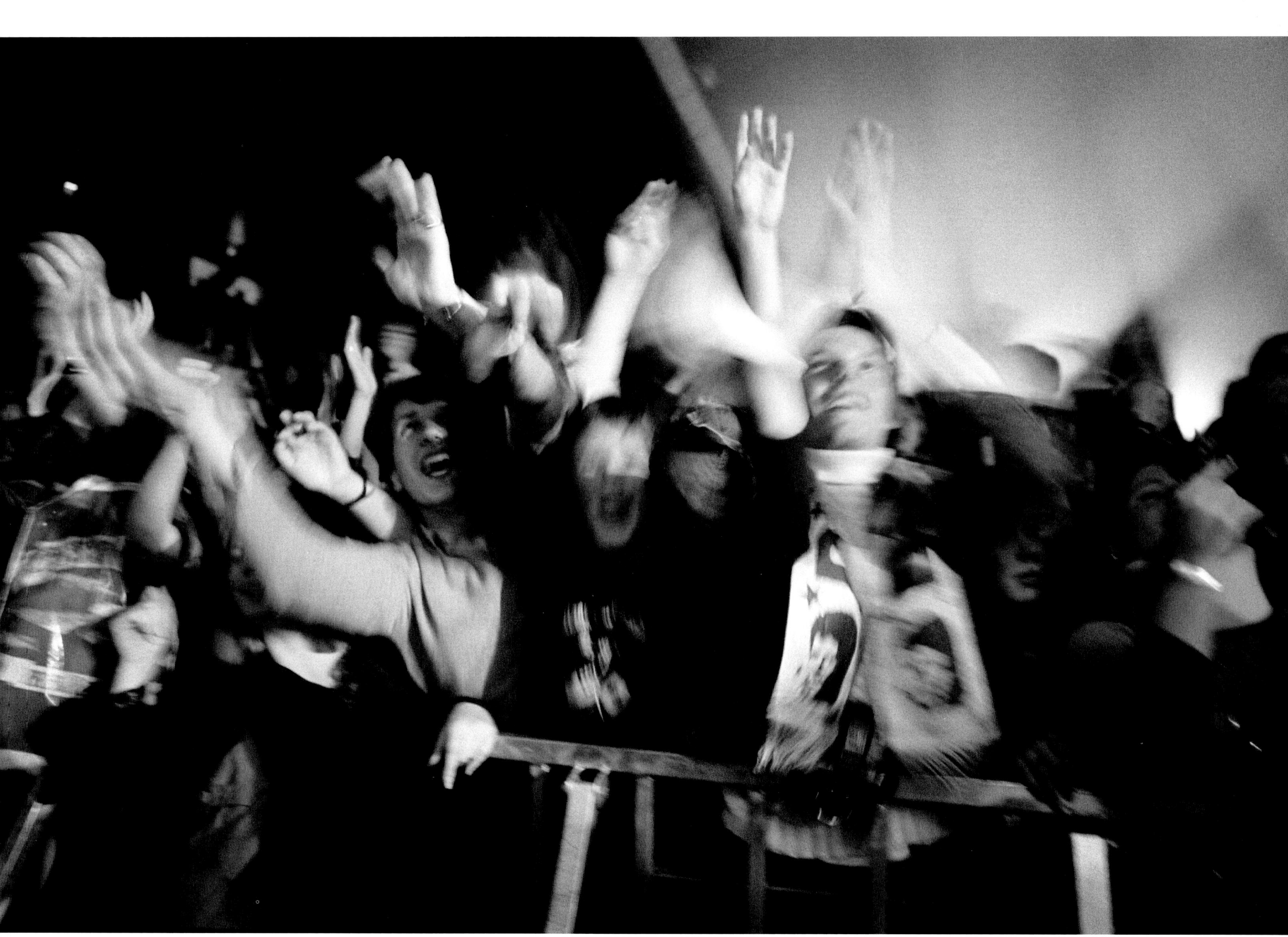

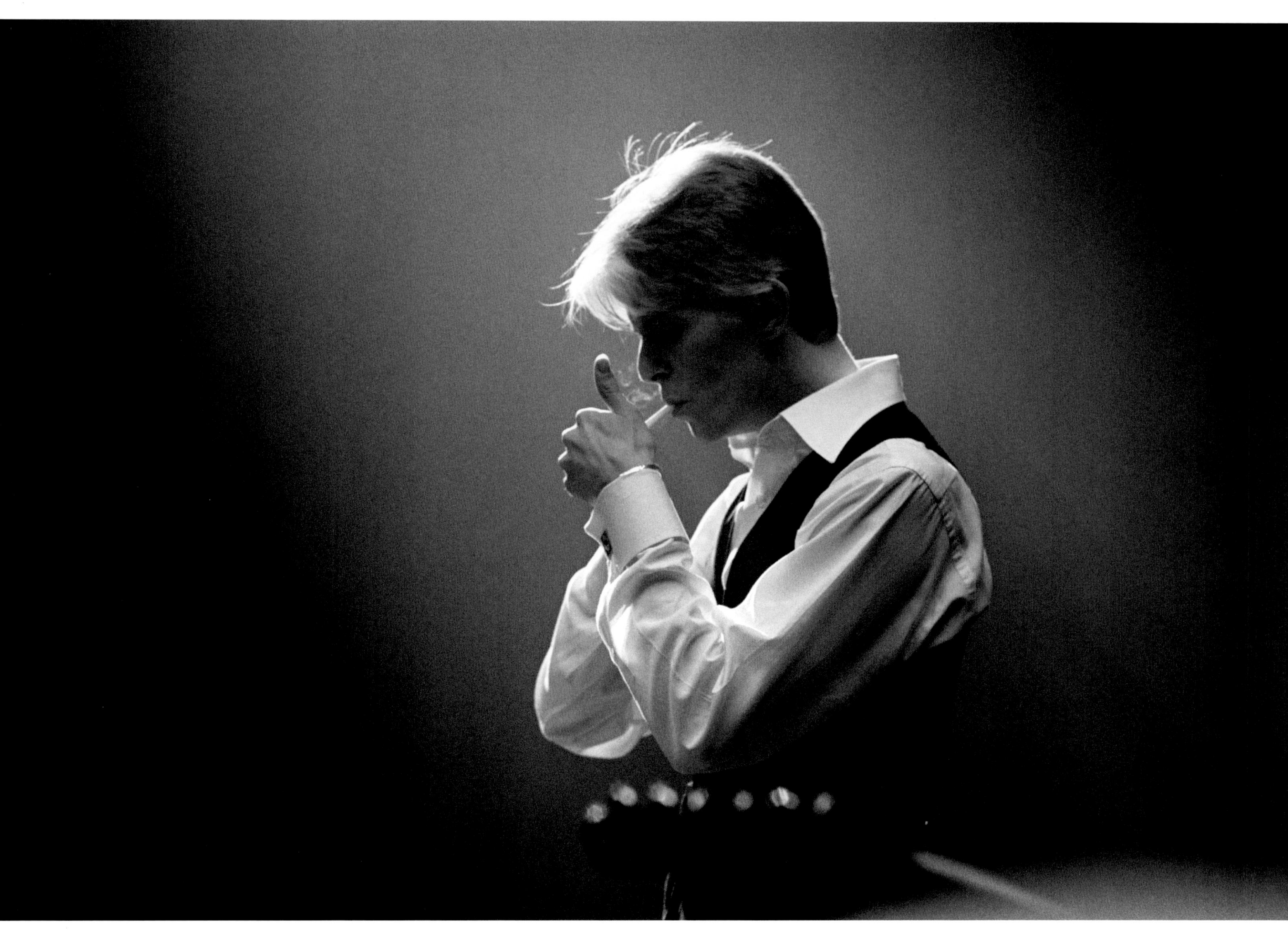

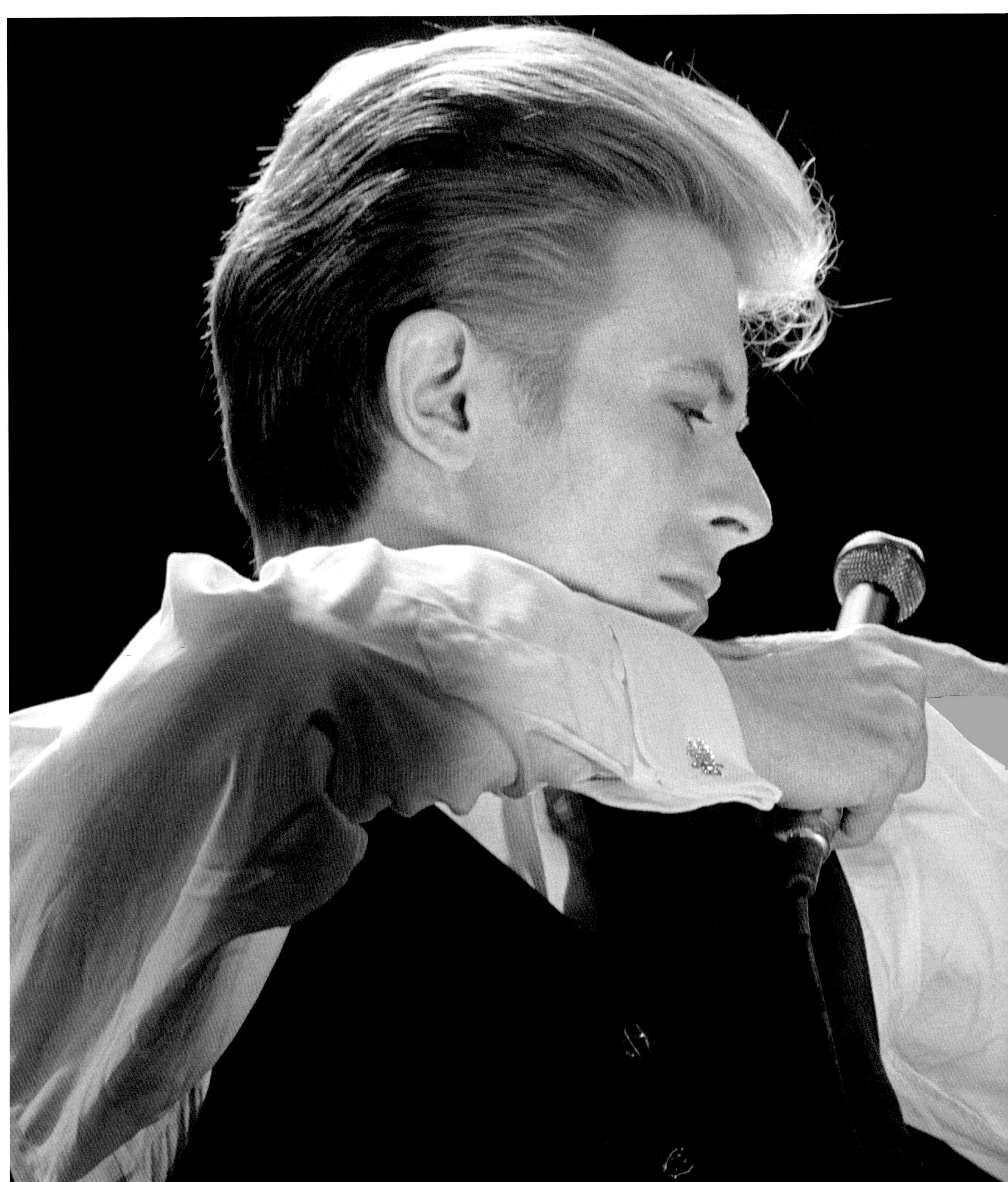

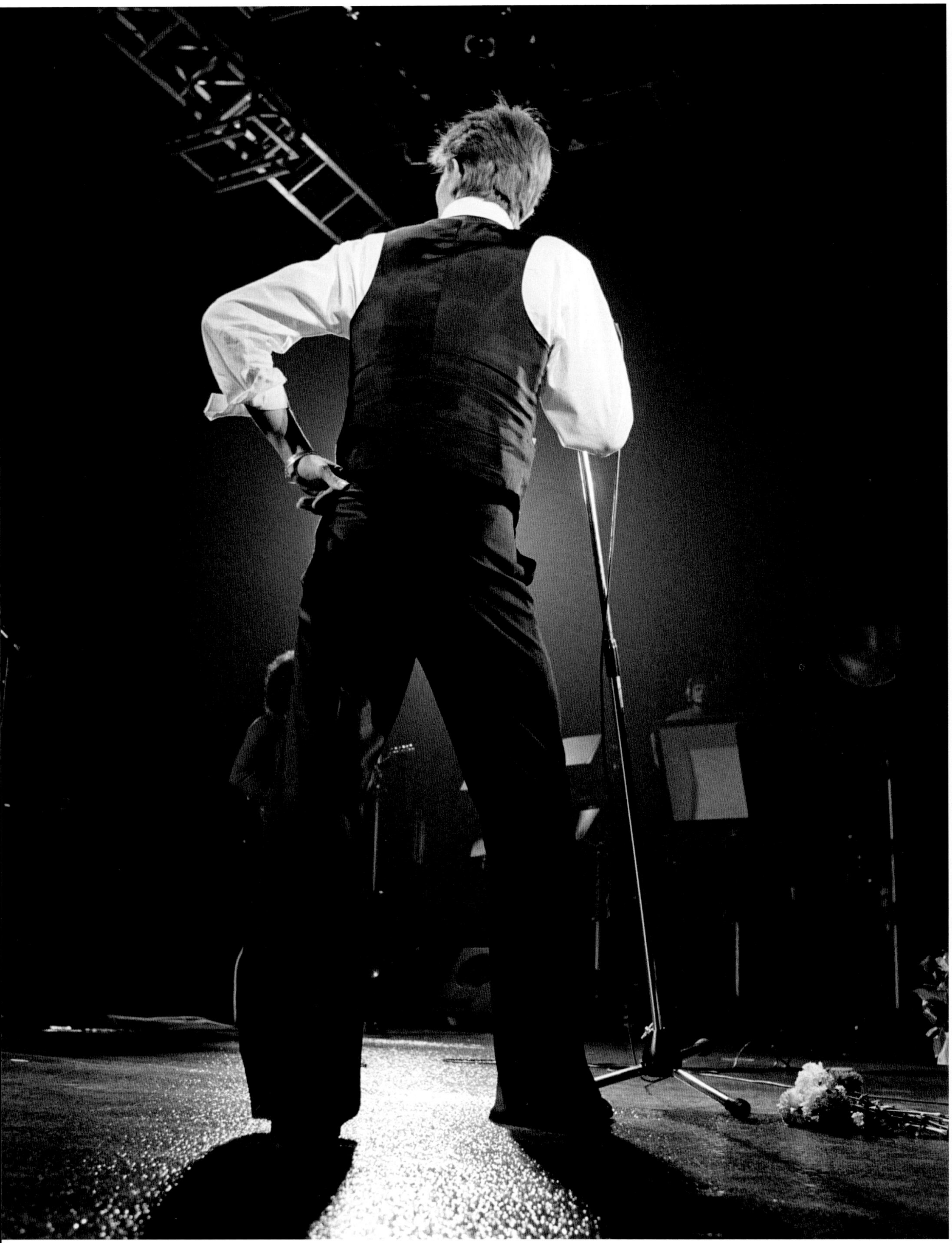

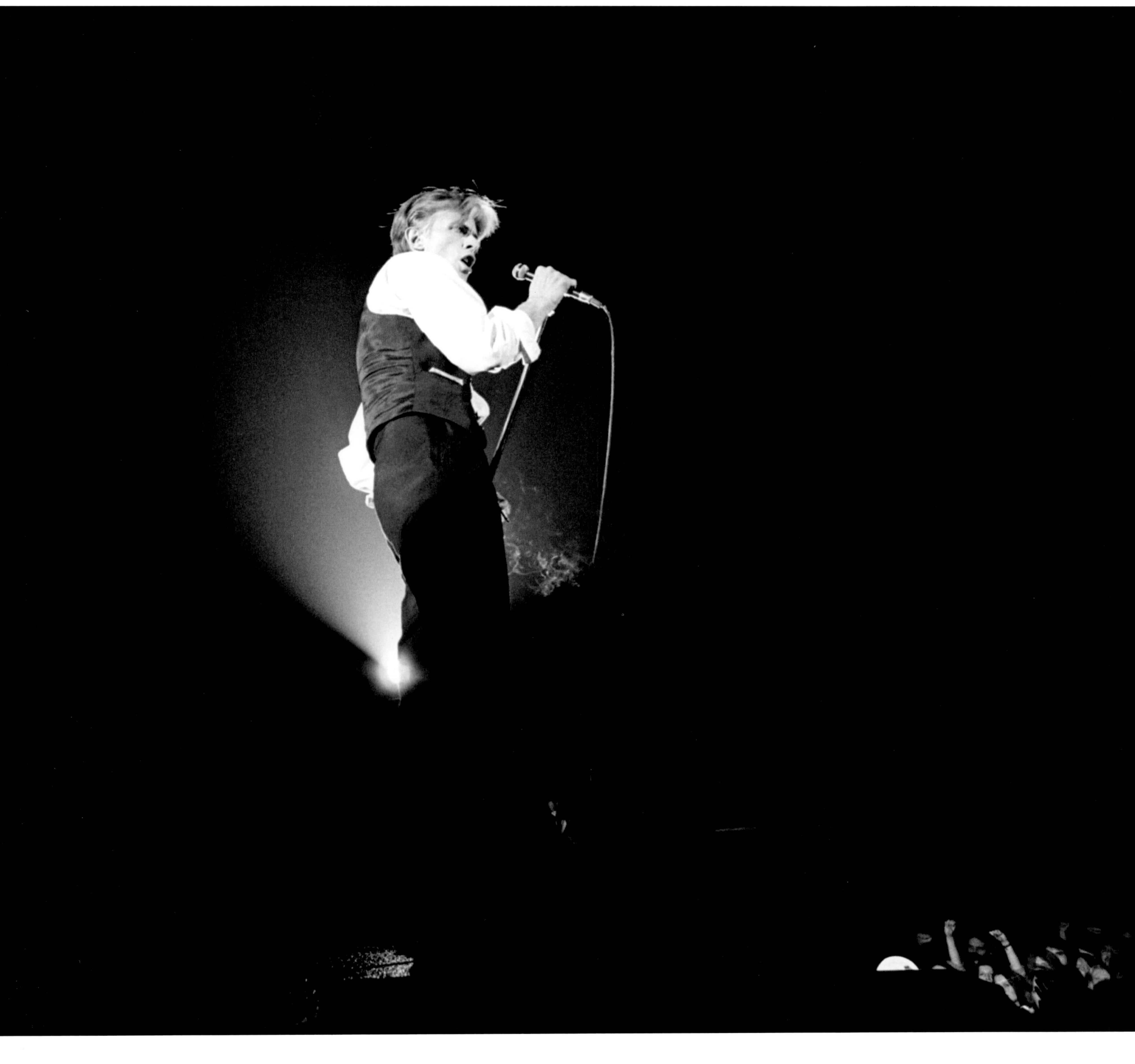

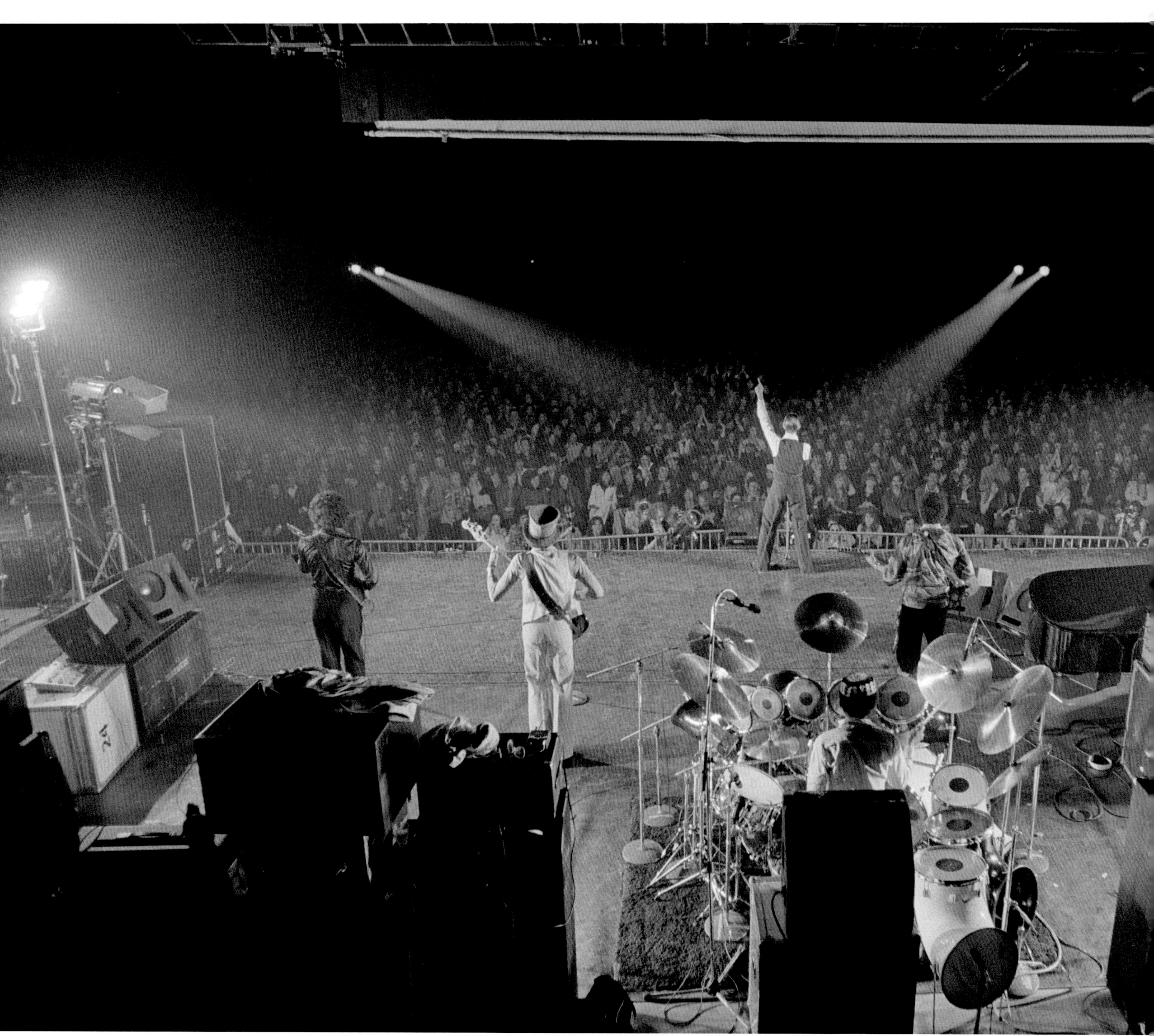

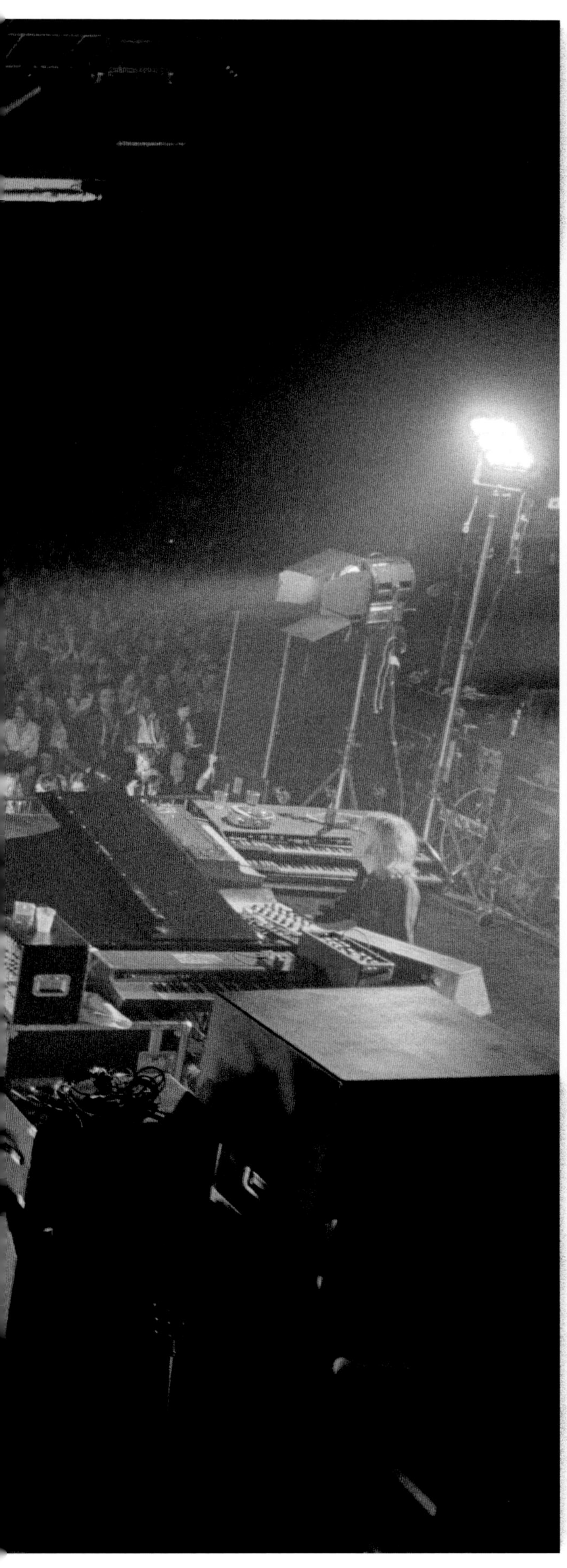

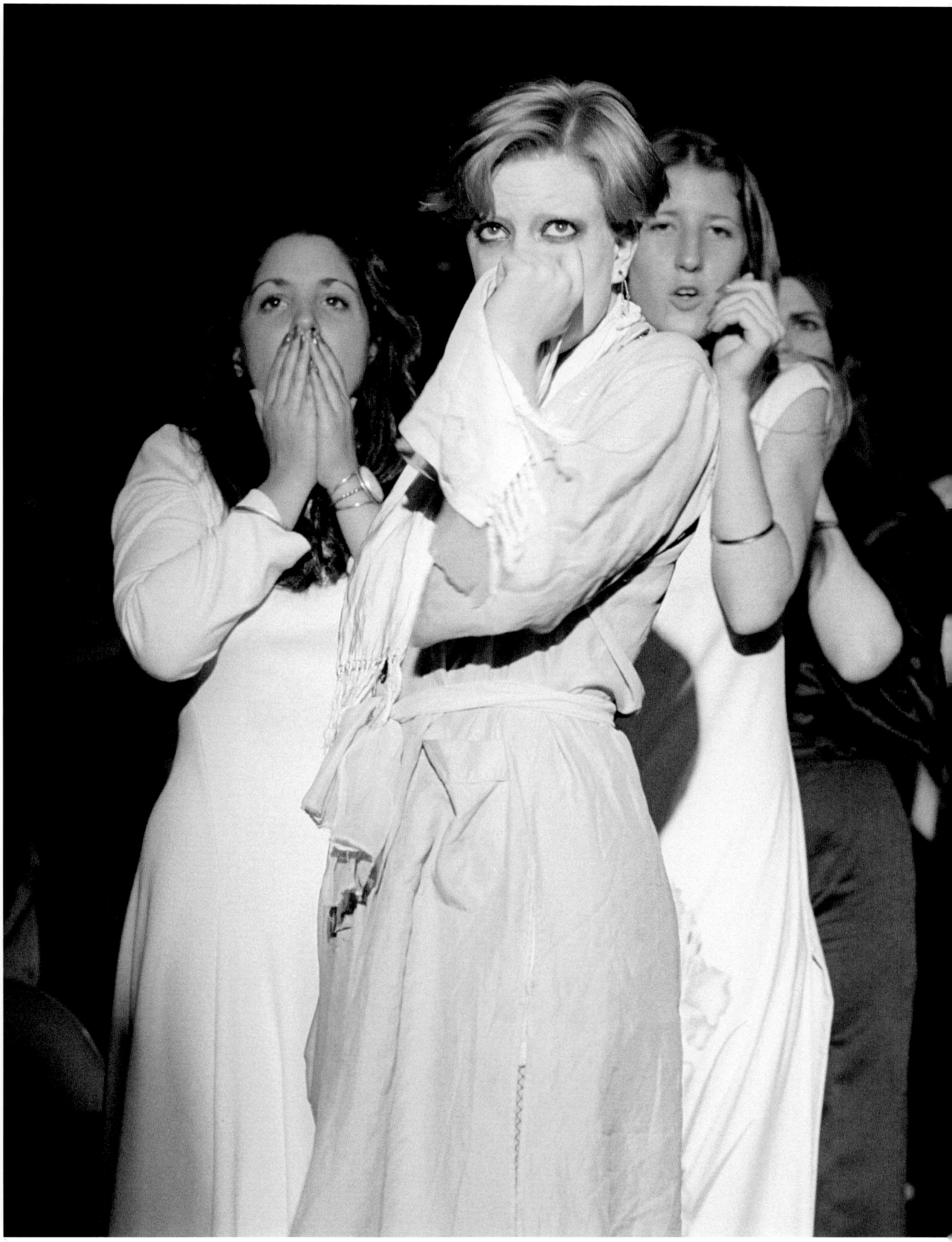

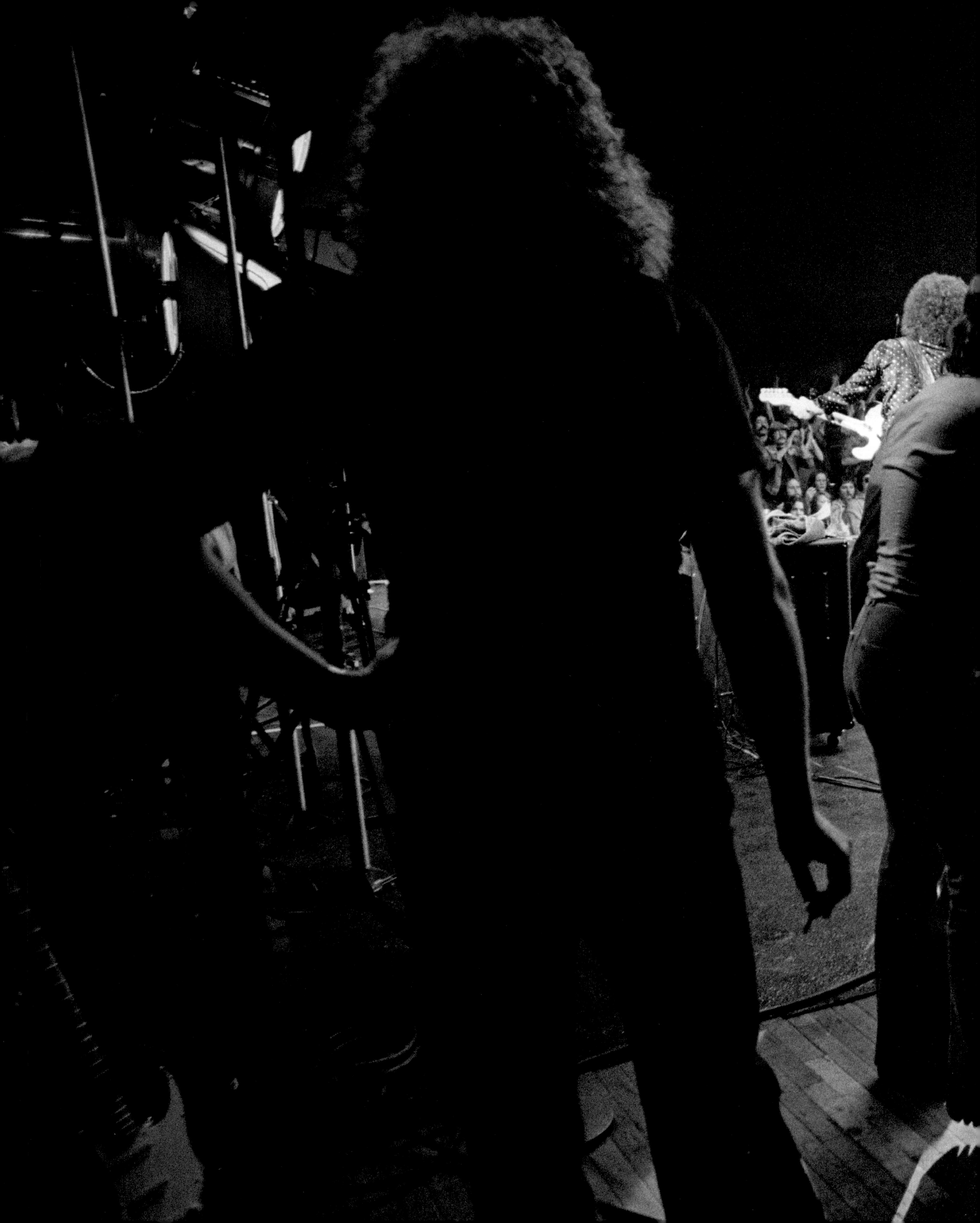

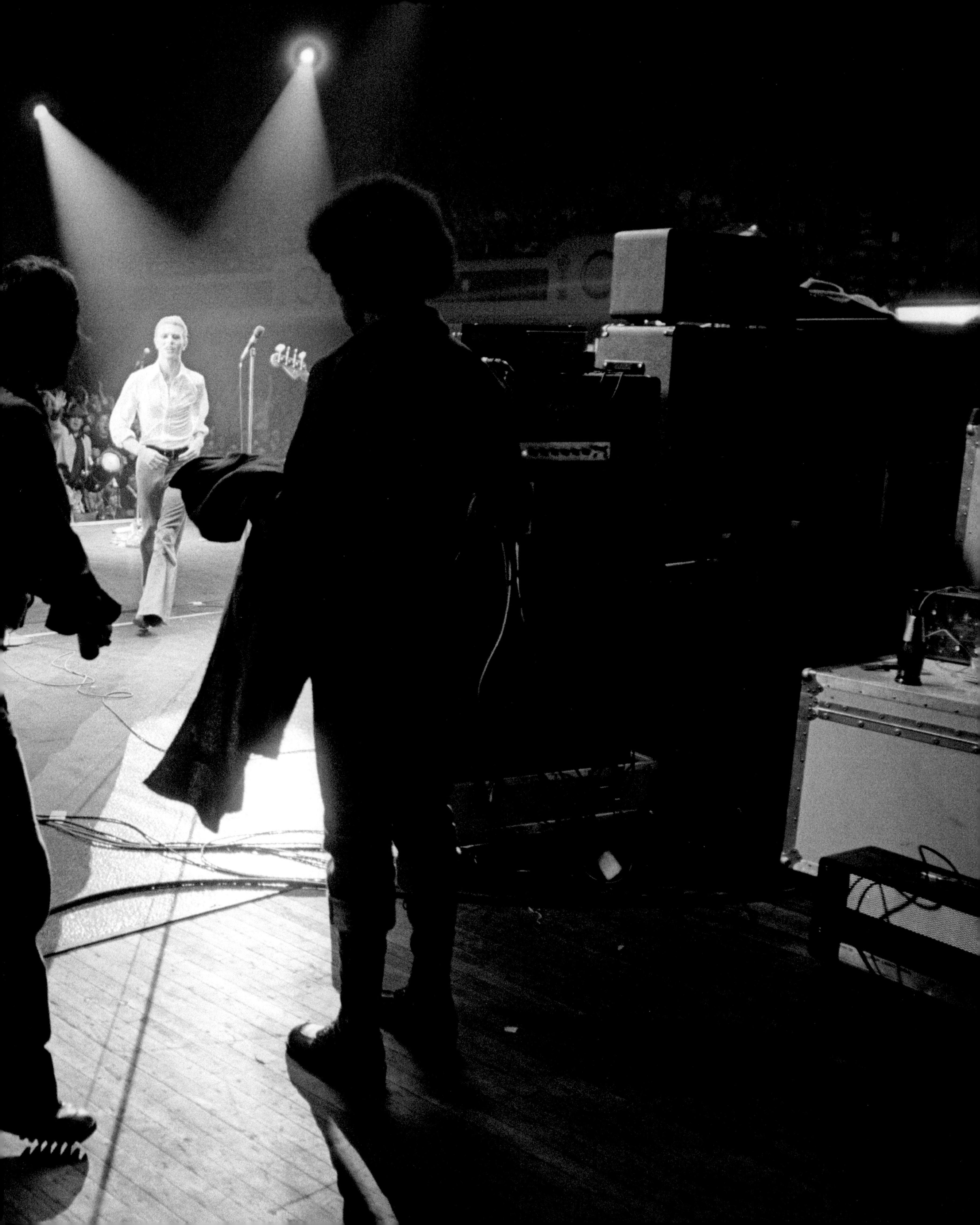

"Antistyle" as Bowie once said, "...it's not what you actually put on the canvas, it's the reason why you did it. Like the Andy Warhol thing. It wasn't why he painted a Campbell's soup can. It was 'What sort of man paints a Campbell's soup can?' That's what aggravates people. That's the premise behind antistyle. And antistyle is the premise behind me."

Bowie in his own wonderfully insane yet deftly calculating manner managed to both define and utterly defy style. The mad aristocrat would endlessly fascinate fans, confound parents, and enrage critics with his wild swings in fashion and persona. All in a days work for the Duke.

"I honestly don't know where the real David Jones is. It's like playing the shell game. Except I've got so many shells I've forgotten what the pea looks like. I wouldn't know it if I found it. Being famous helps put off the problems of discovering myself. I mean that. That's the main reason I've always been so keen on being accepted, why I've striven so hard to put my brain to artistic use. I want to make a mark. In my early stuff, I made it through on sheer pretension. I consider myself responsible for a whole new school of pretensions–they know who they are. Don't you, Elton? Just kidding. No, I'm not. See what I mean?"

To further that point, Bowie said, "I haven't a clue where I'm gonna be in a year. A raving nut, a flower child or a dictator, some kind of reverend - I don't know. That's what keeps me from getting bored."

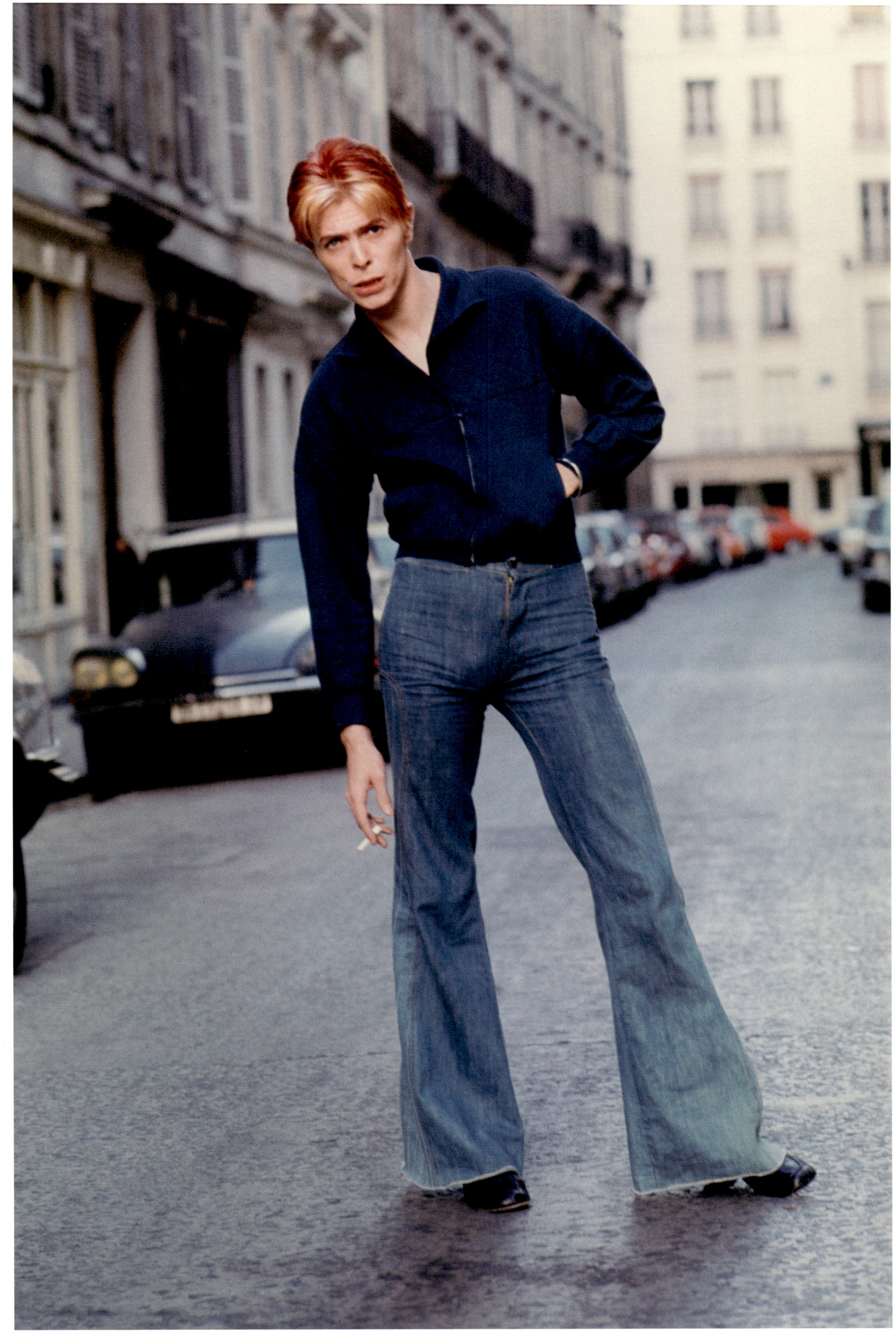

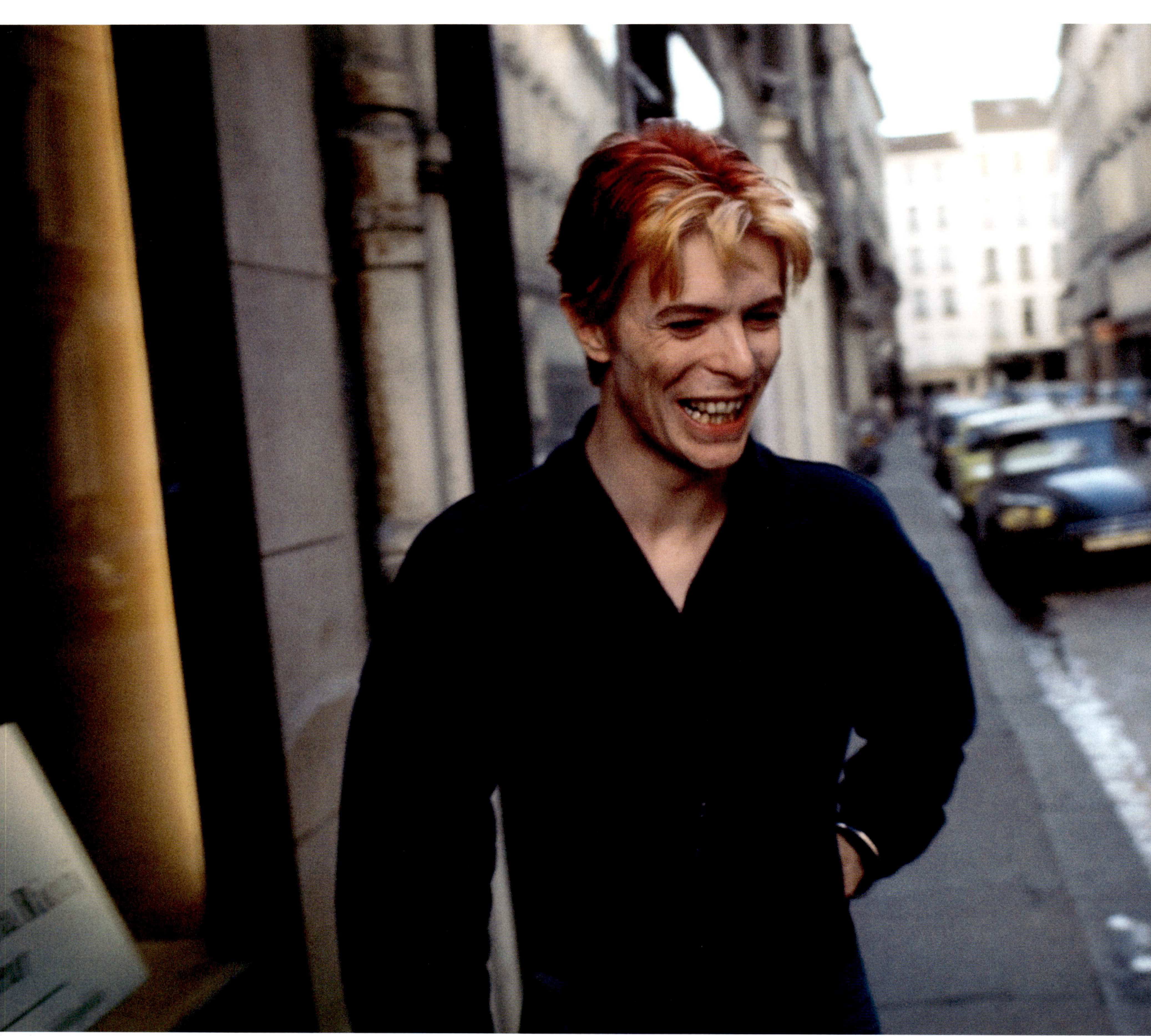

(Previous spread, above, and right)
After calling Andrew to his hotel room, David spontaneously decided to take some photos on the street outside L'Hotel in Paris. The impromptu photo shoot lasted about ten minutes.

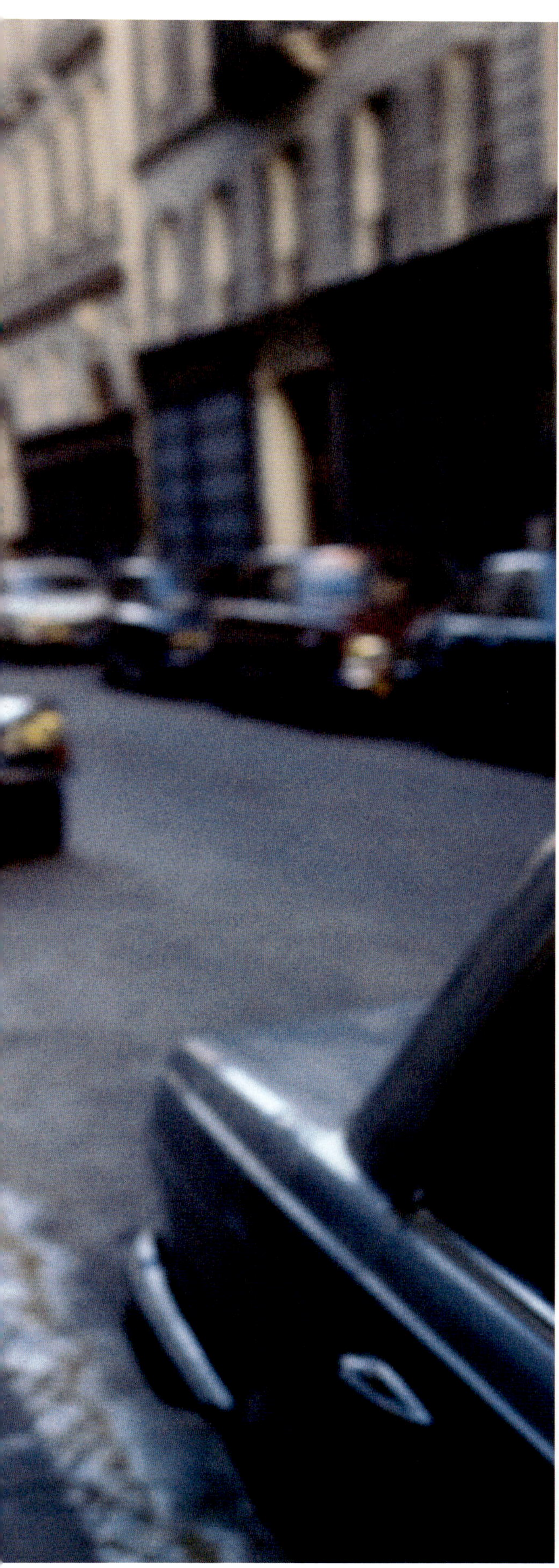

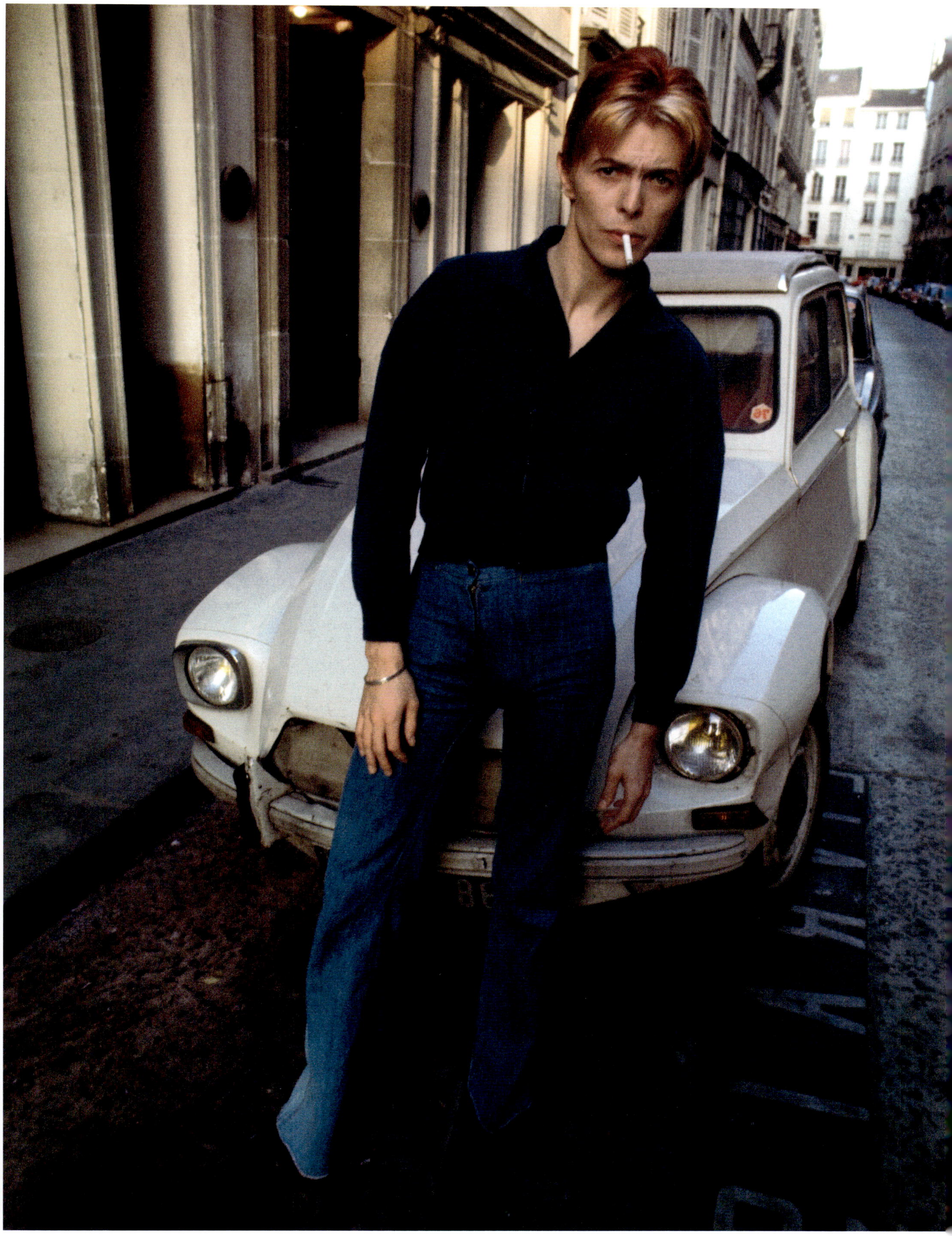

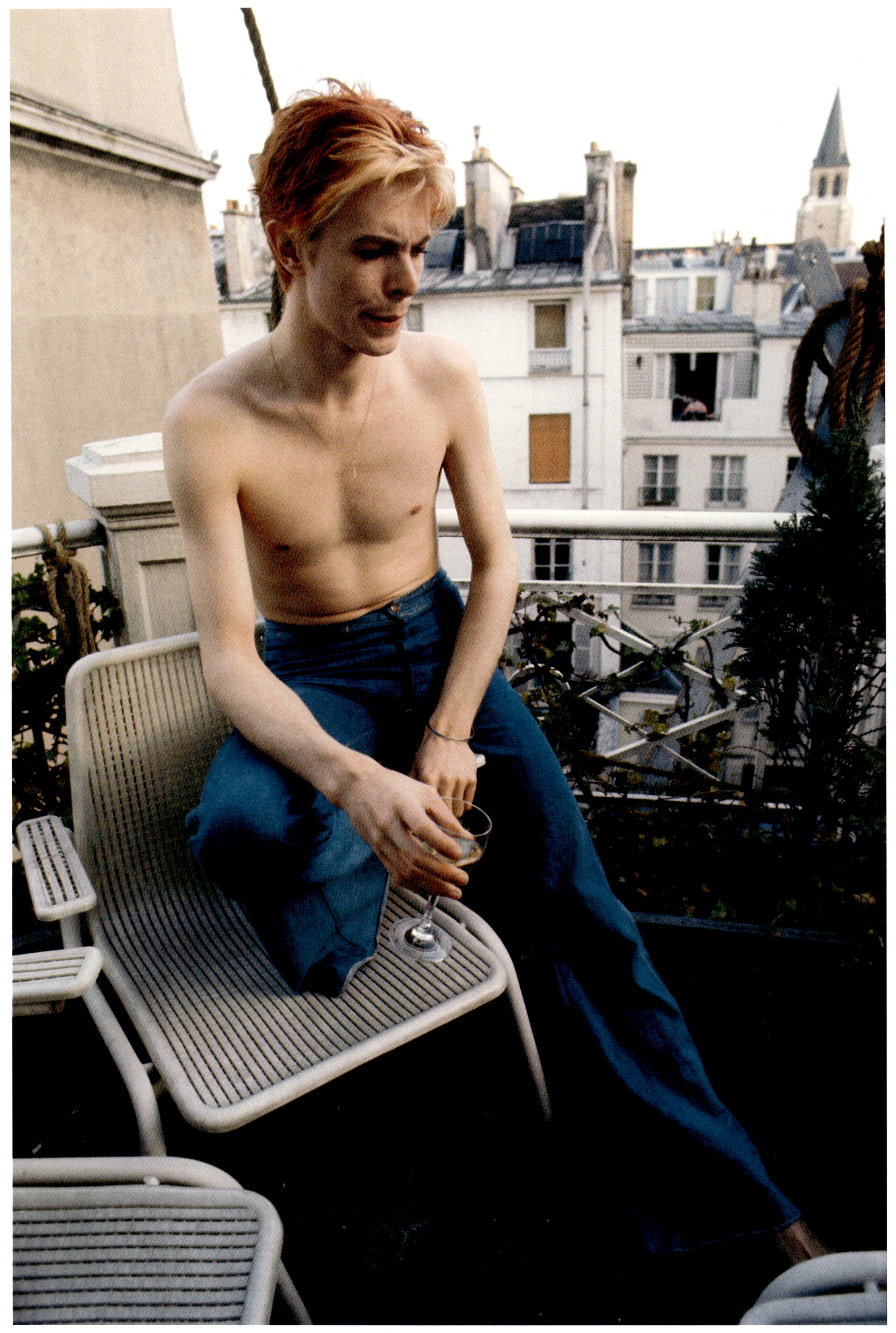

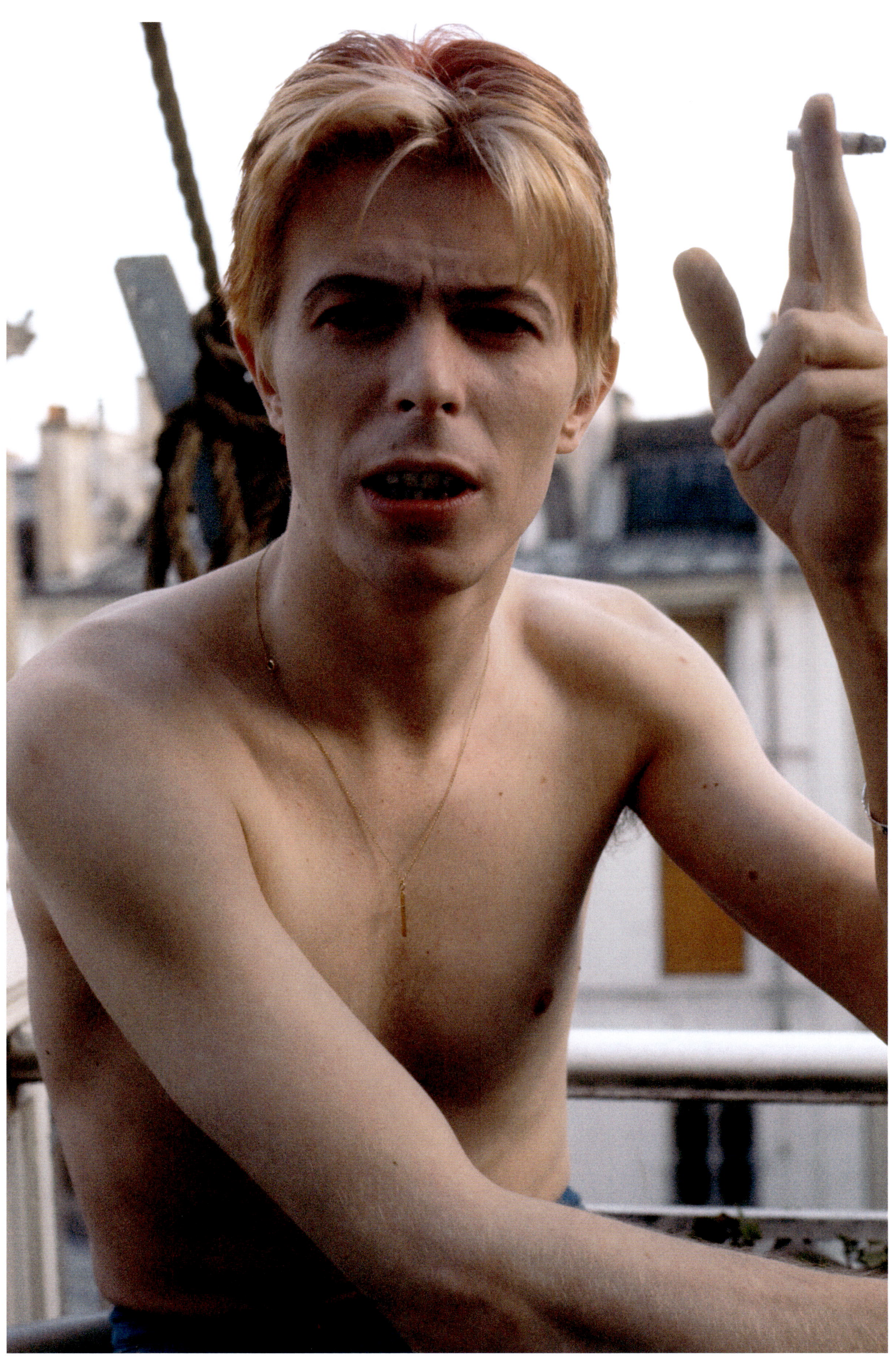

"I HATE SLEEP. I WOULD MUCH PREFER STAYING UP, JUST WORKING, ALL THE TIME.

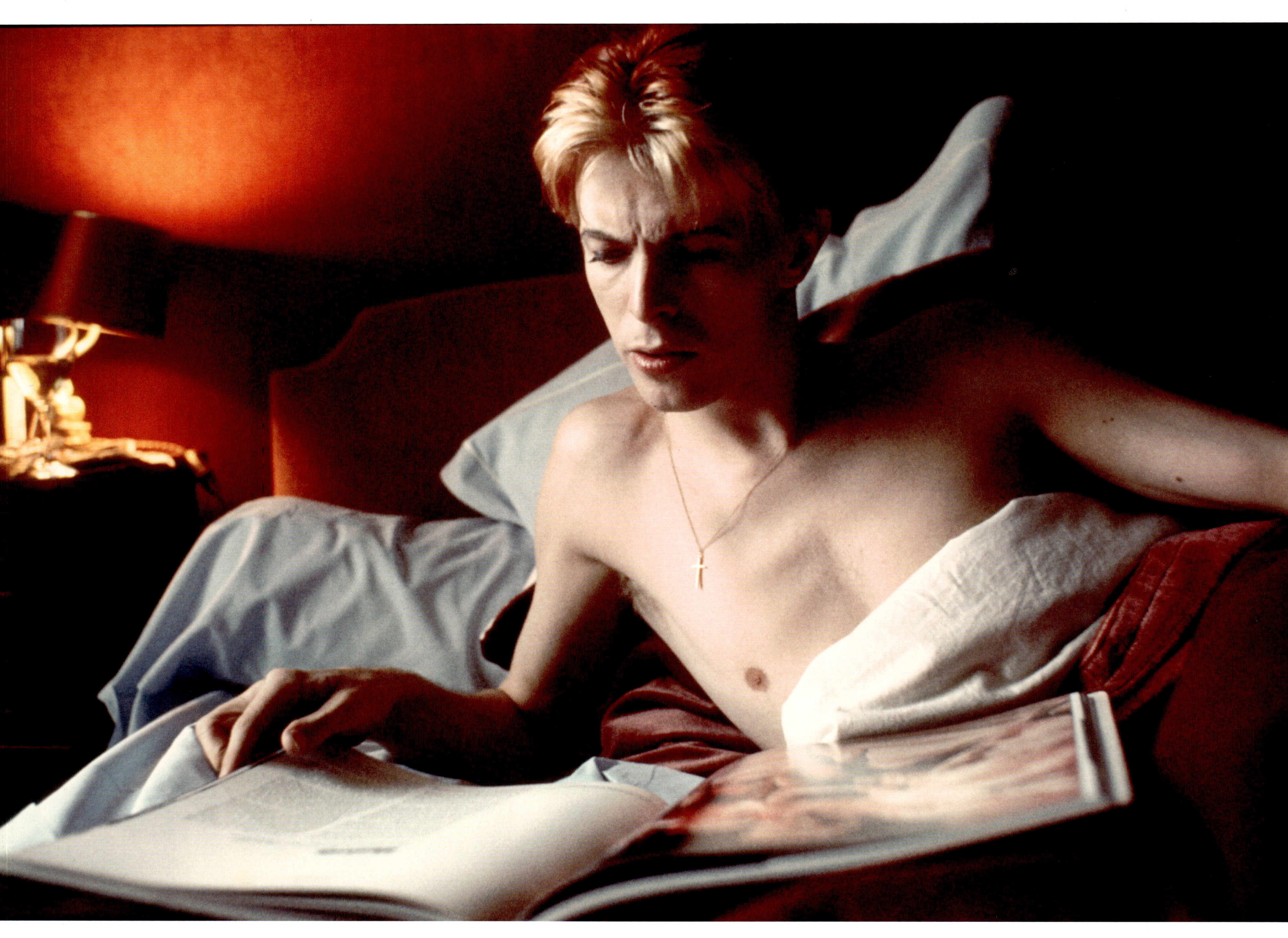

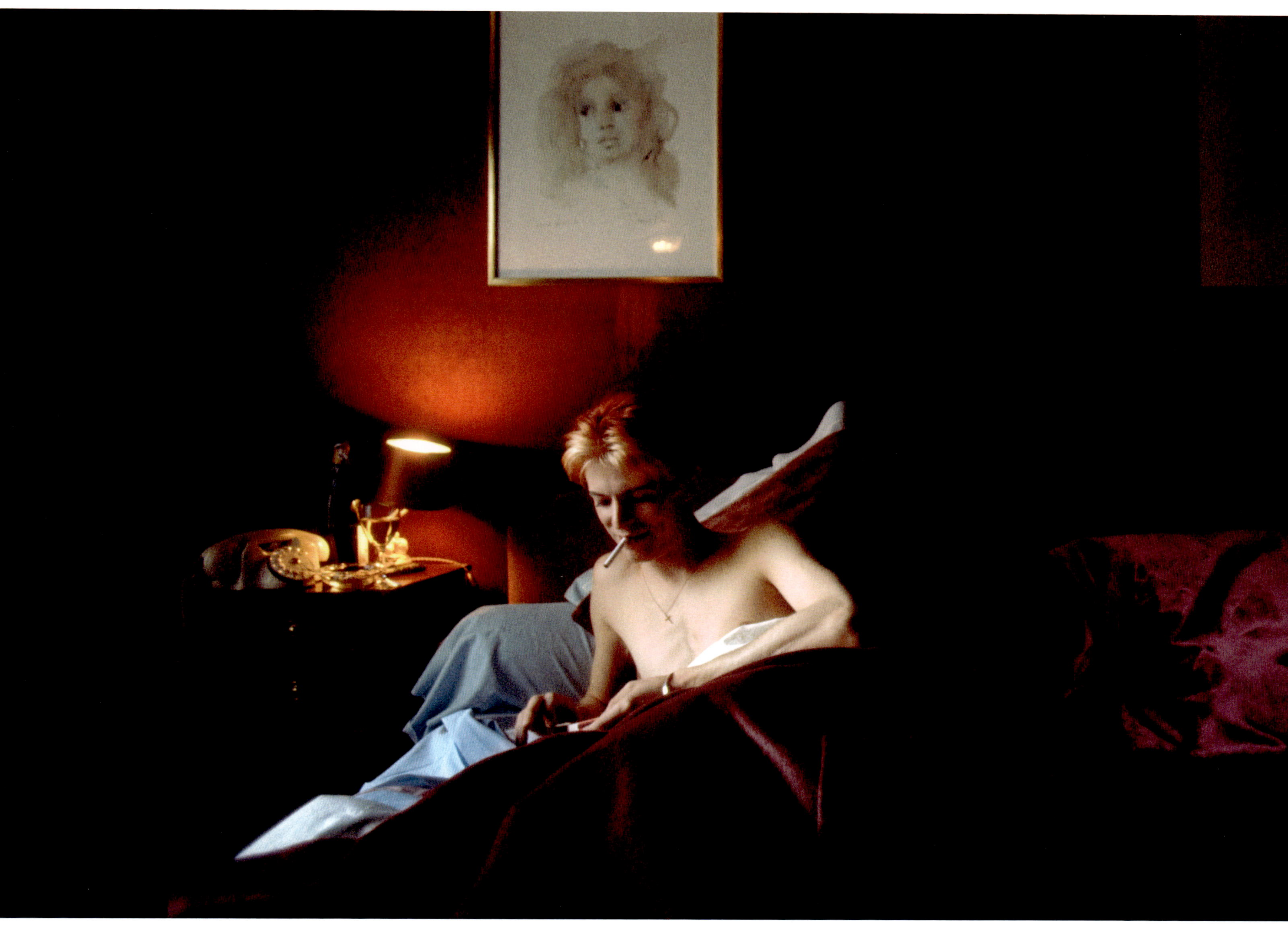

(Previous spread) David has a glass of white wine and a cigarette on the balcony of his suite at L'Hotel in Paris.
(Above and left) David reads through a book in his bed during a rare quiet morning in his suite at L'Hotel in Paris.

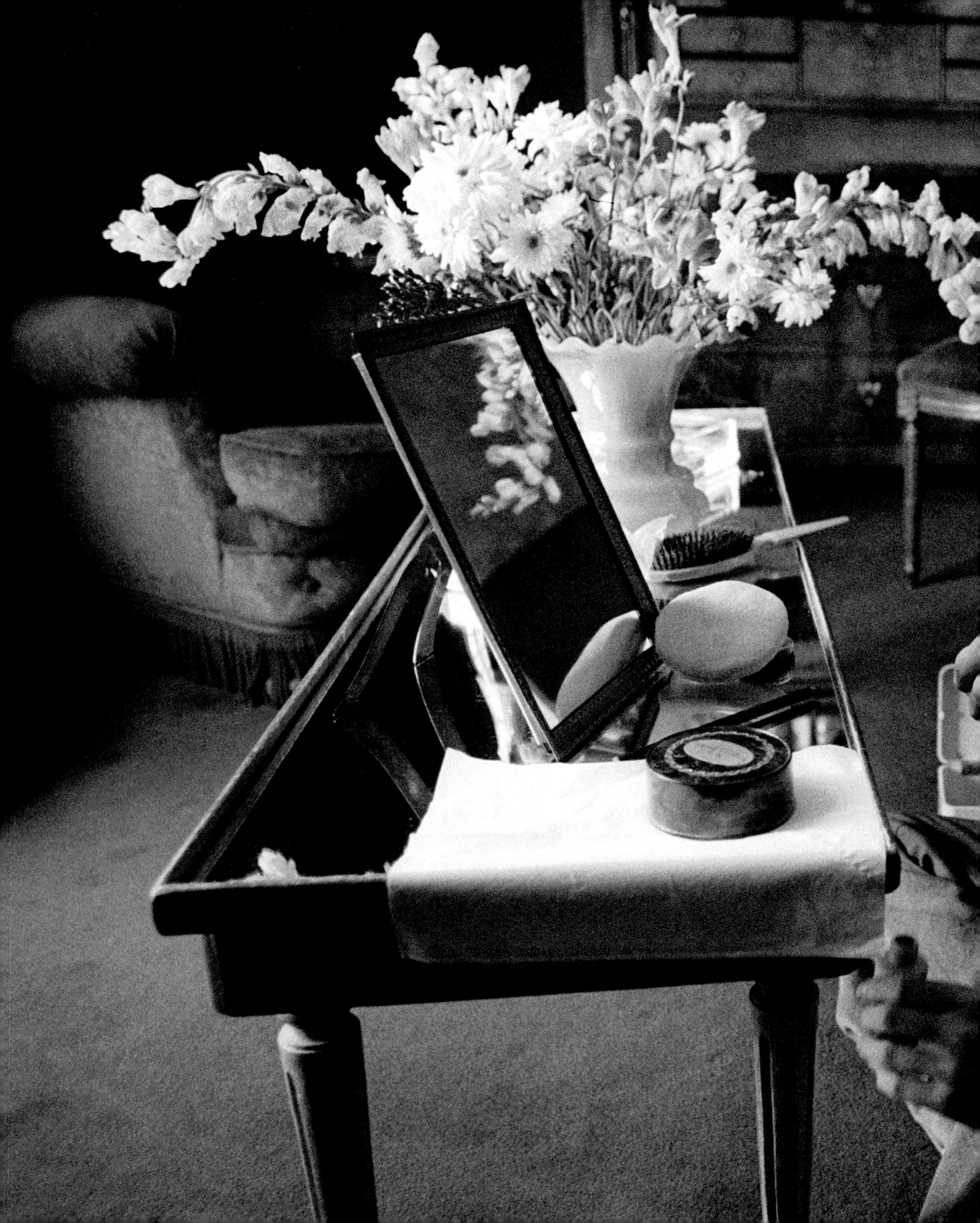

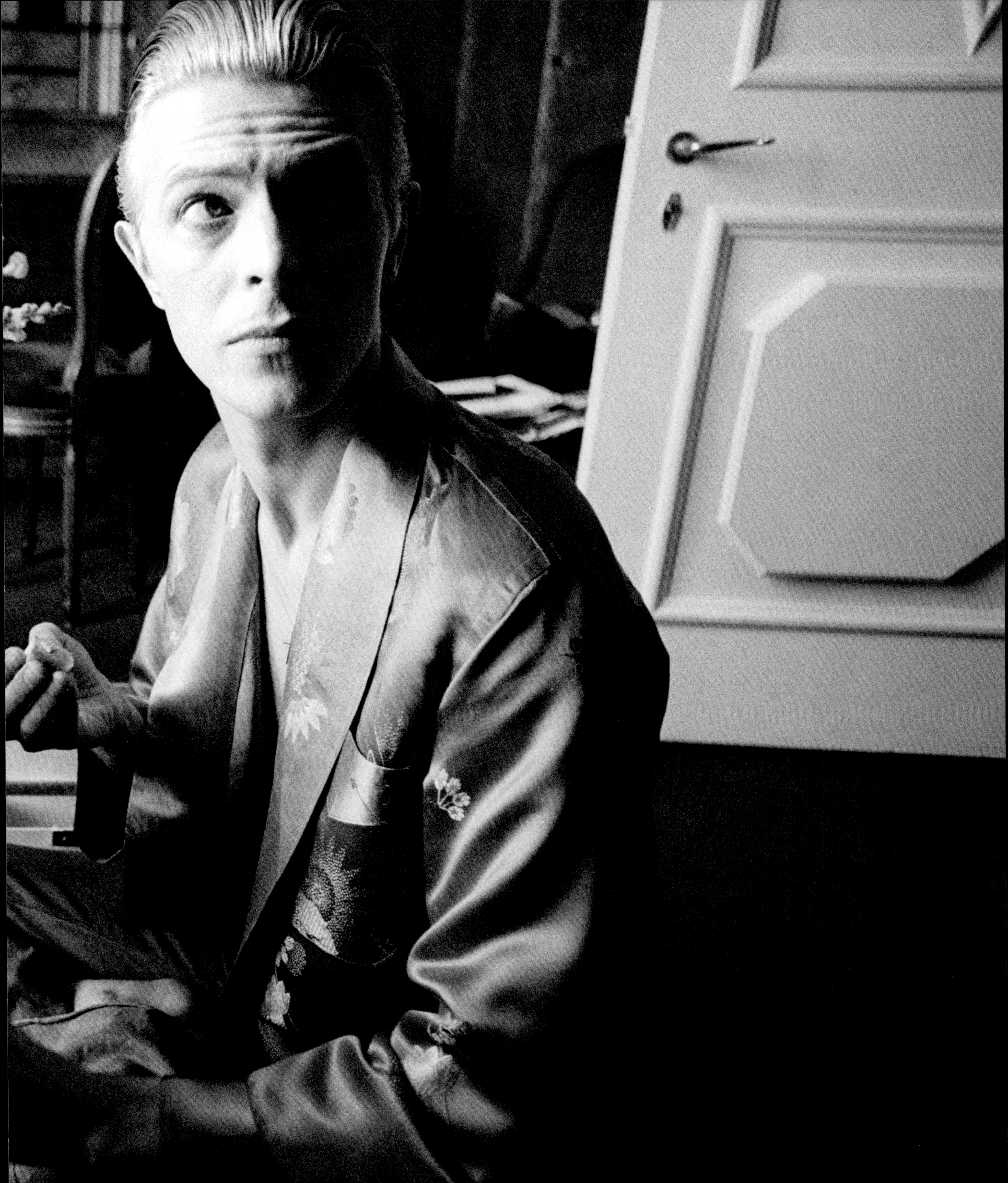

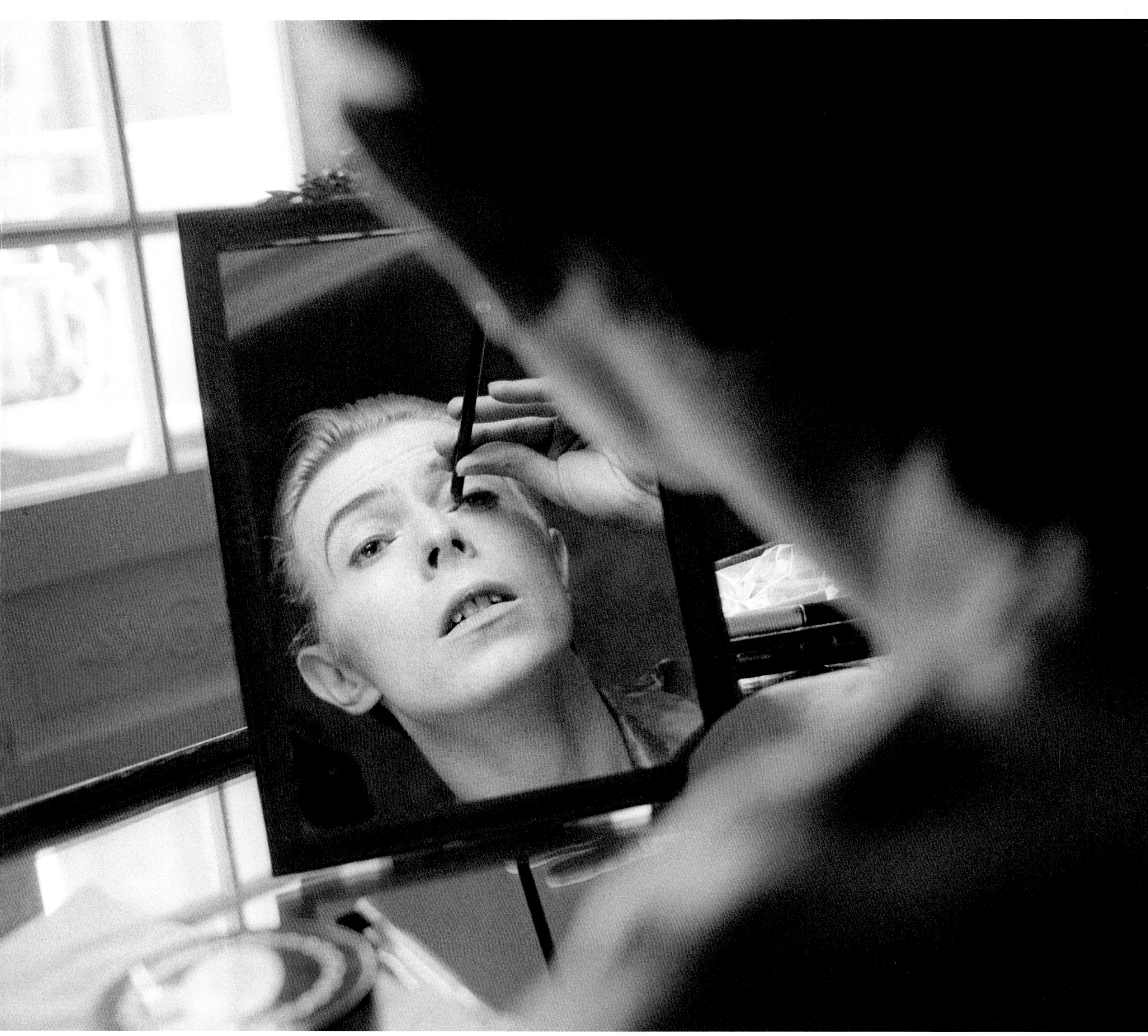

(Previous spread, above, and right)
*David prepares his makeup in his hotel
suite prior to an impromptu photo shoot
that morning in Paris.*

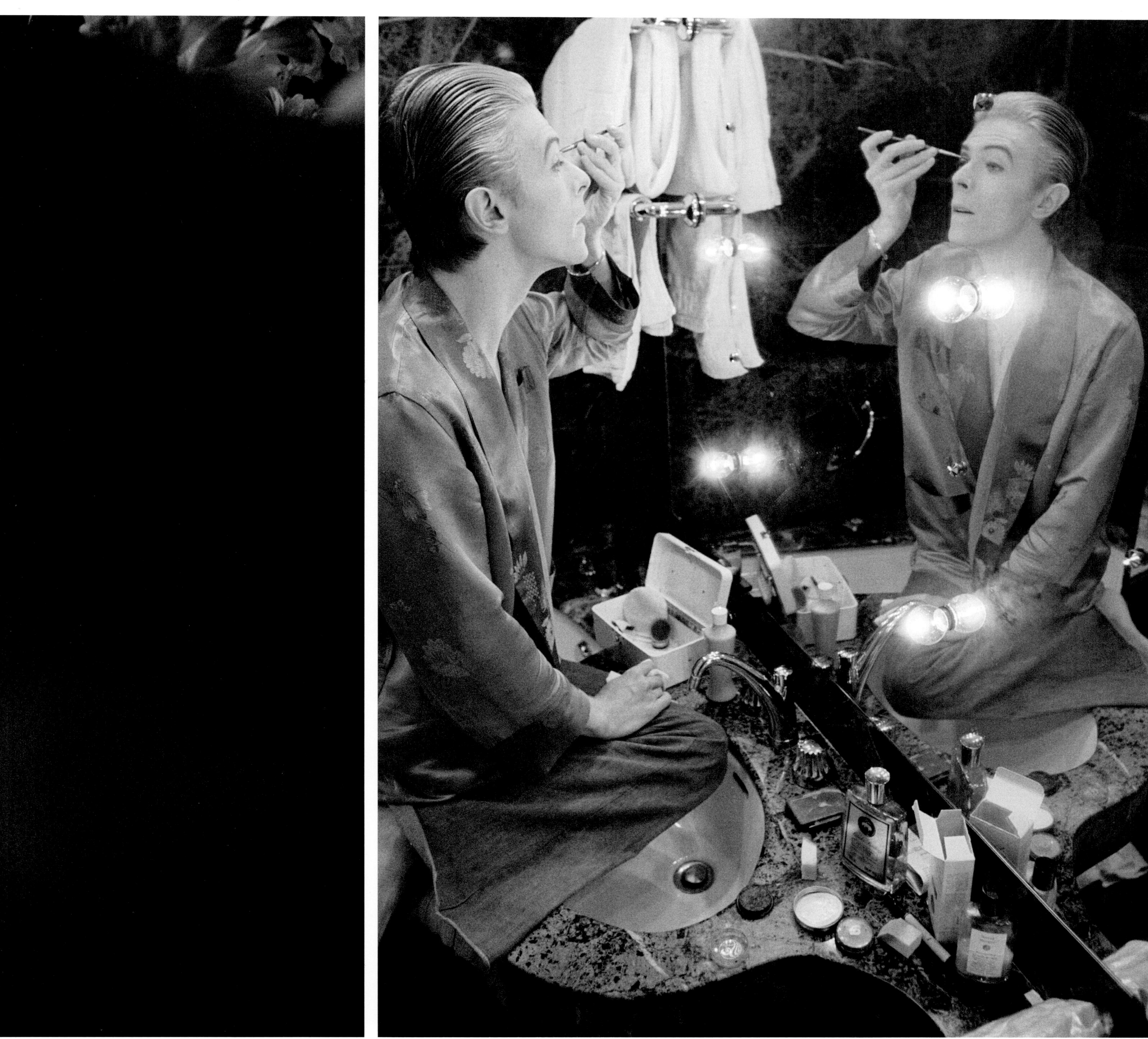

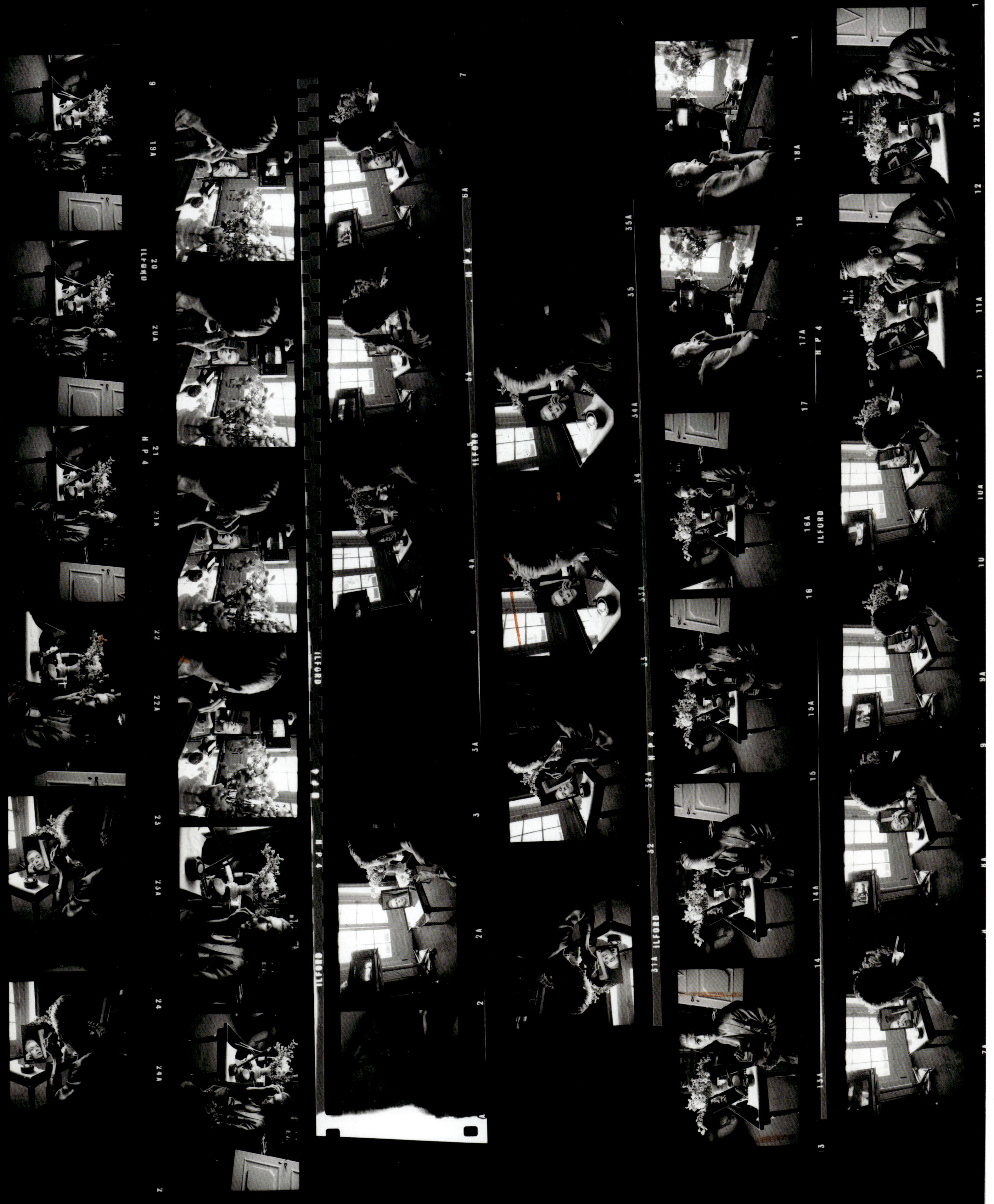

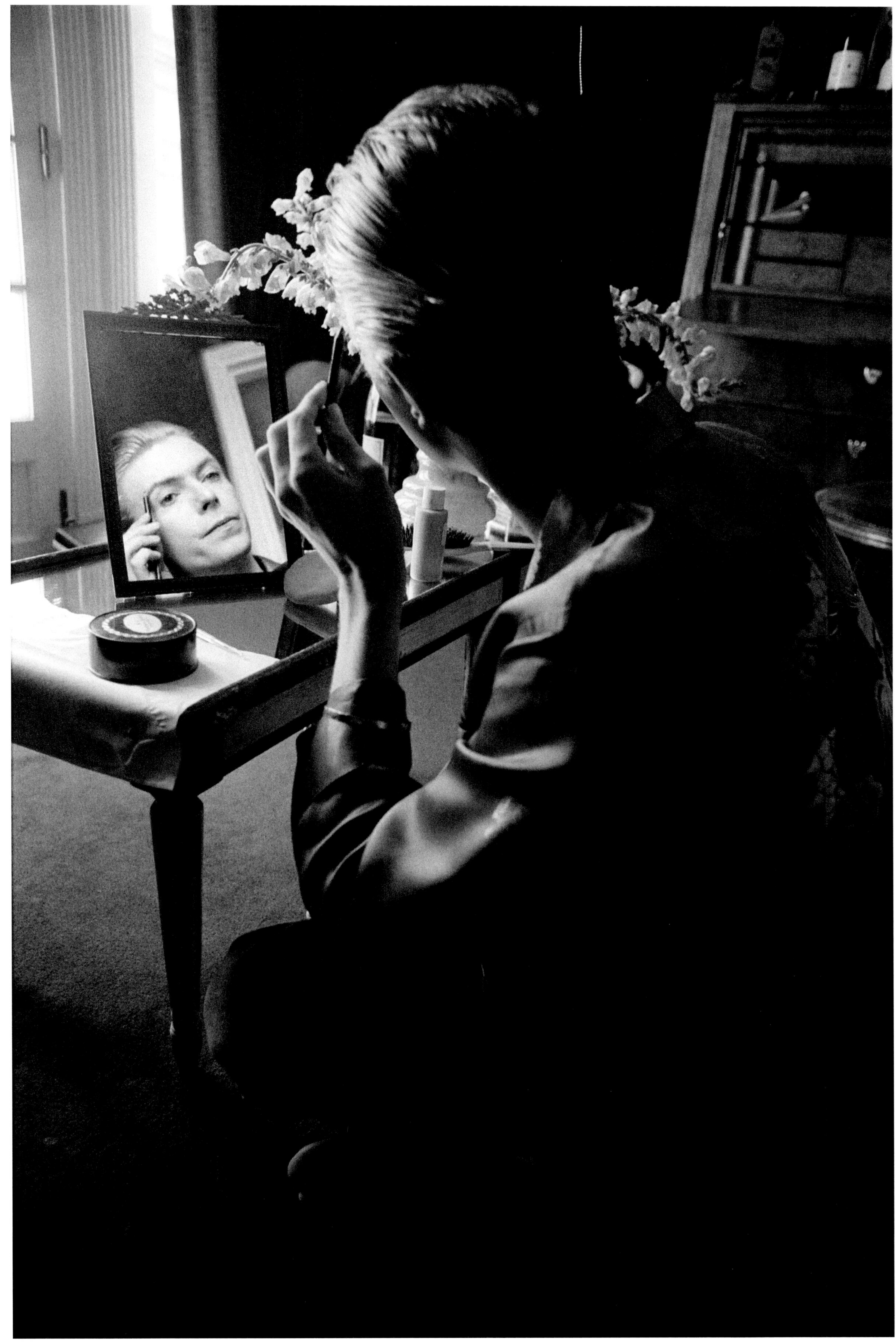

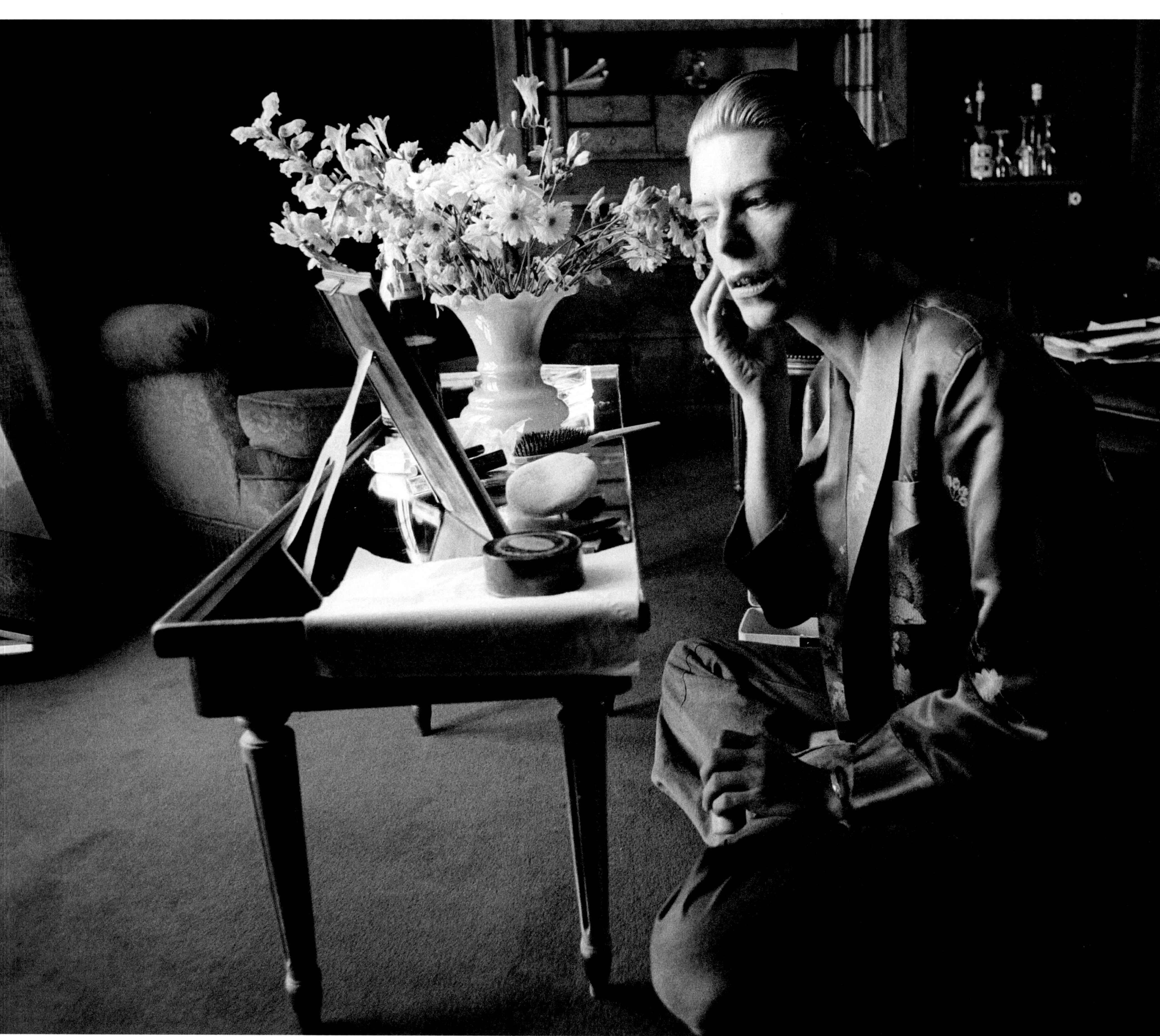

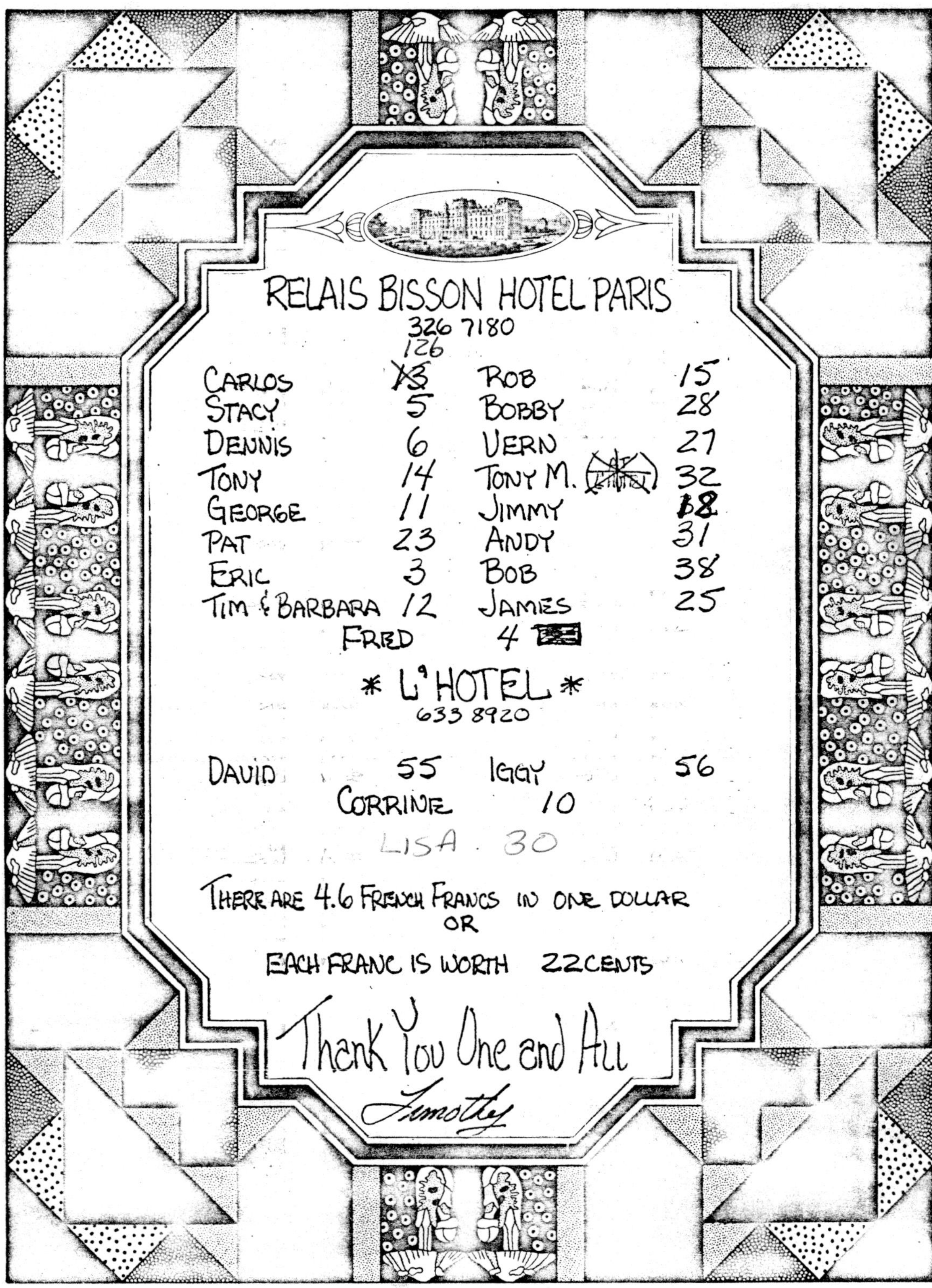

RELAIS BISSON HOTEL PARIS
326 7180
126

CARLOS	18	ROB	15
STACY	5	BOBBY	28
DENNIS	6	VERN	27
TONY	14	TONY M.	32
GEORGE	11	JIMMY	18
PAT	23	ANDY	31
ERIC	3	BOB	38
TIM & BARBARA	12	JAMES	25
	FRED	4	

* L'HOTEL *
633 8920

DAVID	55	IGGY	56
CORRINE	10		
LISA	30		

THERE ARE 4.6 FRENCH FRANCS IN ONE DOLLAR
OR
EACH FRANC IS WORTH 22 CENTS

Thank You One and All

Timothy

(Above) Assistant tour manager, Tim De-Witte, prepared room assignment sheets for each city on the tour. Often times he would find unique stationary for each separate hotel. The above example is the room assignment sheet for L'Hotel in Paris, 1976.
(Left) David finds time to prepare his make up during a rare quiet moment in his suite at L'Hotel in Paris.

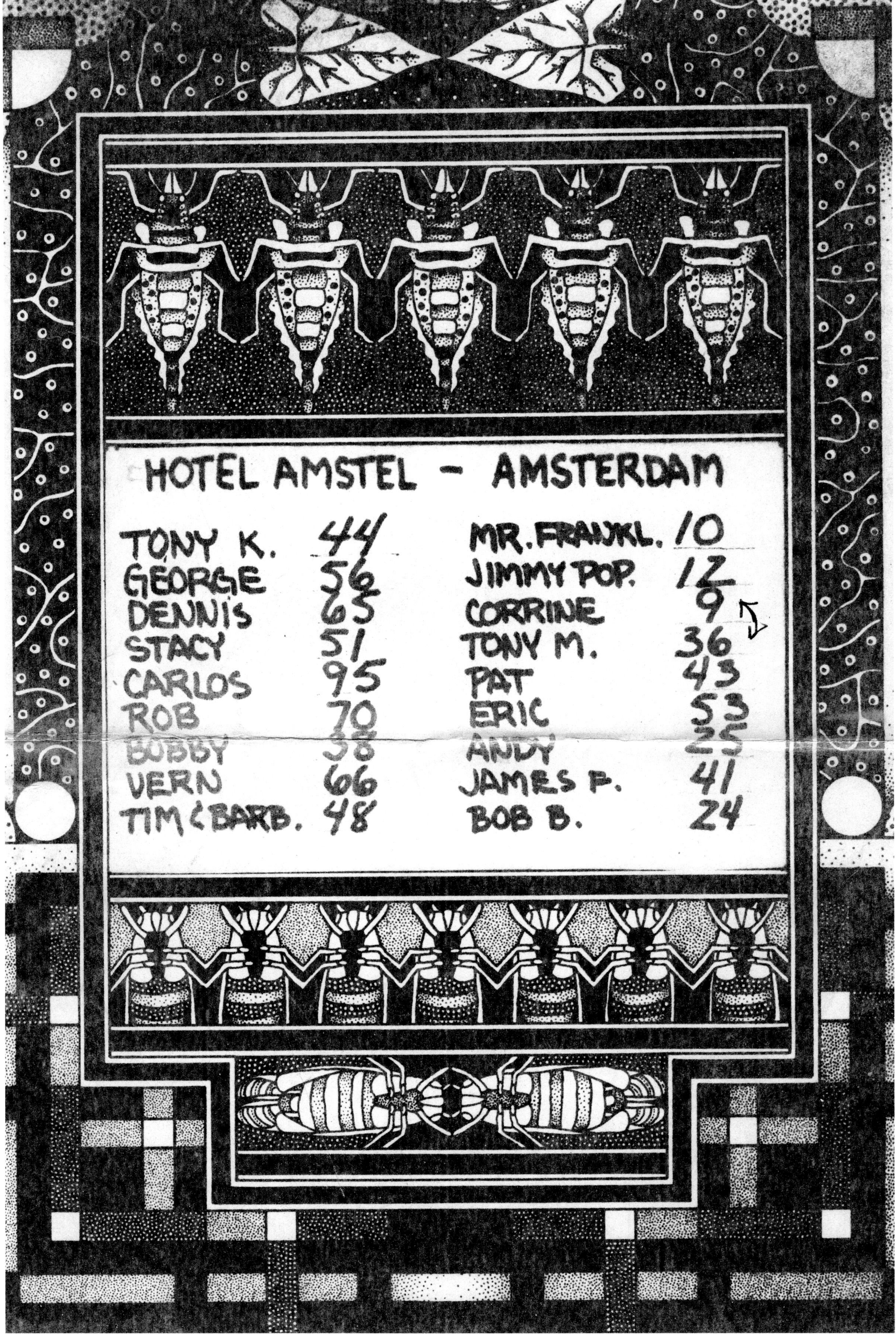
HOTEL AMSTEL - AMSTERDAM
TONY K.   44   MR. FRANKL.   10
GEORGE   56   JIMMY POP.   12
DENNIS   65   CORRINE   9
STACY   51   TONY M.   36
CARLOS   95   PAT   43
ROB   70   ERIC   53
BOBBY   38   ANDY   25
VERN   66   JAMES P.   41
TIM & BARB.   48   BOB B.   24

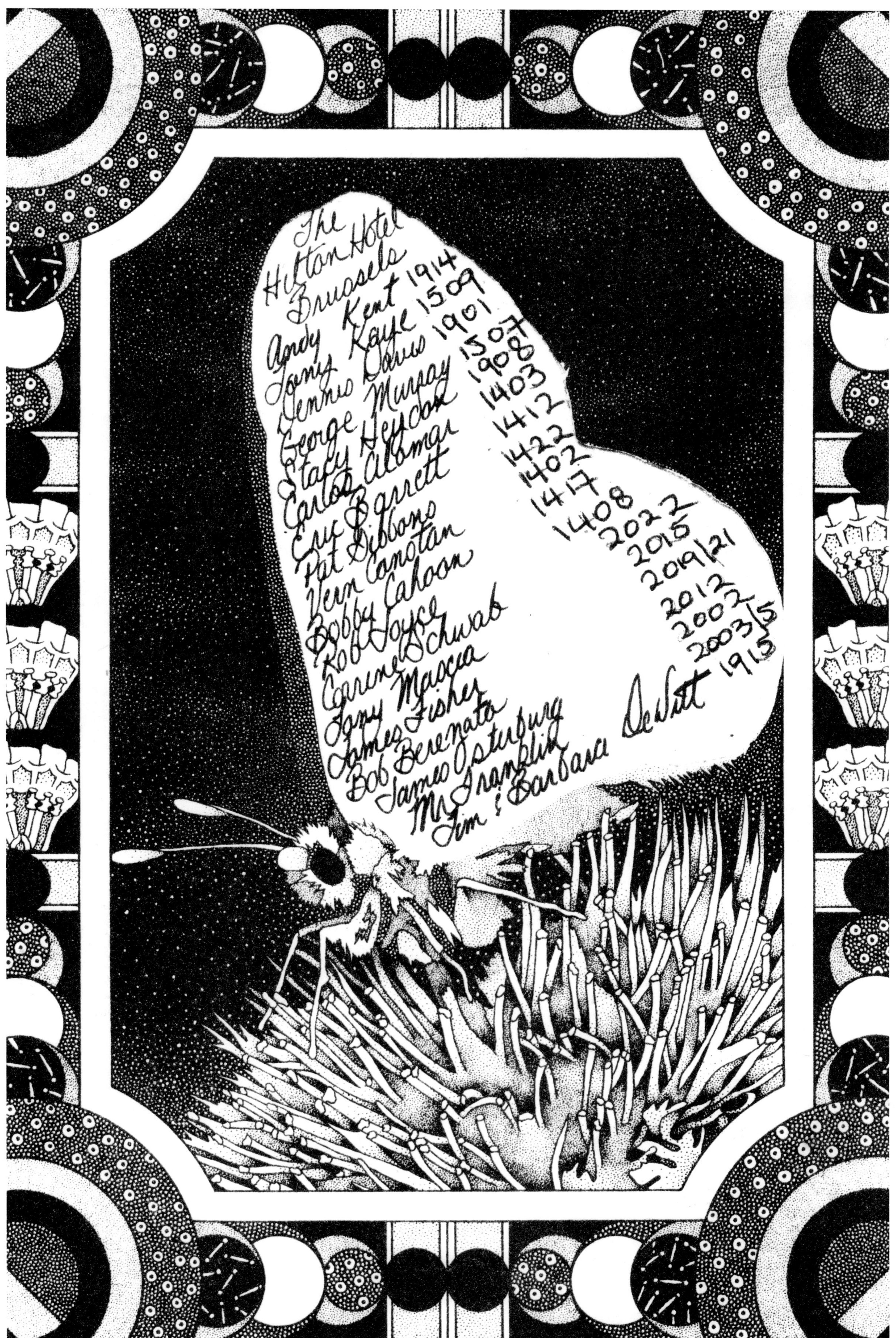

The Hilton Hotel
Brussels
Andy Kent 1914
Jamie Kaye 1509
Dennis Davis 1901
George Murray 1507
Stacy Heycox 1908
Carlos Alomar 1403
Eric Barrett 1412
Pat Gibbons 1422
Vern Canotan 1402
Bobby Cahoon 1417
Rob Joyce 1408
Carine Schwab 2022
Tony Mascia 2015
James Fisher 209/21
Bob Berenato 2012
James Ostburg 2002
My Franklin 2003/5
Jim & Barbara DeWitt 1915

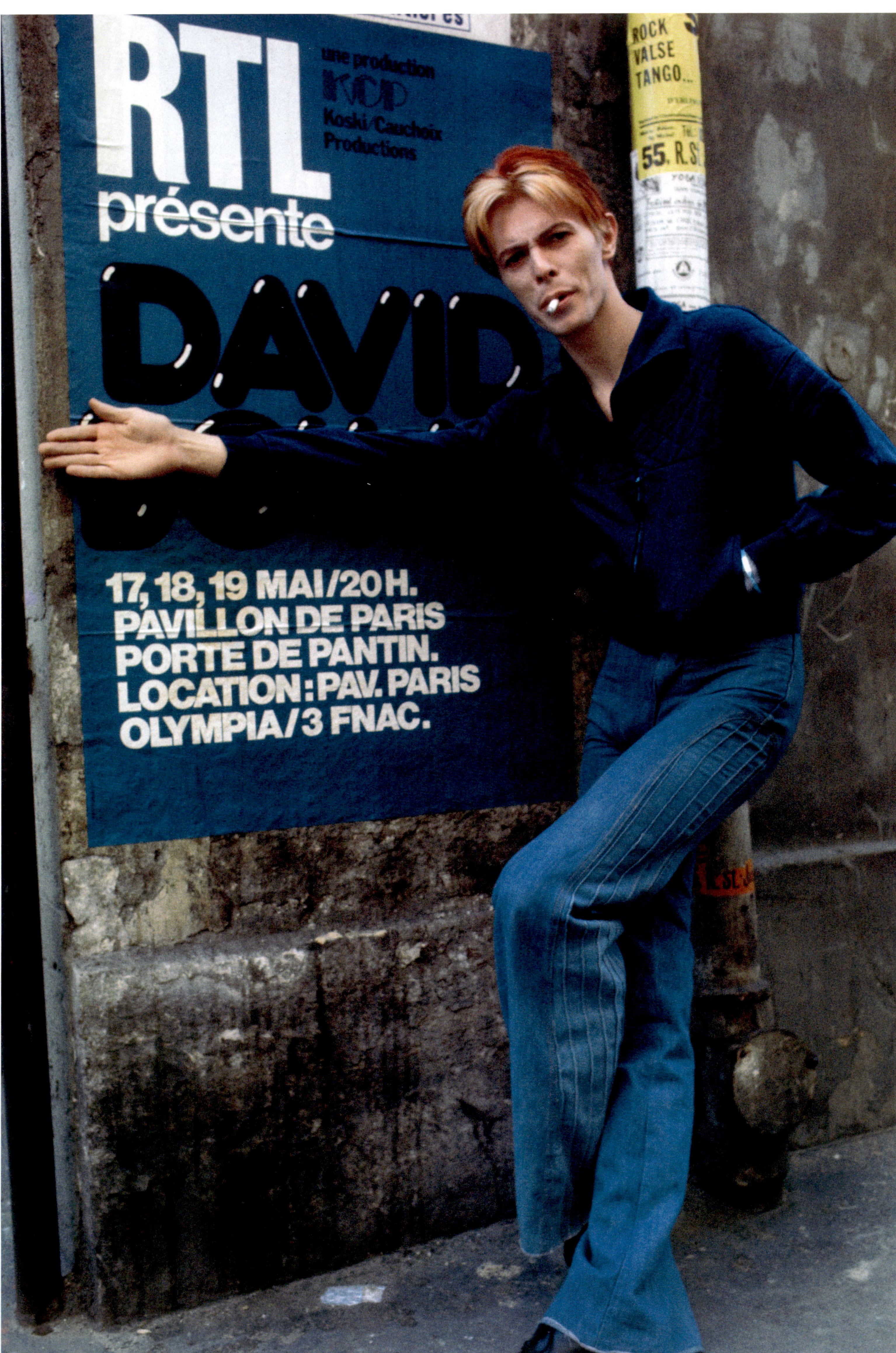

RTL
une production
Koski/Cauchoix
Productions
présente
DAVID
17, 18, 19 MAI/20 H.
PAVILLON DE PARIS
PORTE DE PANTIN.
LOCATION : PAV. PARIS
OLYMPIA/3 FNAC.
ROCK
VALSE
TANGO...
55, R.ST

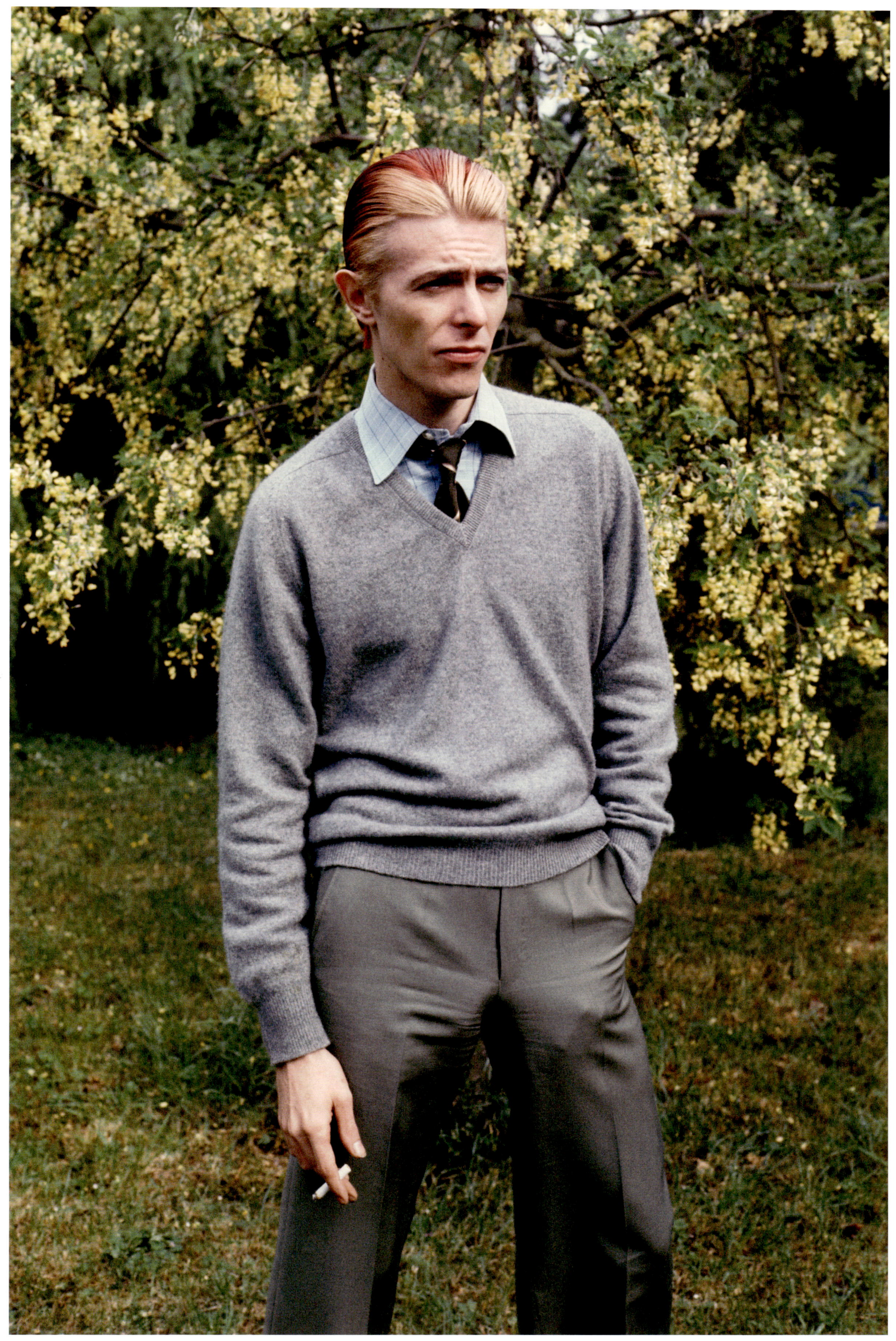

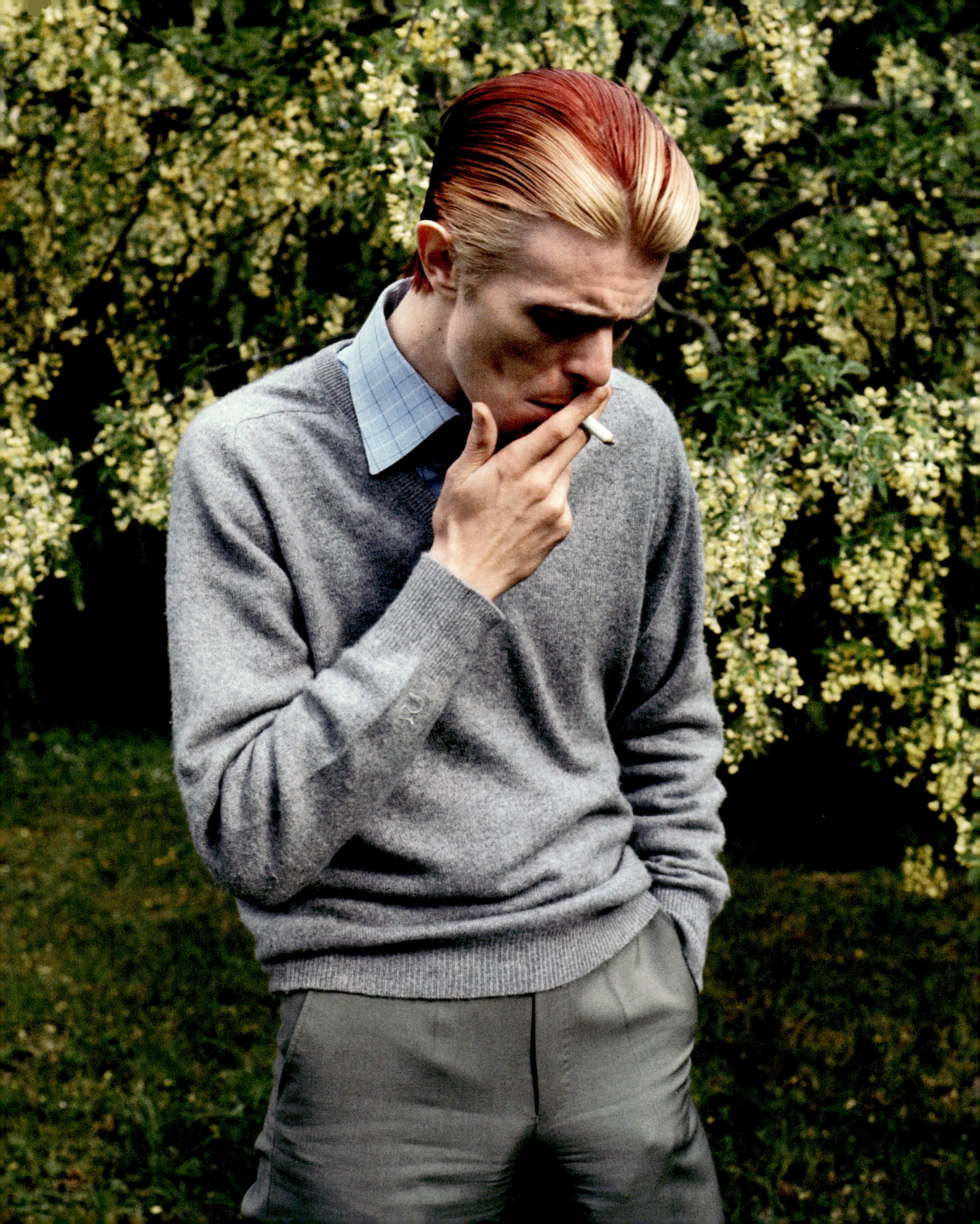

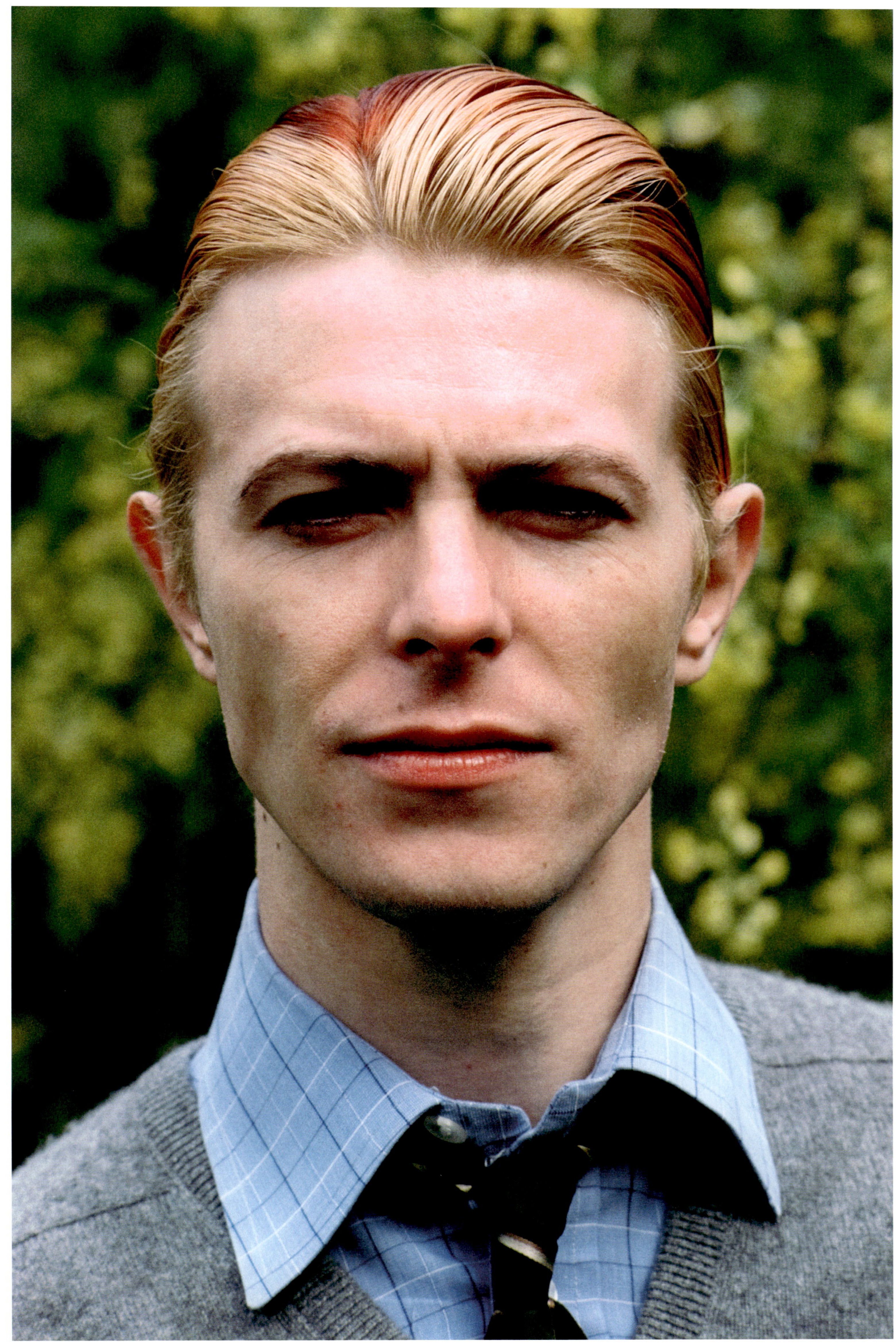

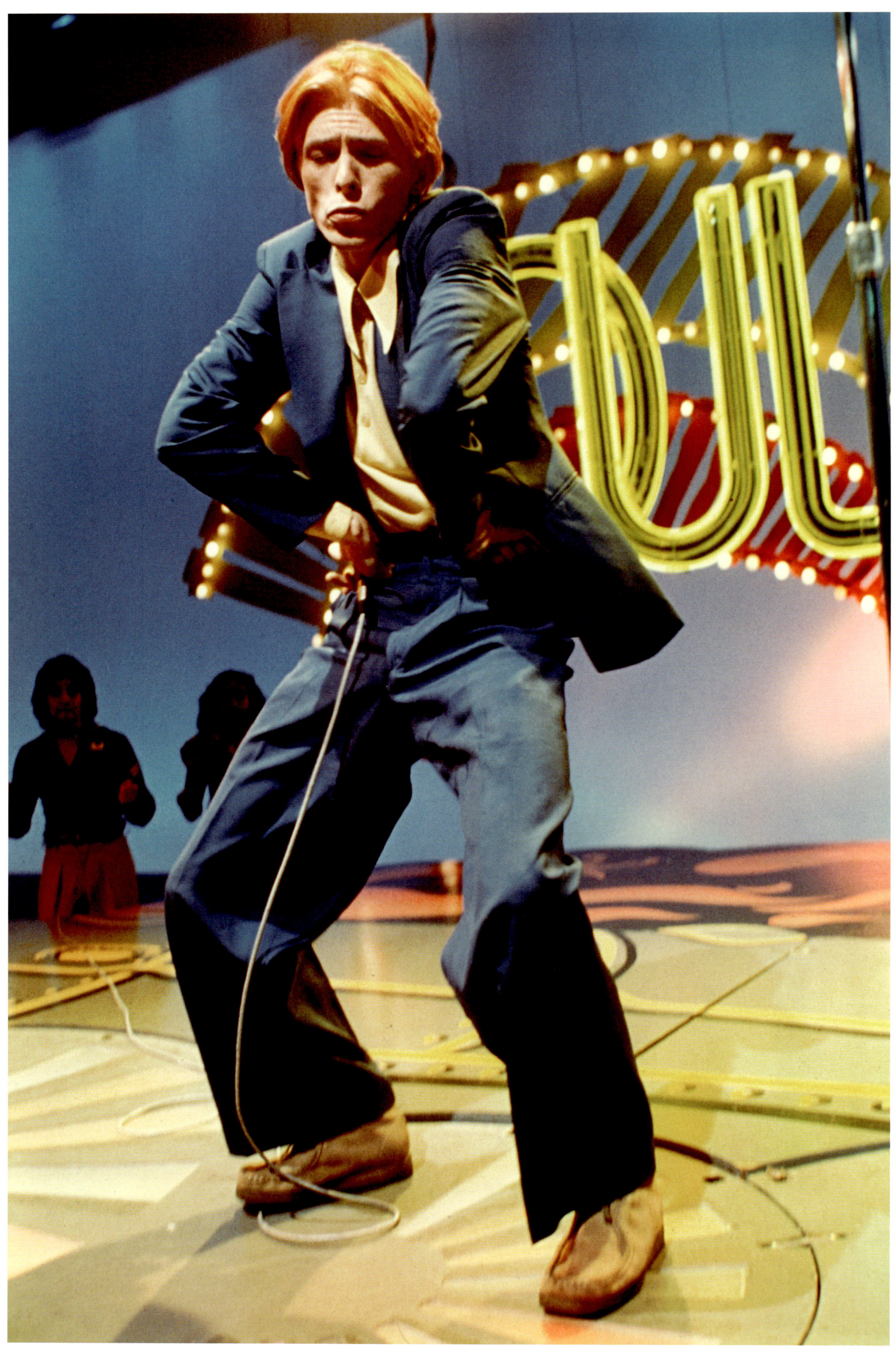

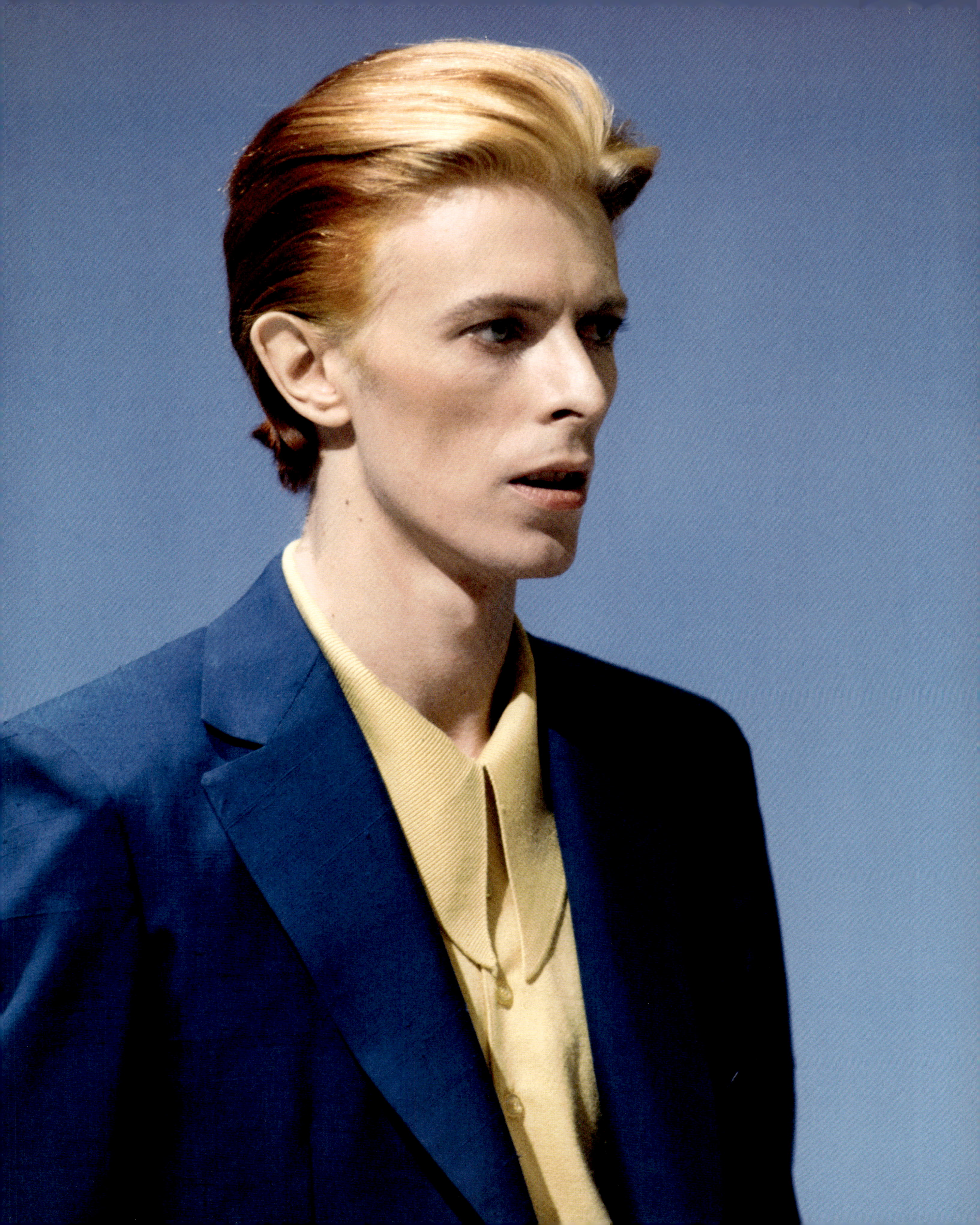

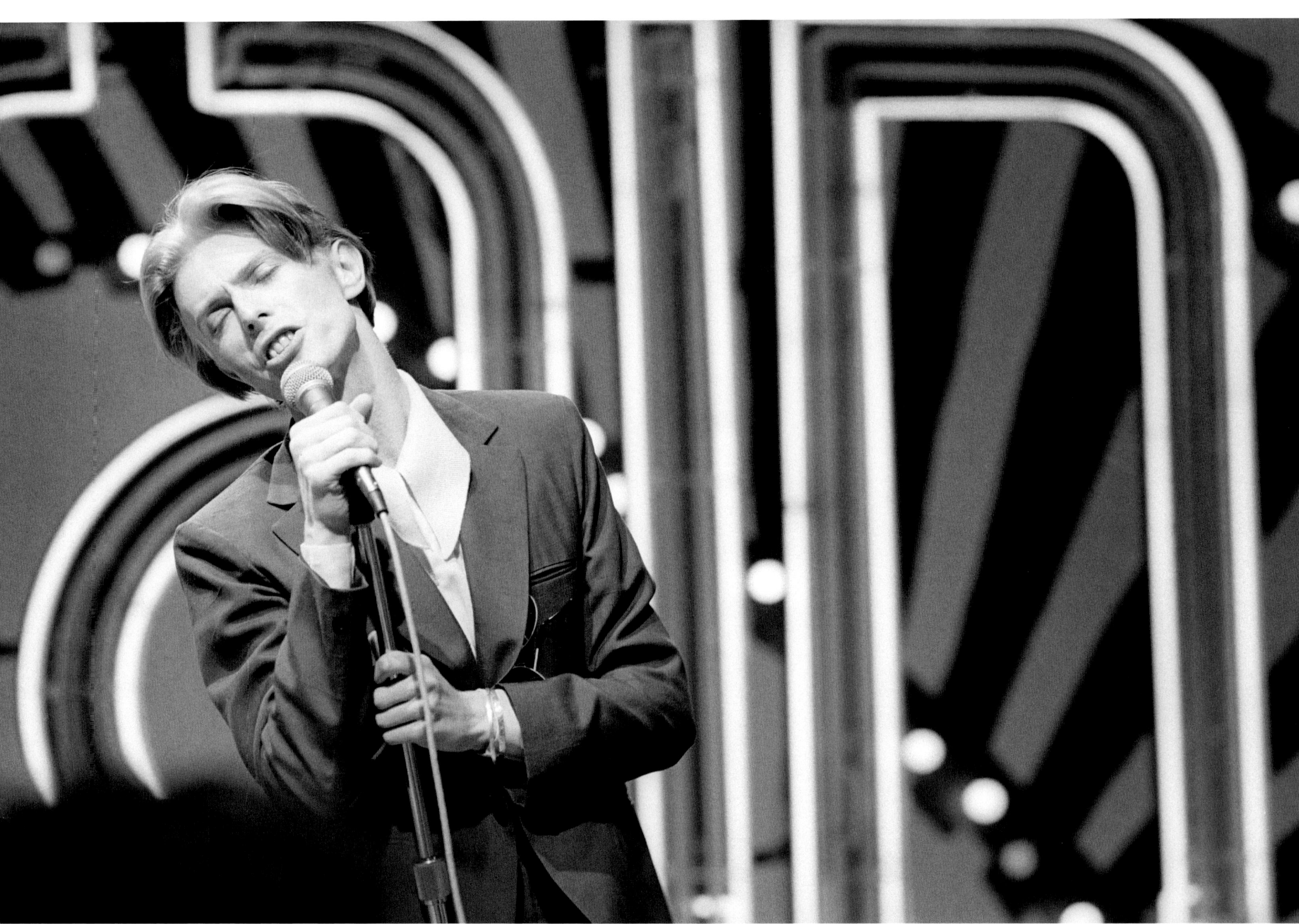

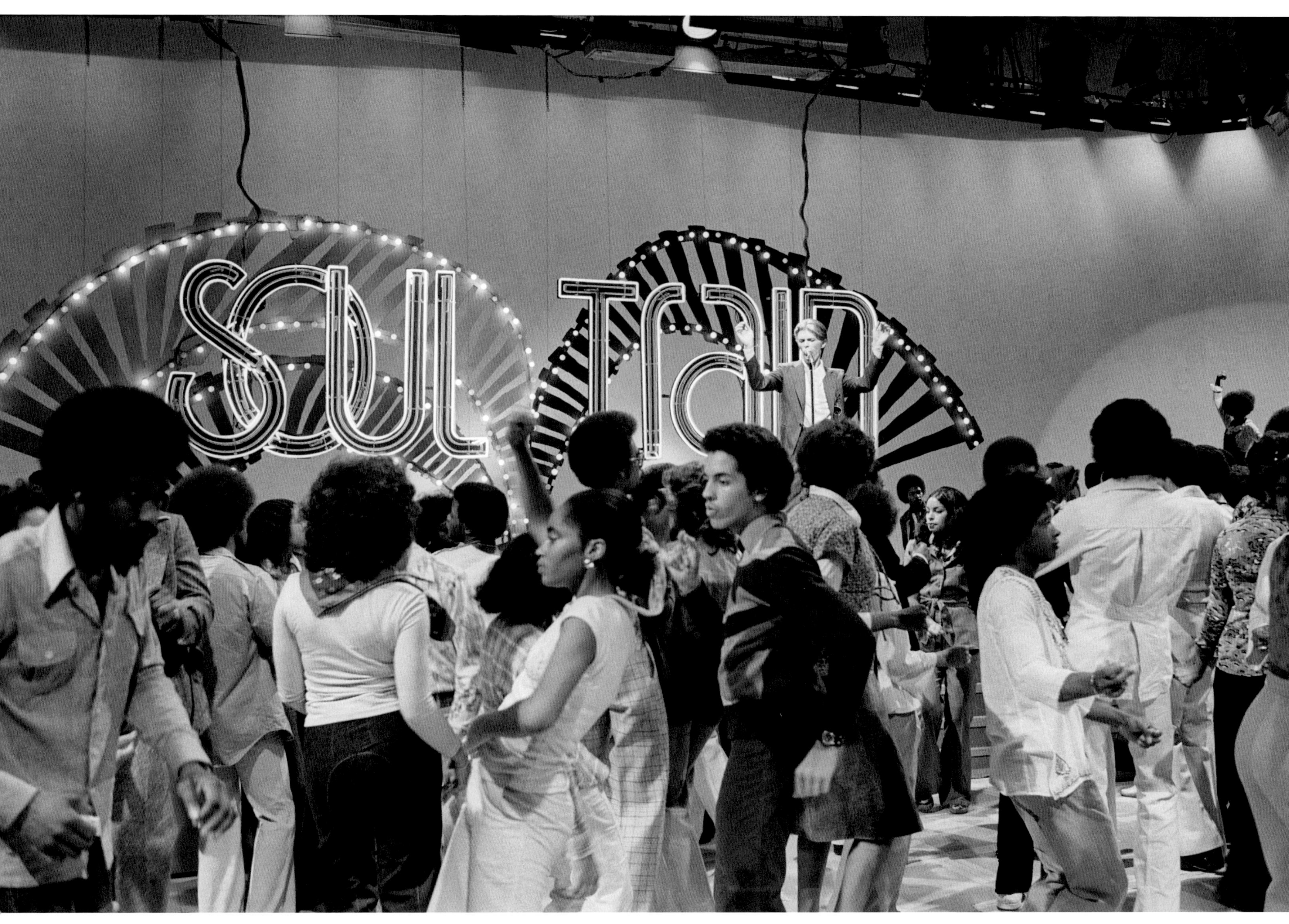

(Previous spread and above) In 1975 David was, at the time, one of very few white artists invited to perform on the legendary television dance show, *Soul Train*. He performed "Golden Years" in support of his *Station to Station* album.
(Next spread) David was interviewed by *Playboy* in Los Angeles in 1976.

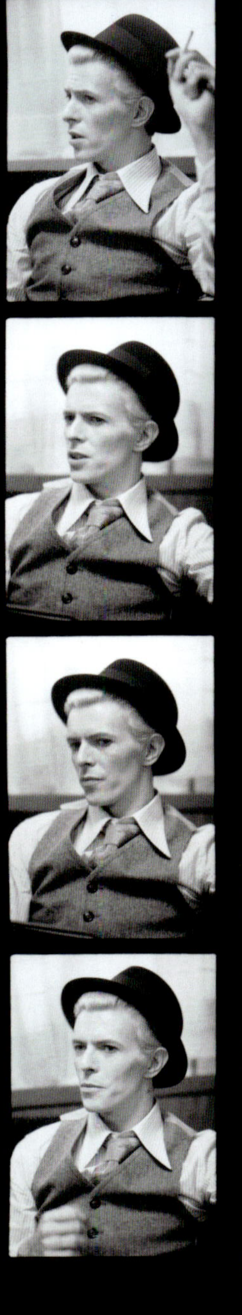
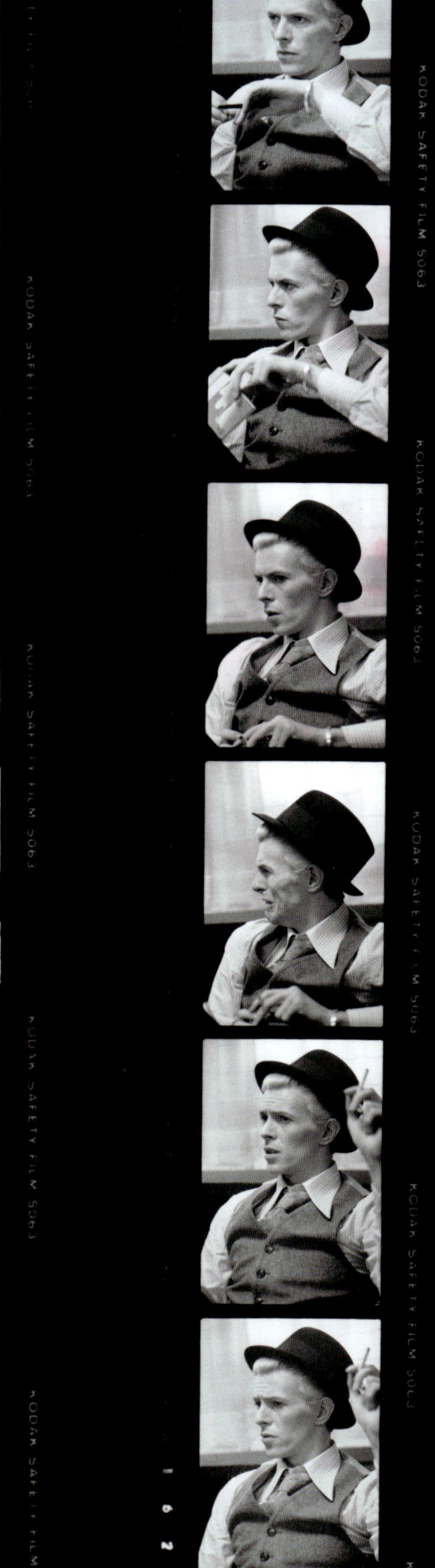
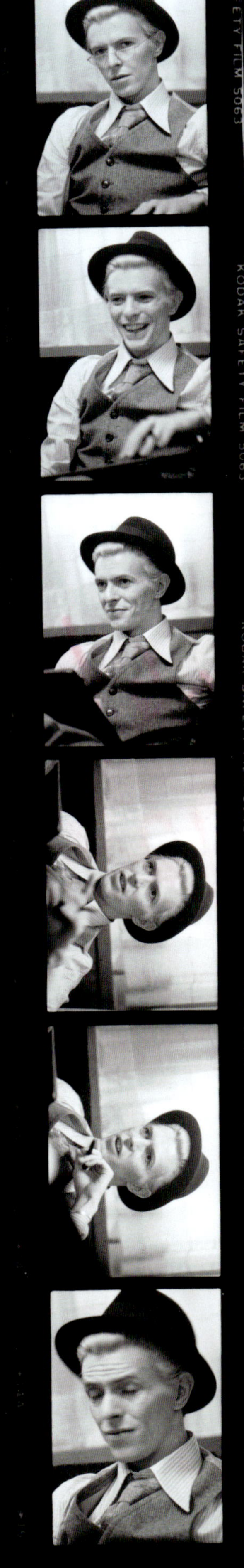
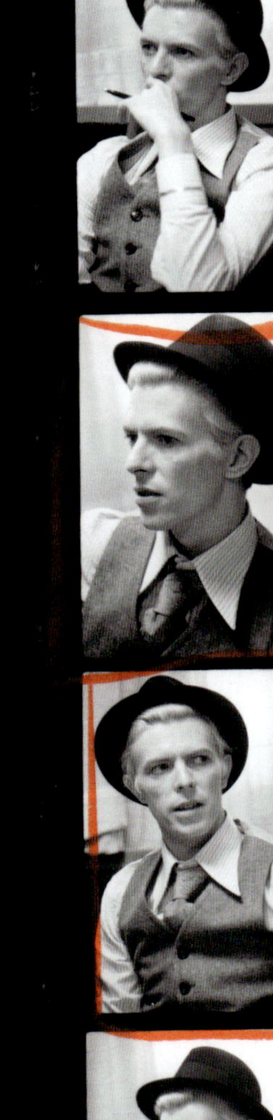

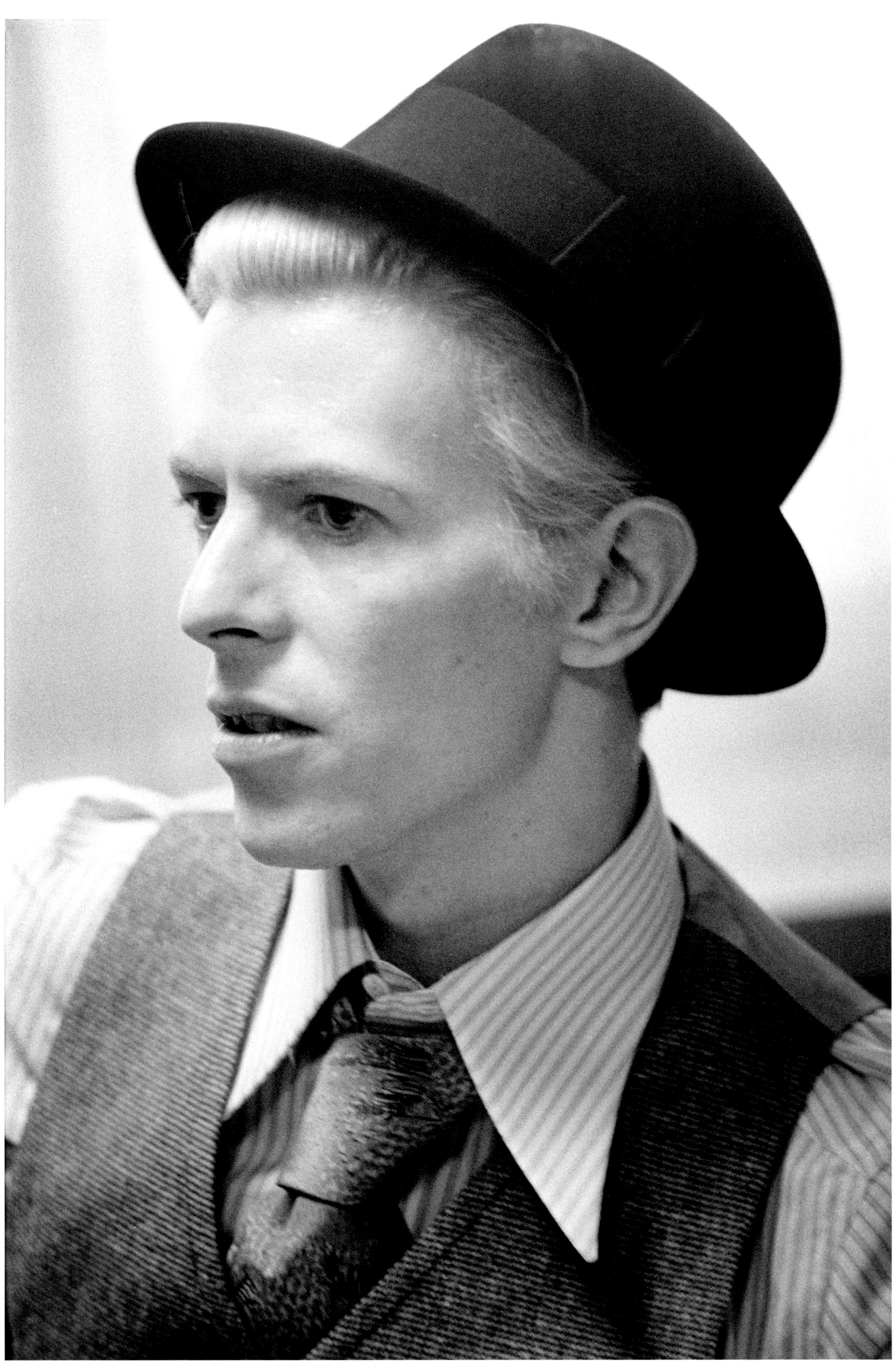

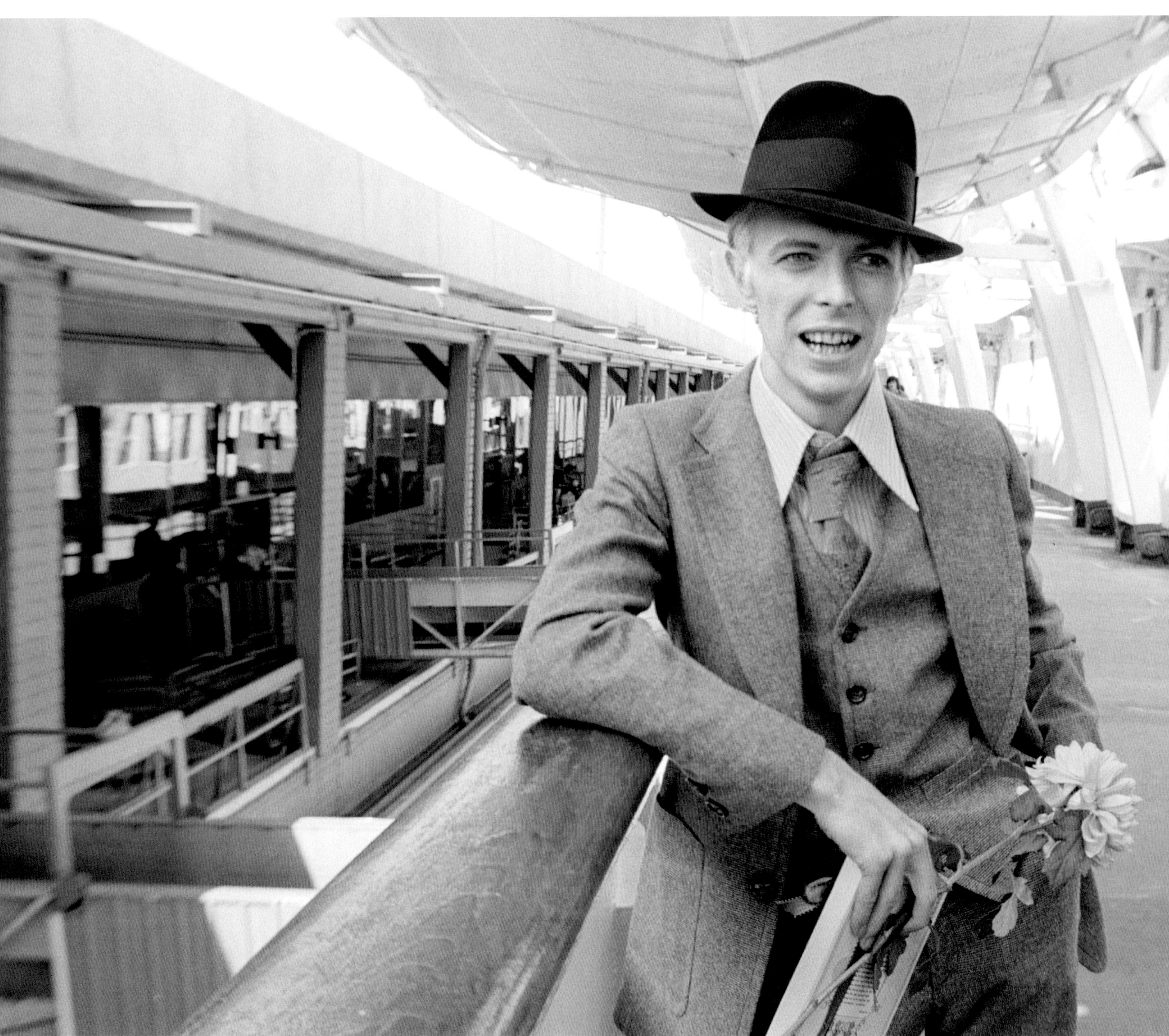

David prepares to take a cruise aboard the SS Leonardo Da Vinci from New York to London in 1976. Accompanying him on the journey was his assistant, Coco.

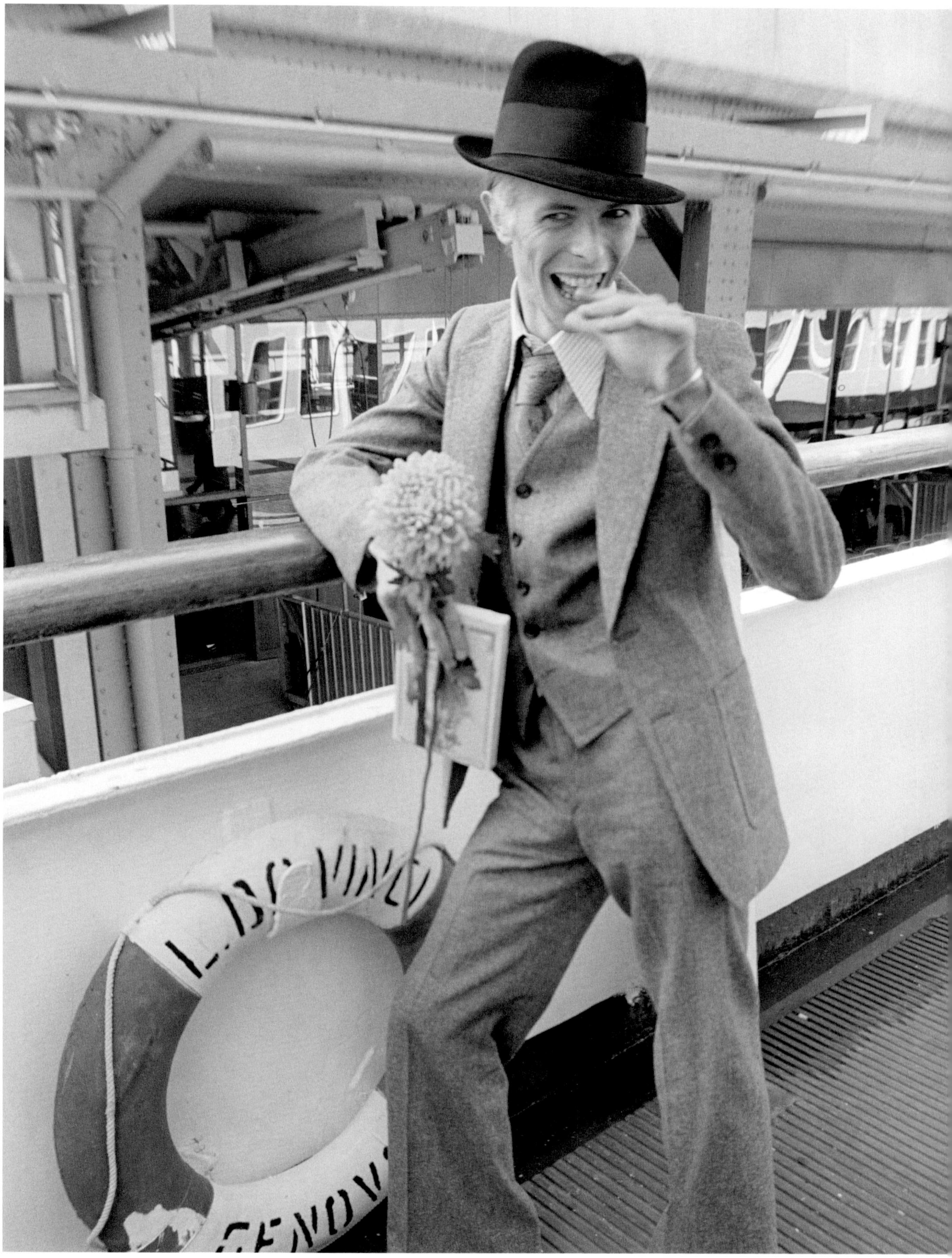

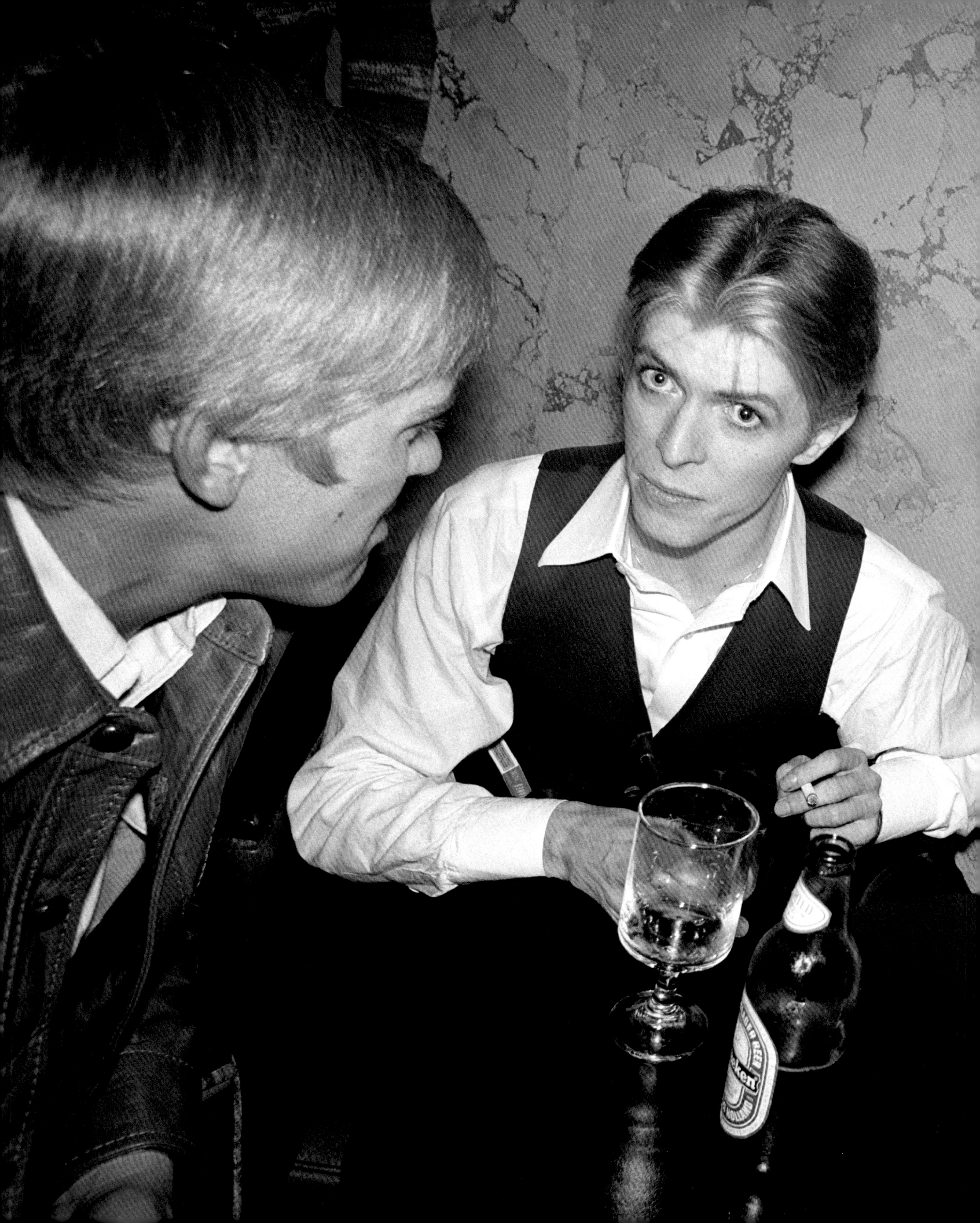

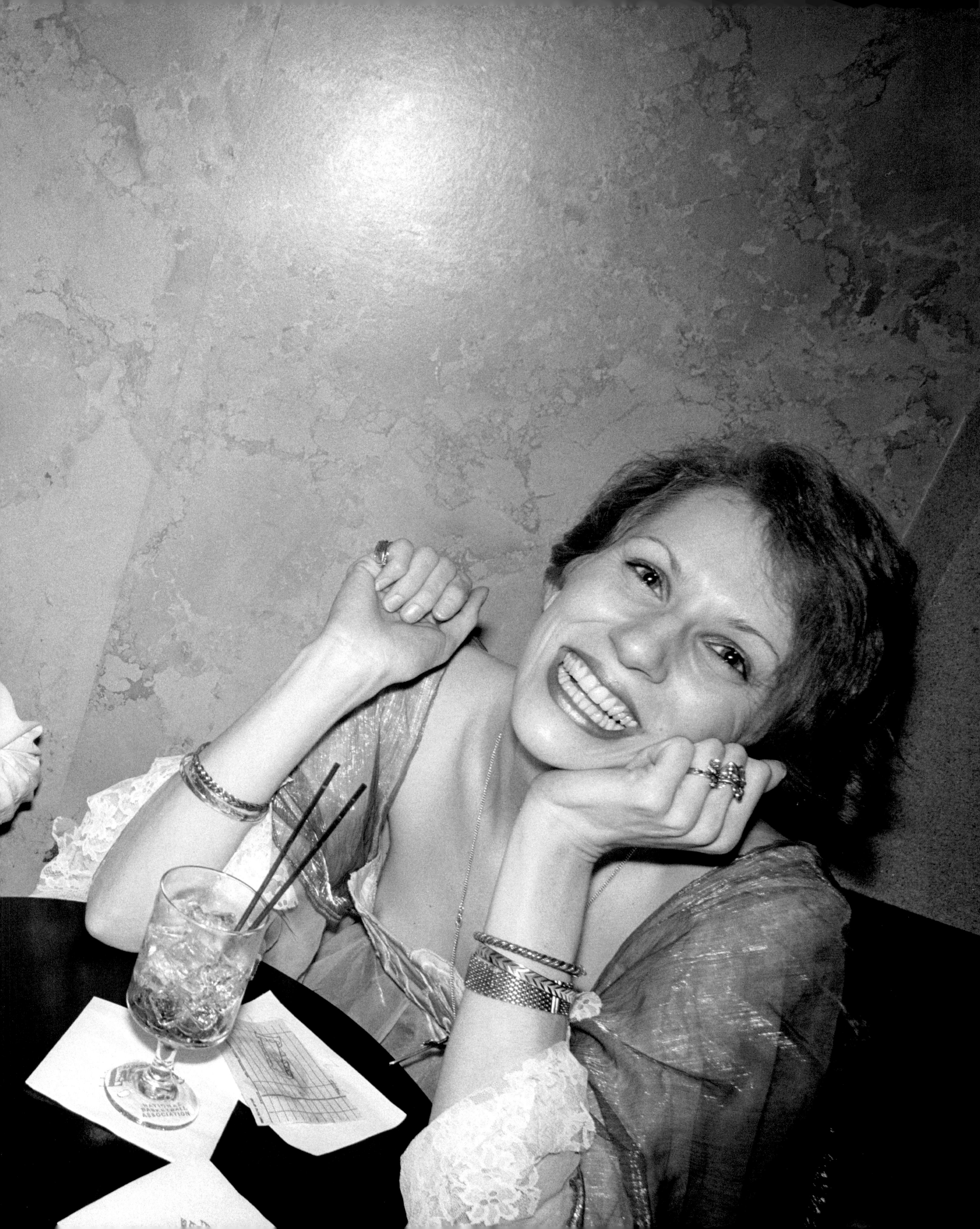

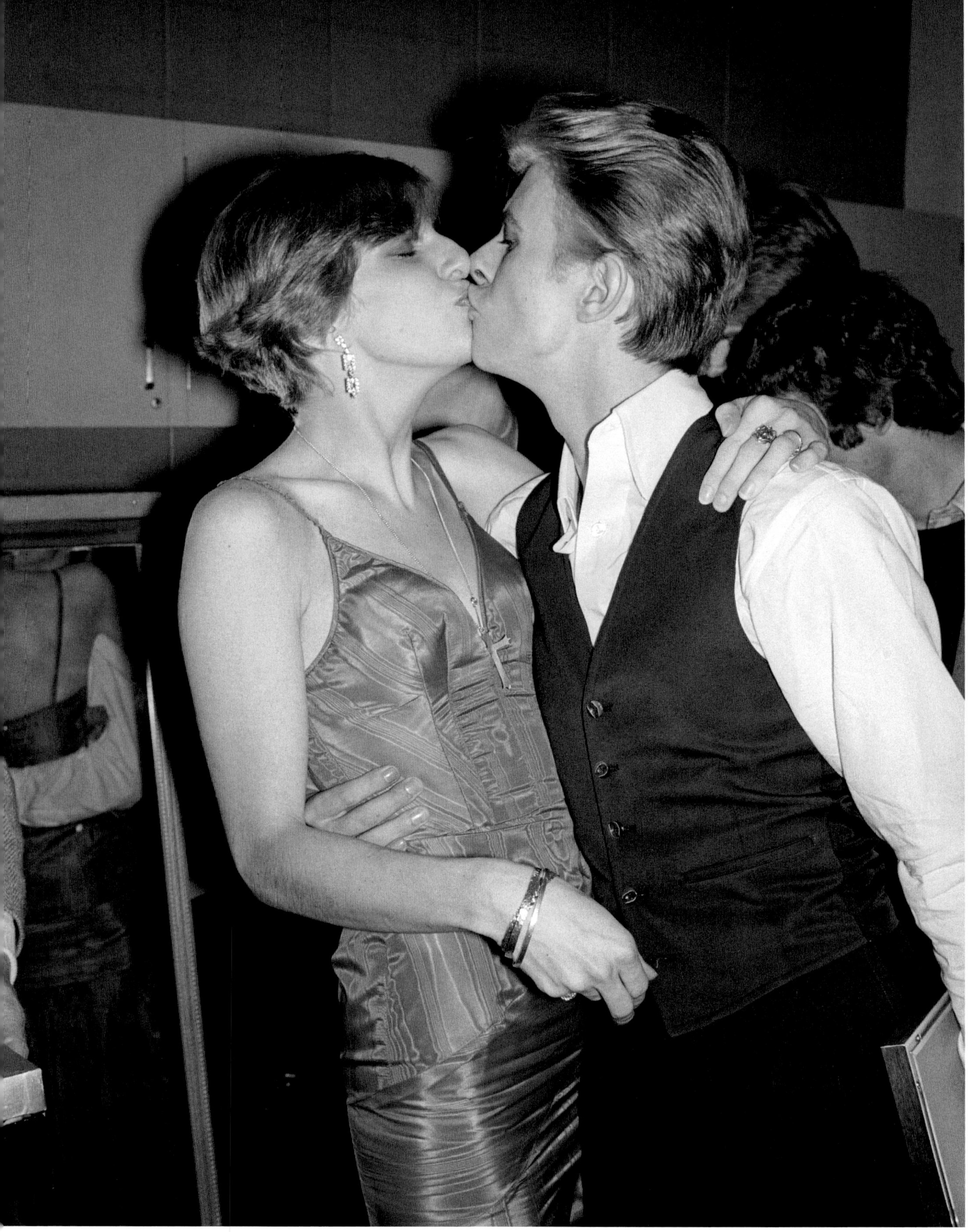

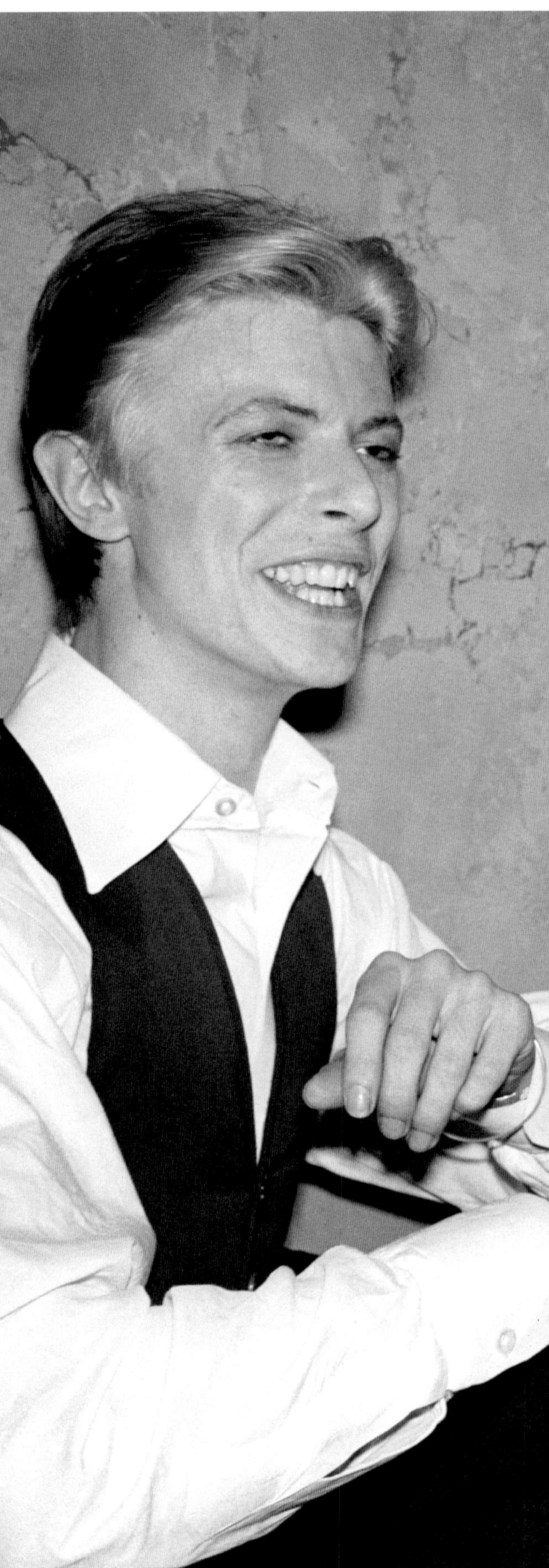

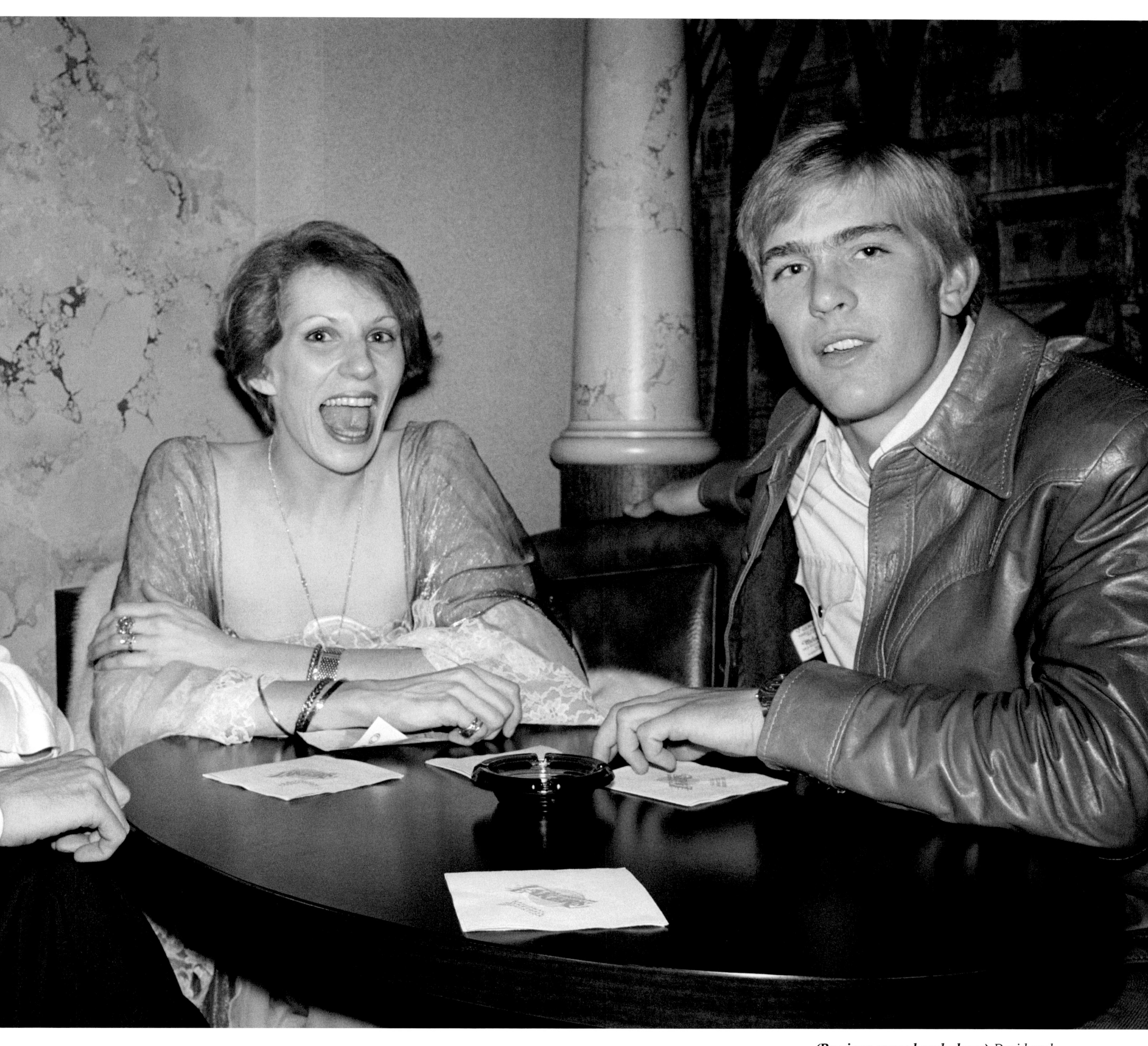

(Previous spread and above) David and his wife, Angela, with President Gerald Ford's son, Steven, at a party in Los Angeles celebrating "Fame" being certified a gold record.

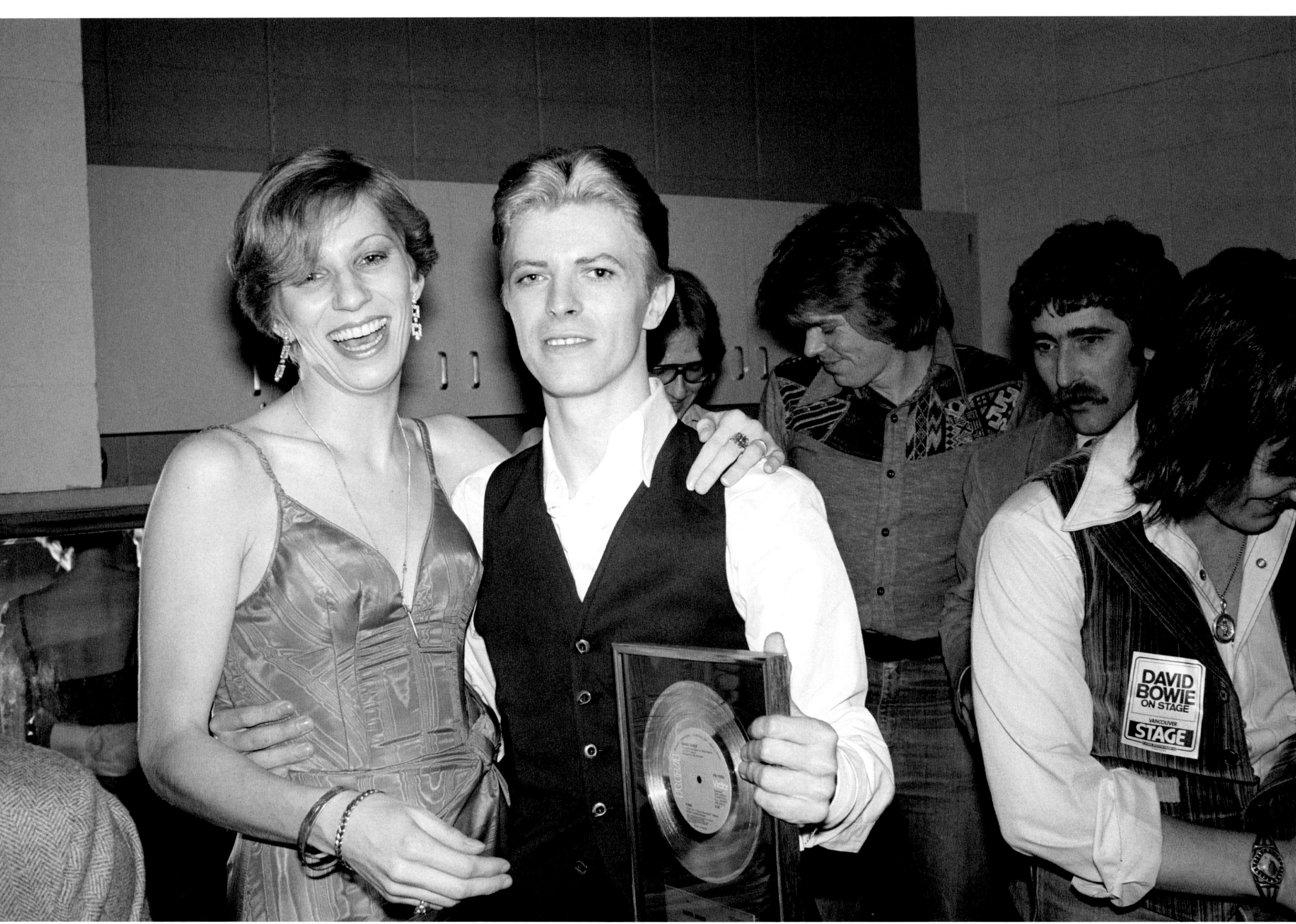

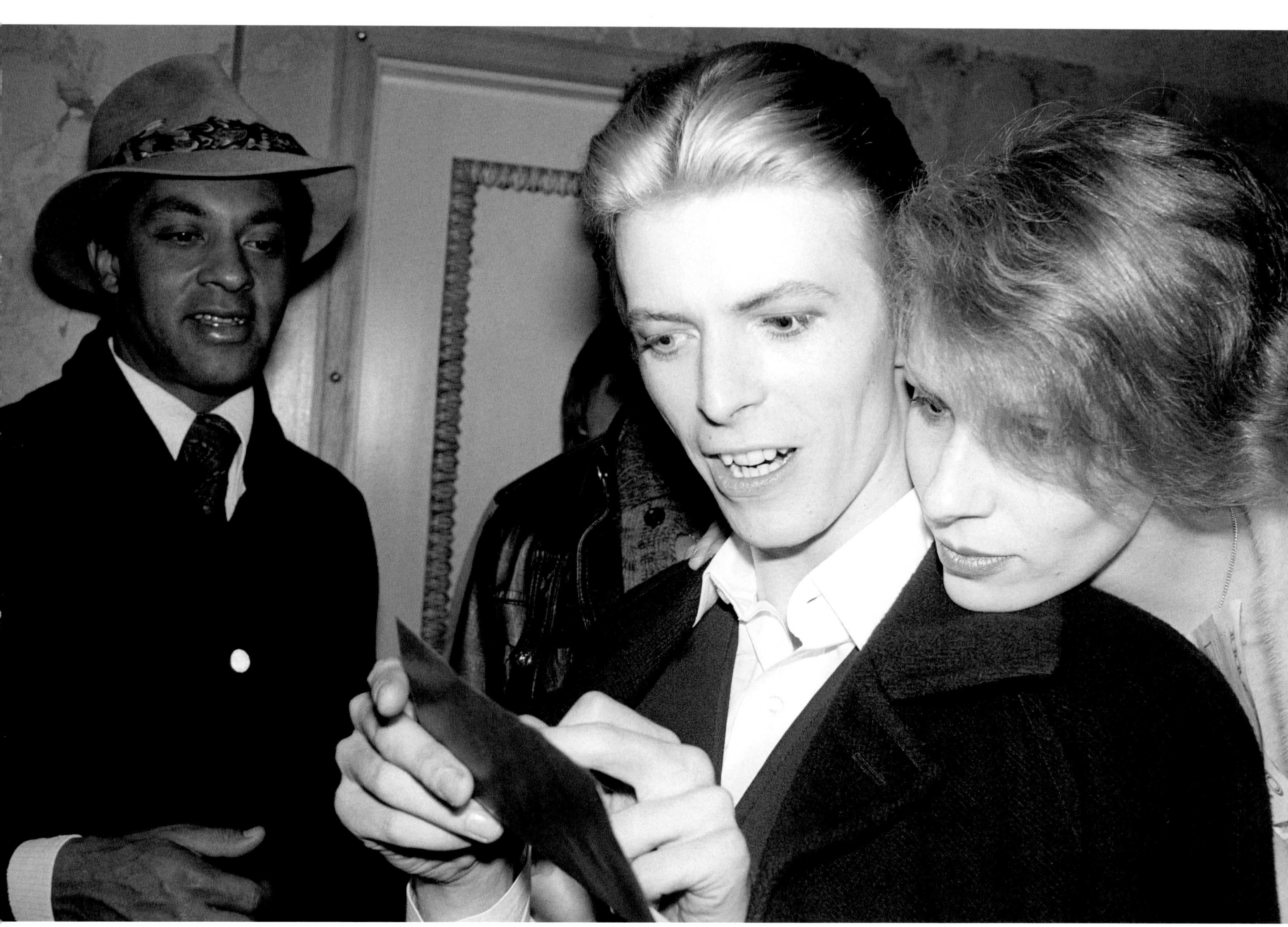

(Above and left) David and Angela together at a party celebrating "Fame" being certified a gold record.

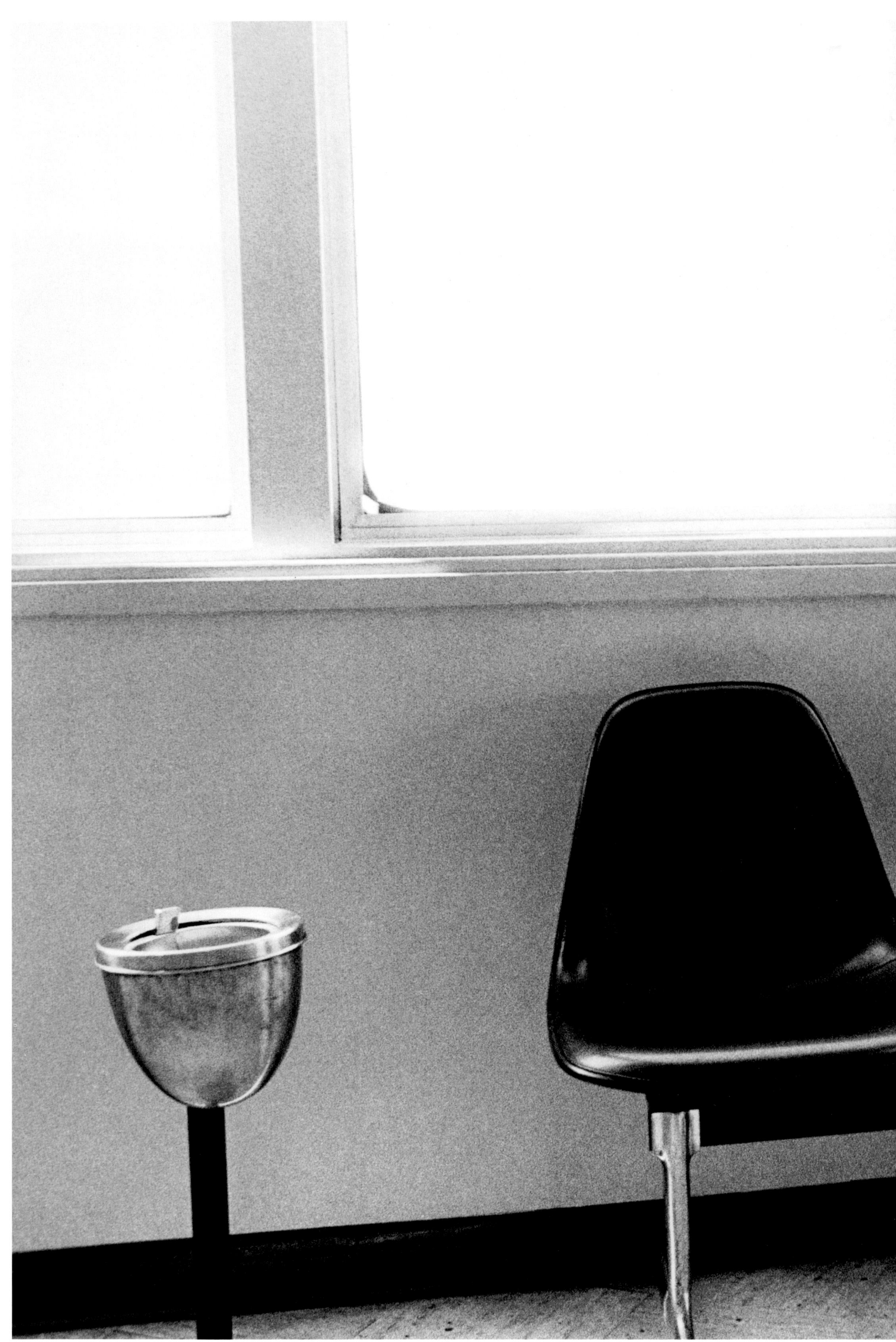

Five year old Zowie (Duncan Jones) plays with his action figure in an airport lounge between stops on the Isolar tour.

"I think Zowie's a survivor. He's very definitely an independent person, of his own choosing, it seems." said David to Rolling Stone in 1976.

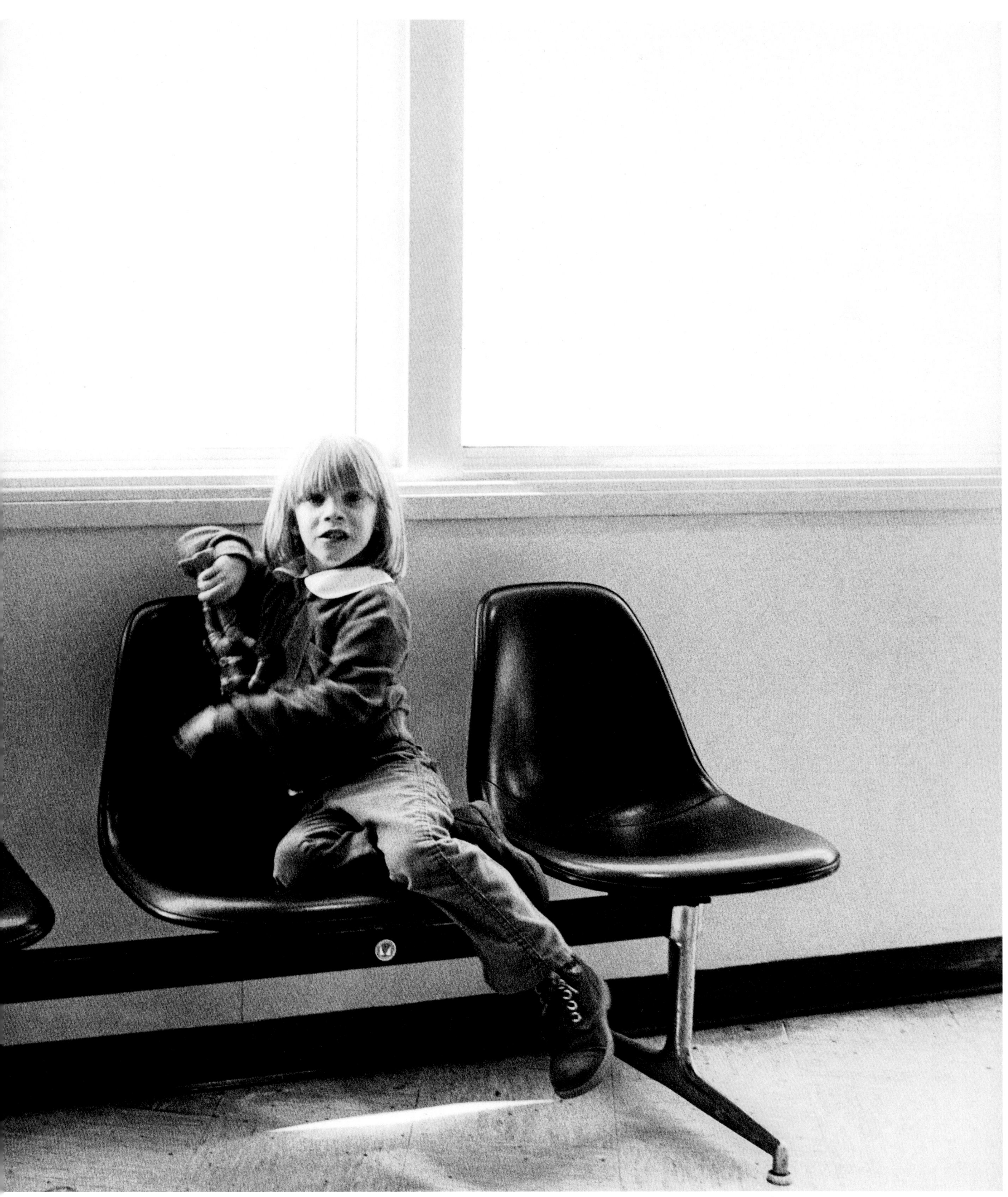

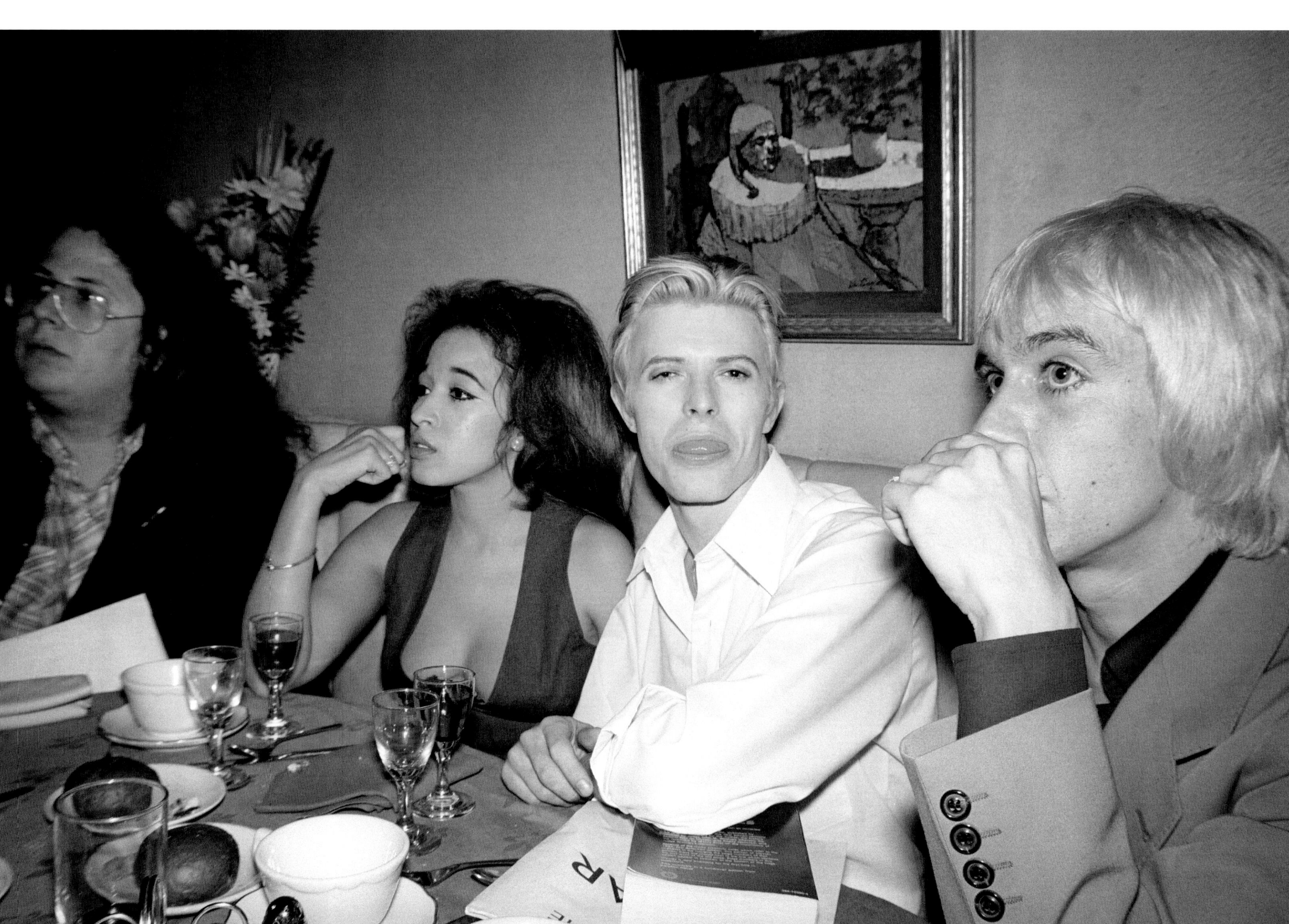

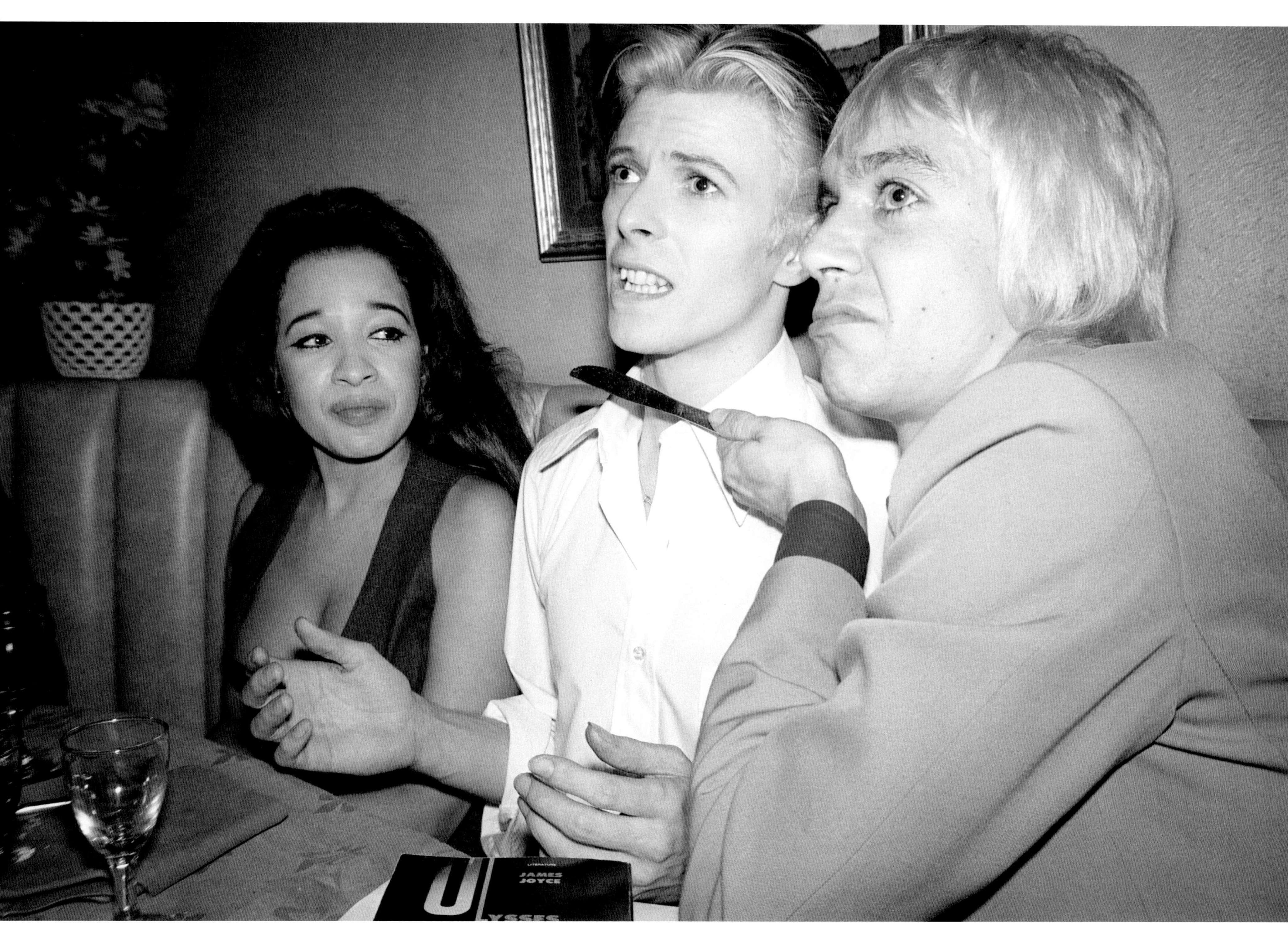

(Left) David with Iggy, Ronnie Spector, and Mark Volman of the Turtles at a party backstage following David's performance at Madison Square Garden in New York.
(Above) Iggy jokingly threatens to cut David's throat as Ronnie Spector looks on.

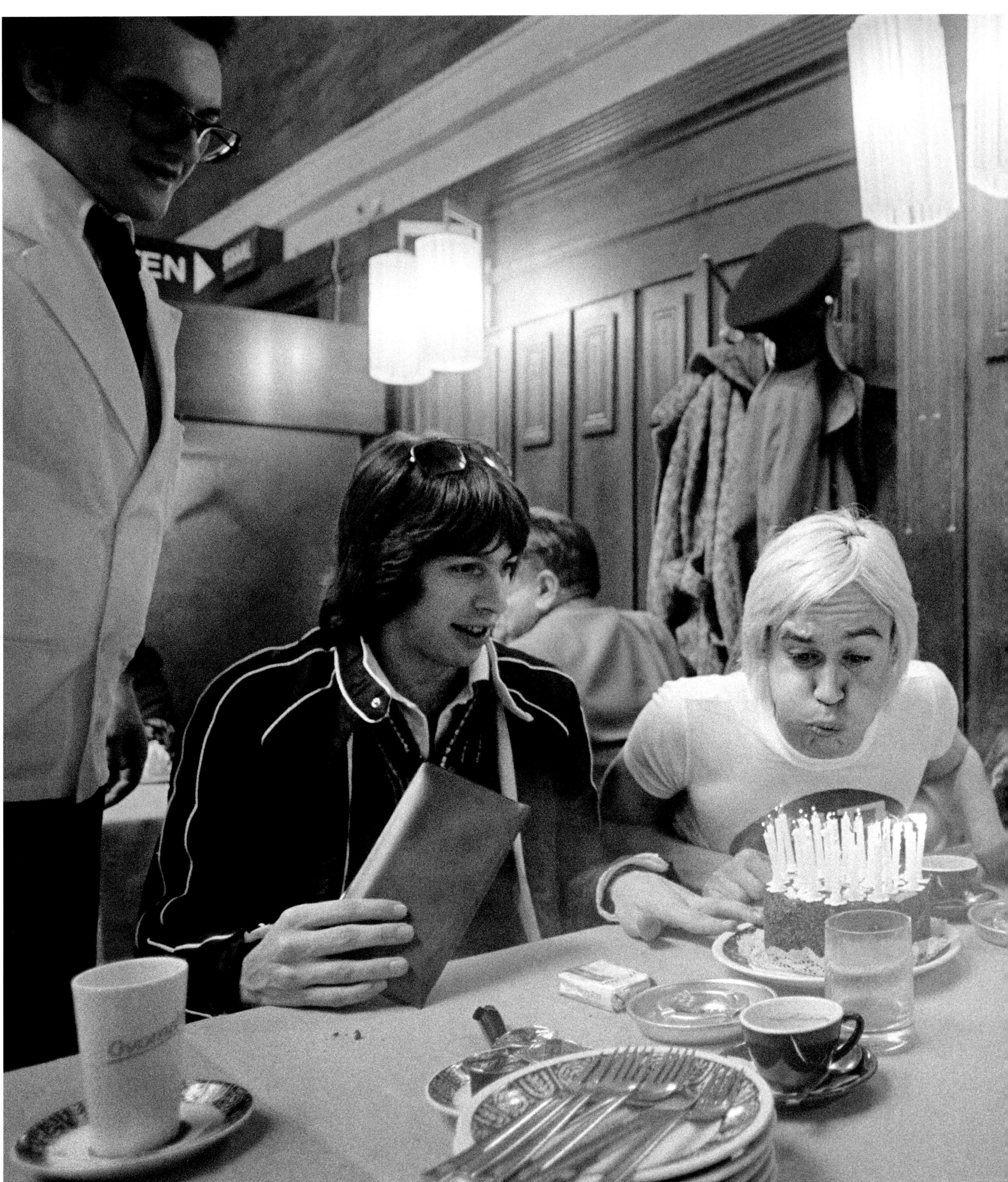

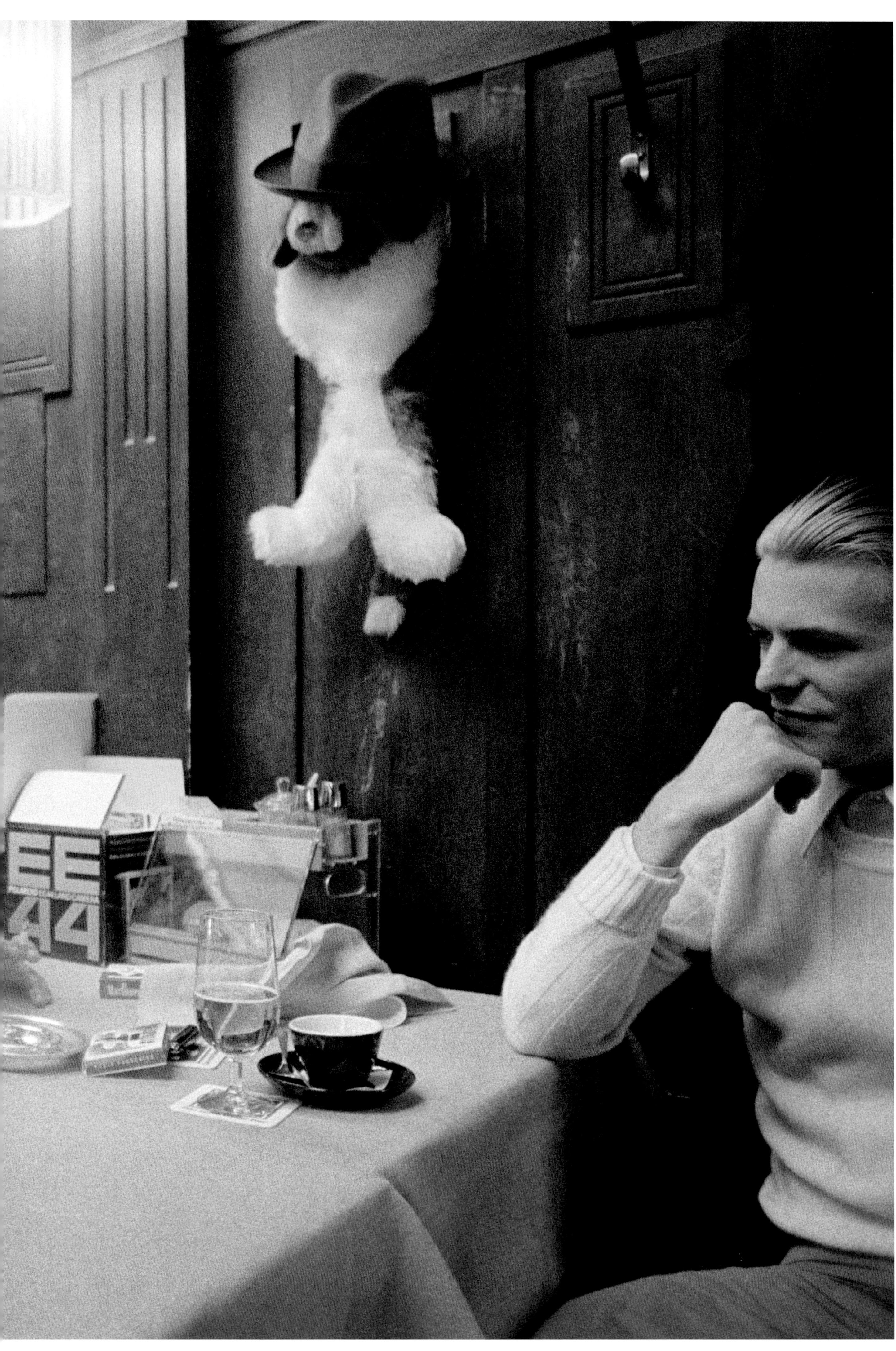

Iggy blows out the candels on his birthday cake as David and Pat Gibbons look on at a restaurant in the Basel, Switzerland train depot prior to departing for the Soviet Union.

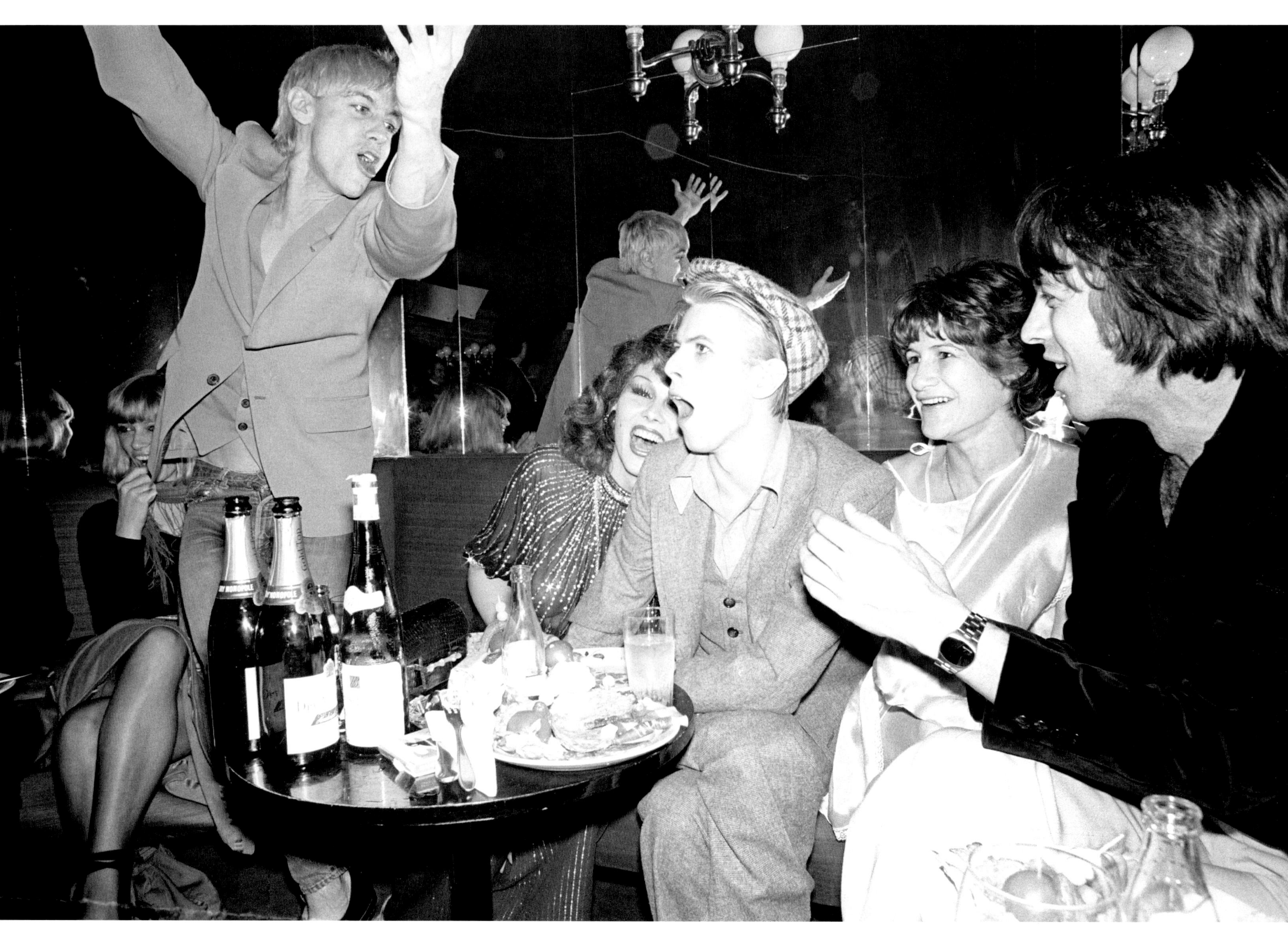

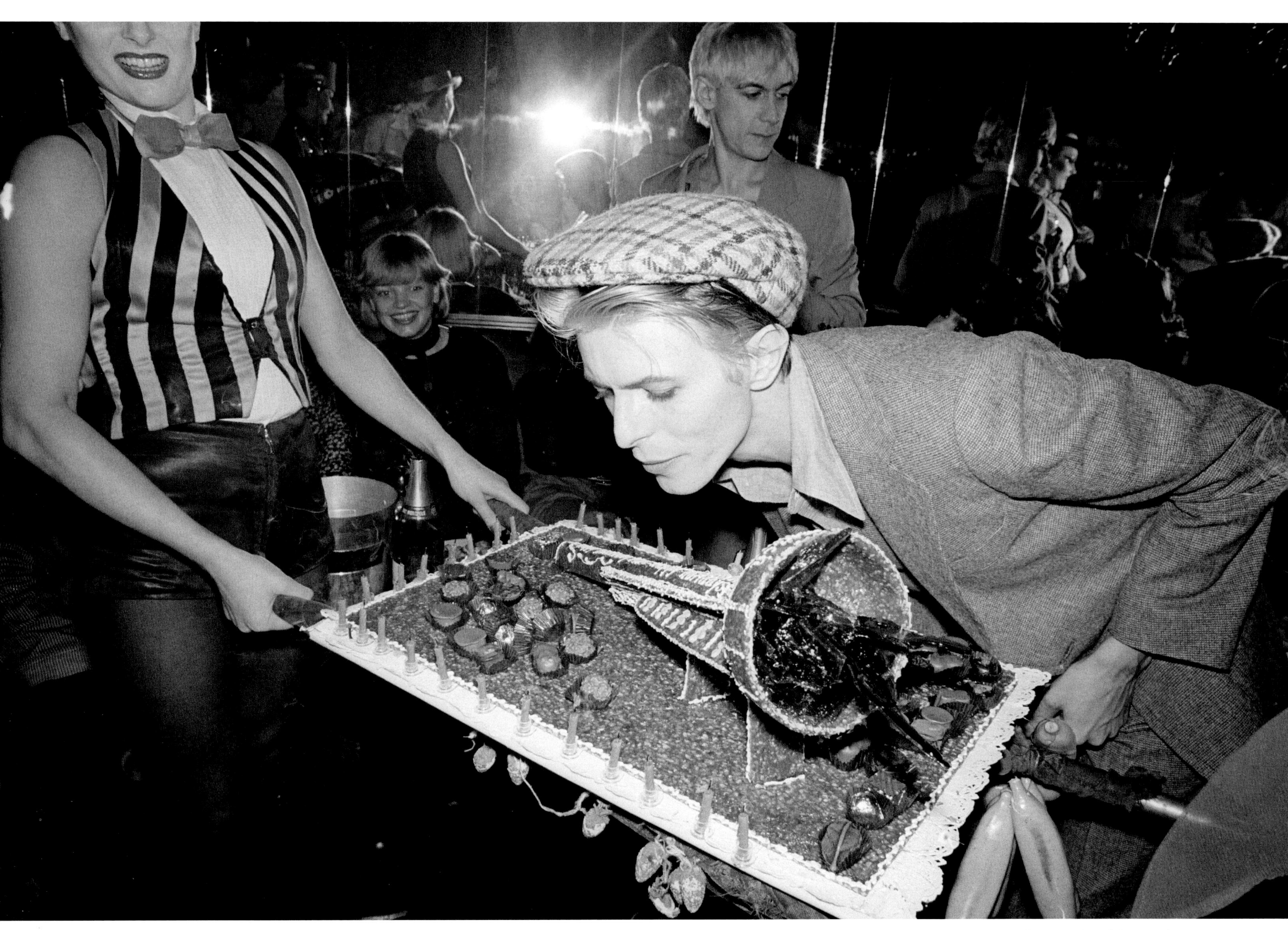

(Above and left) David celebrates his birthday and the end of the Isolar tour at L'Ange Bleu in Paris with (from left to right) Iggy, Romy Haag (David's good friend and a noted transgender European cabaret performer of some fame), Coco Schwab, and Pat Gibbons.

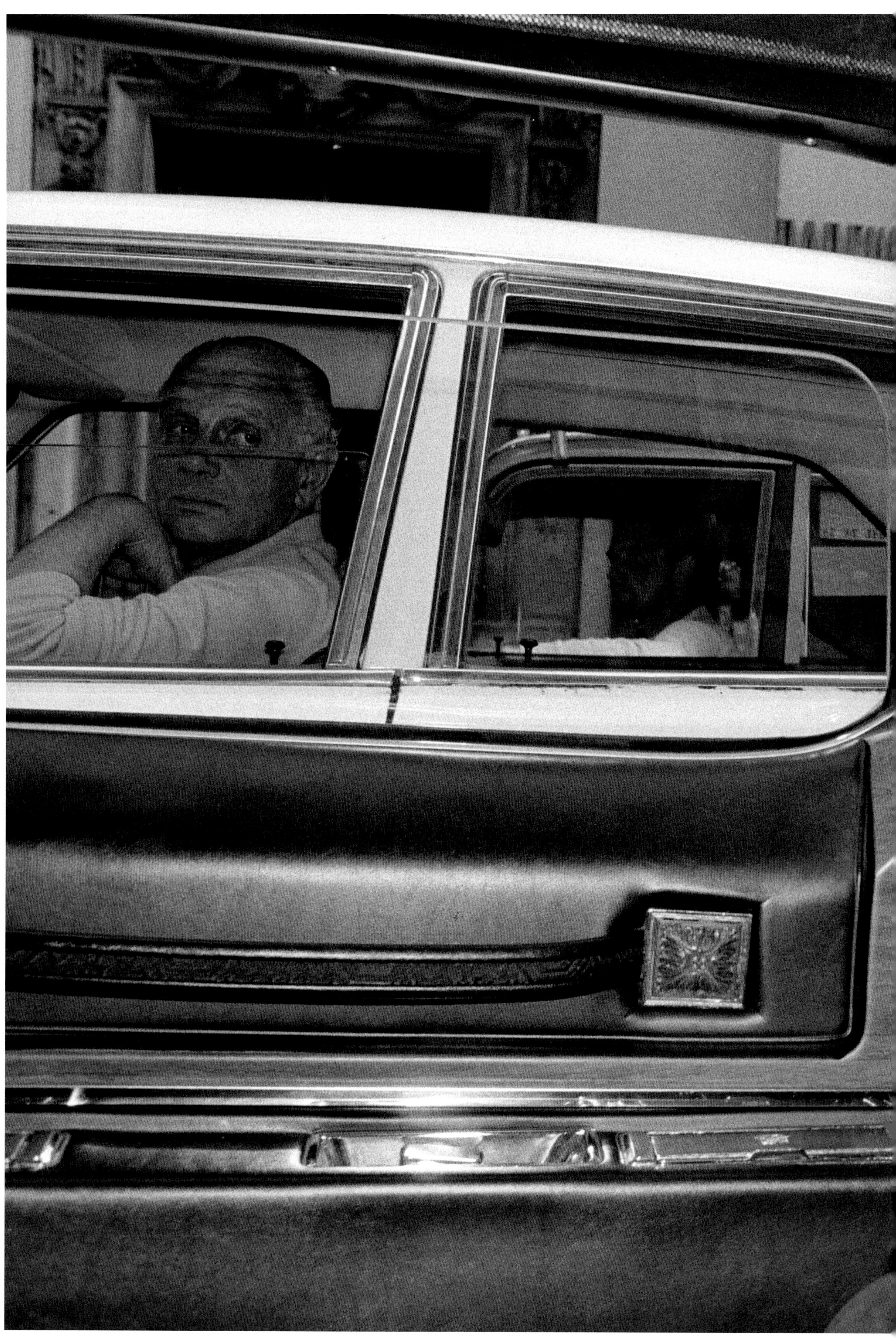

(Right) The driver of the car next to David's limo notices the star as they are stuck in afternoon Parisian traffic.
(Next spread) David, always dressed for the occasion, takes a walk about East Berlin dressed in a full length black leather trench coat and hat.

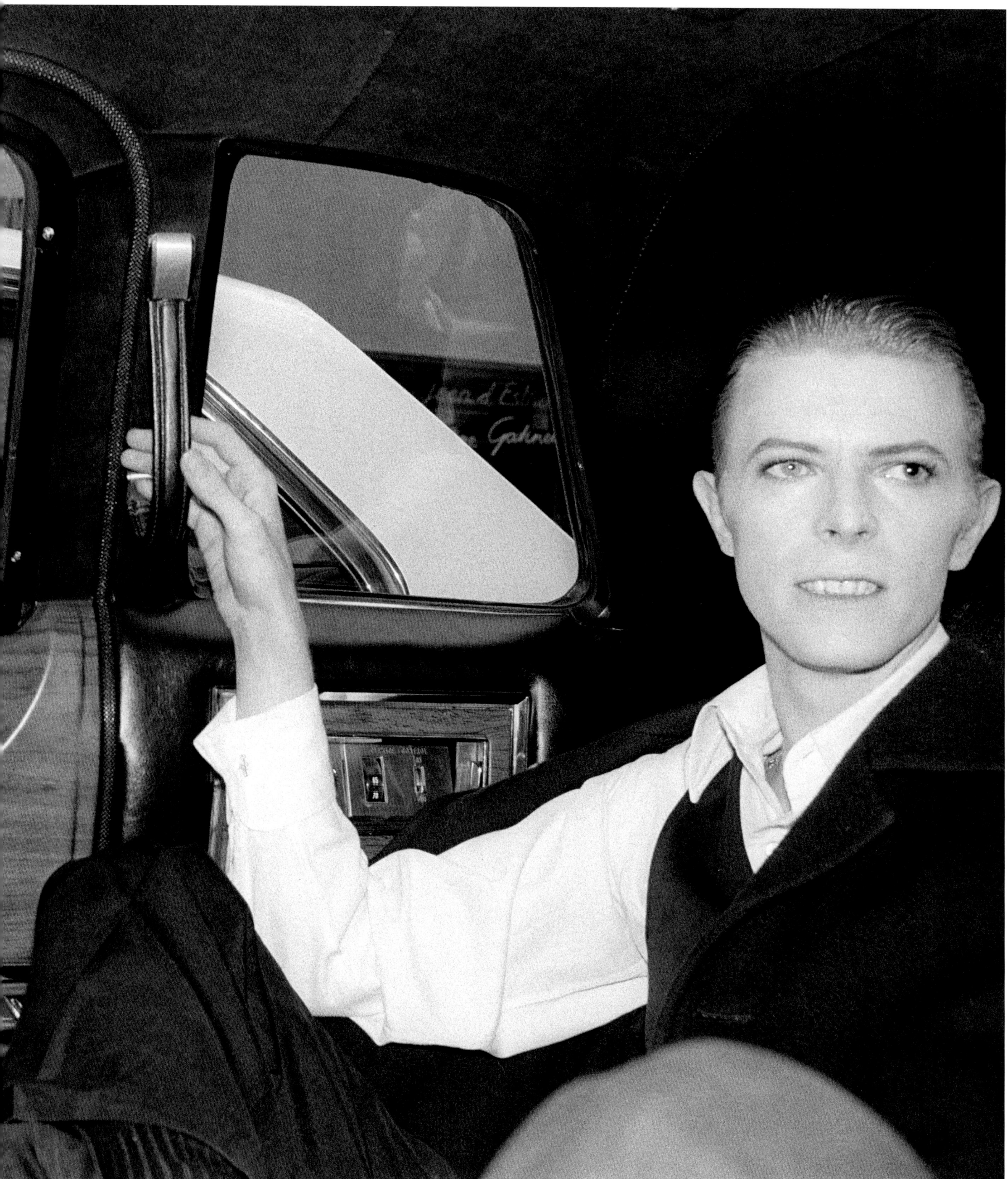

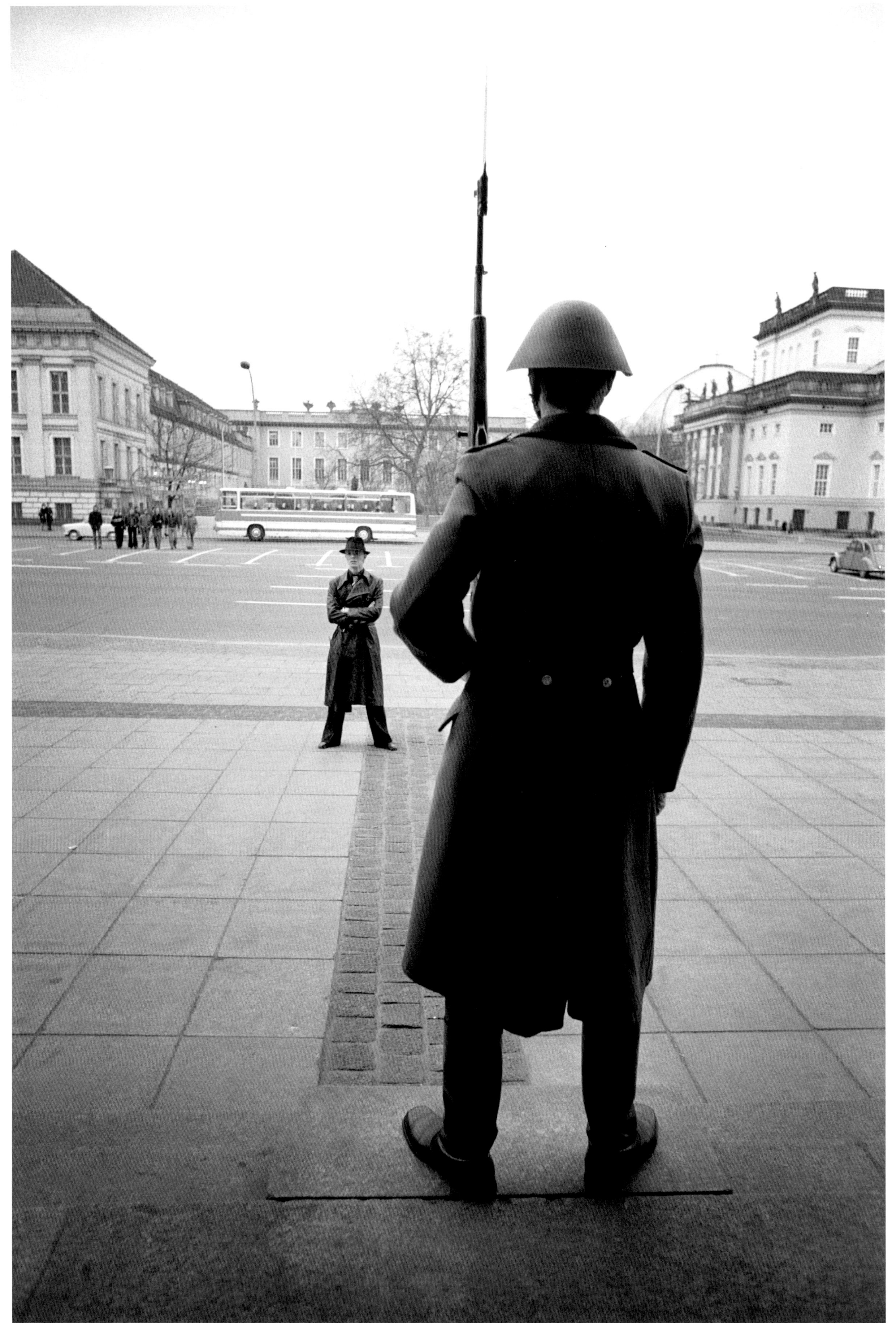

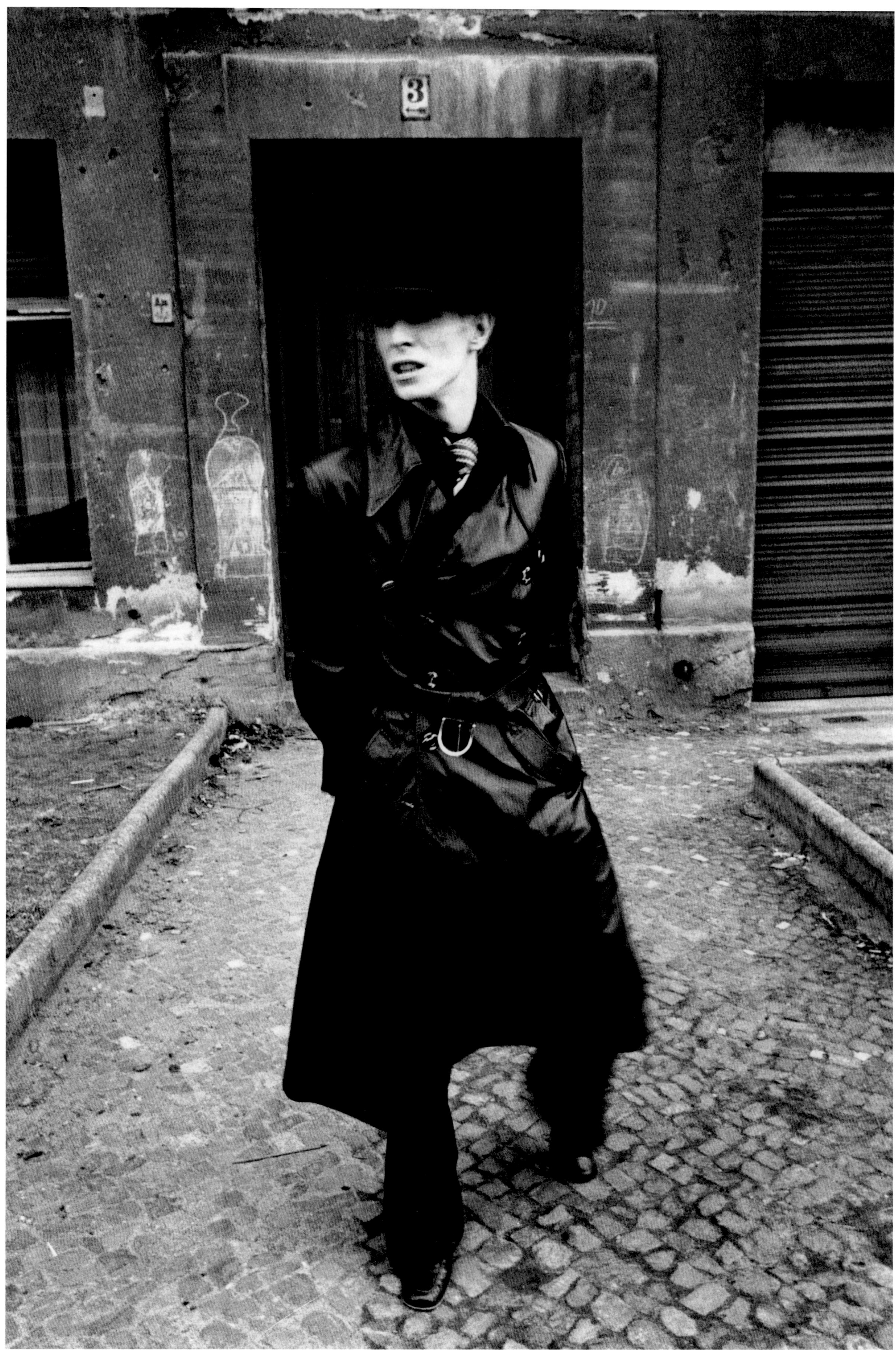

"We had a week off in Zurich and they had elected me to be the, 'getter of visas and documentation' to go through Russia on a transit visa from Basel to Warsaw to Moscow to Helsinki. We didn't really get off the trains in any of those places except Moscow.

We got to Brest, Belarus, at the Russia / Belarus border and we were taken off our train, and our luggage, and it was really sorta like totalitarian state. X (shaped) fluorescent lights on the wall. You know... big room. They came up to us and said, 'We weren't expecting you'. I had done all this preliminary work that said that everything would be prepared for us and I'd done everything correct except there's, like, no line of communication there particularly.

So they took a Playboy away from me, some books away from David. They didn't really tell us what was going on. They didn't tell us why we were taken off the train. We thought we were going to be left in Brest. You know... we didn't know. We were there for quite a while and it turns out that my World War Two history was not quite up to snuff. The train tracks in Russia are different sized from those in Eastern Europe so people could not invade by trains. We had to switch trains.

The guy that came into our compartment was an albino KGB guy, which scared the piss out of us! Eventually they put all our stuff on the new train. We didn't know any of that was supposed to happen. They sent us on our way... to Moscow where they said they'd have people meet us at the train. There was nobody.

David had been there once before so he knew sort of his way around a little bit. He knew that we could get help at Aeroflot so we went to Aeroflot and spoke to them because he knew they would speak english. There wasn't must english speaking going on in Russia in the 70's. So we rented a truck and went to the Metropol hotel, took our stuff out of the truck, had dinner... that's where I got some of the best pictures, that evening.

Then probably the scariest moment of my life was we were separated. Being the low man on the totem pole I went with all the luggage on the truck to the train station. Which we knew was a different train station but we didn't know anything . They drove away and I'm sorta looking around going, 'I'm fucking lost in Russia, here!' If they have a flat tire I"m dead. But it all worked out.

It was icons that they (Soviet authorities) were really concerned with. What was negotiable was blue jeans and chewing gum. So I didn't want to trade anything for anything. I didn't bring any extra blue jeans but I did bring several packs of chewing gum which I gave to all the porters. I had a ring of people around me and I'm passing out chewing gum to them for nothing, that was a nice little moment.

We're moving along at the pace we were expecting, there was no loss of time. We were in Moscow for 7 hours. Walked around Red Square, GUM department store, then had dinner at the Metropol, Lenin's tomb, the whole walk around.

So we go catch the train and get to the Helsinki border. I always carry a swiss army knife with me so I can unscrew things, bathroom signs, little this-and-that. I got this wonderful little plaque (from the mens room) that says toilet paper in four languages, none of which is english. So I unscrewed it from the wall. (At the border) David and Jimmy get strip searched. I get nothing. I had it sorta stashed under my seat.

We knew that it took us 4 days to make the trip. We knew where we would be and so on. But the train schedules were mismarked. They were wrong, completely wrong. So Barbara DeWitt and Tim, her husband, had gotten all the Scandinavian press into Helsinki awaiting for us to come and the train comes in and we're not there. So the headlines were "Bowie Lost in Soviet Union!"

BOWIE LOST
IN SOVIET UNION!

The Soviet adventure as told in Andrew's words during a conversation at his home in Sun Valley, Idaho.

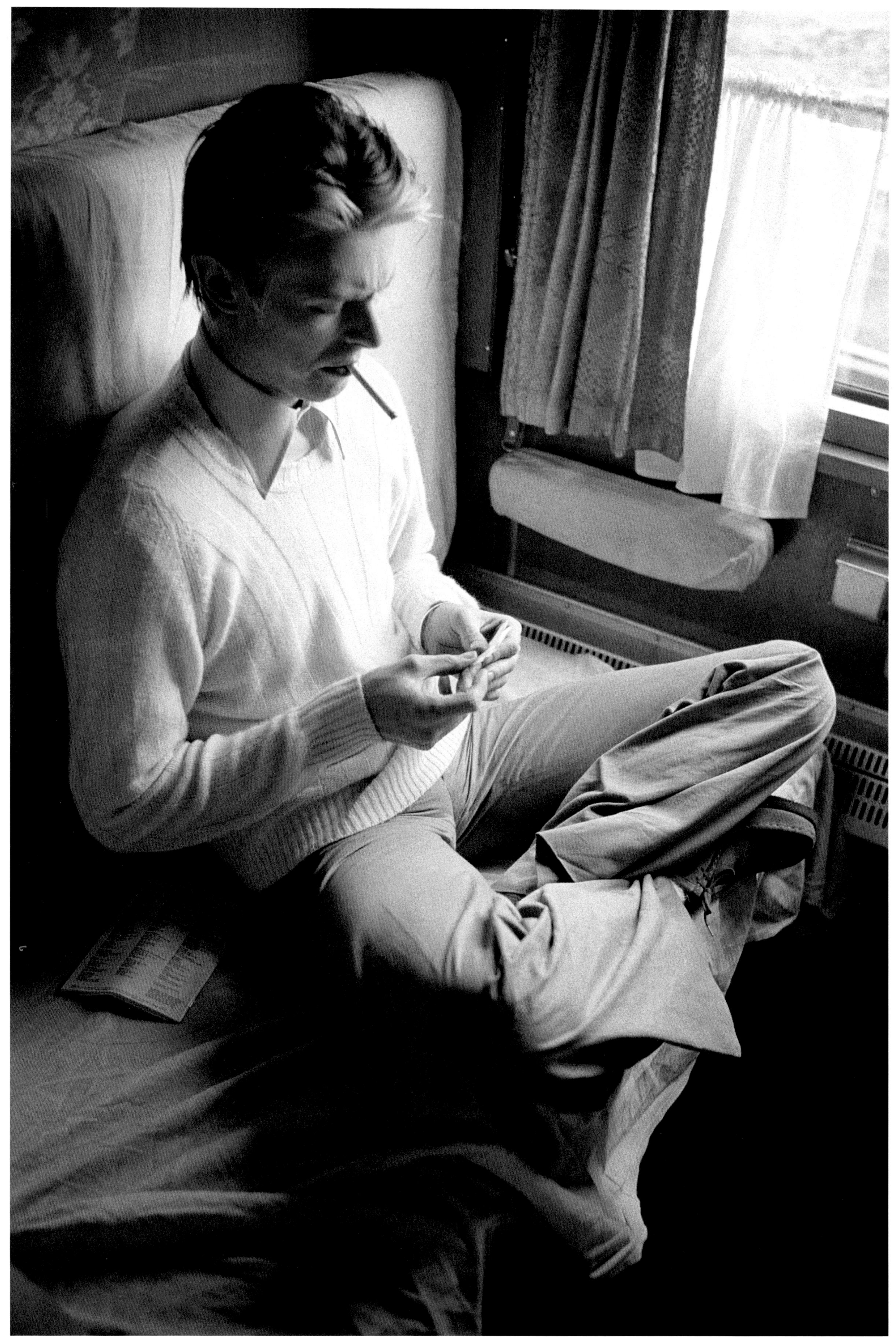

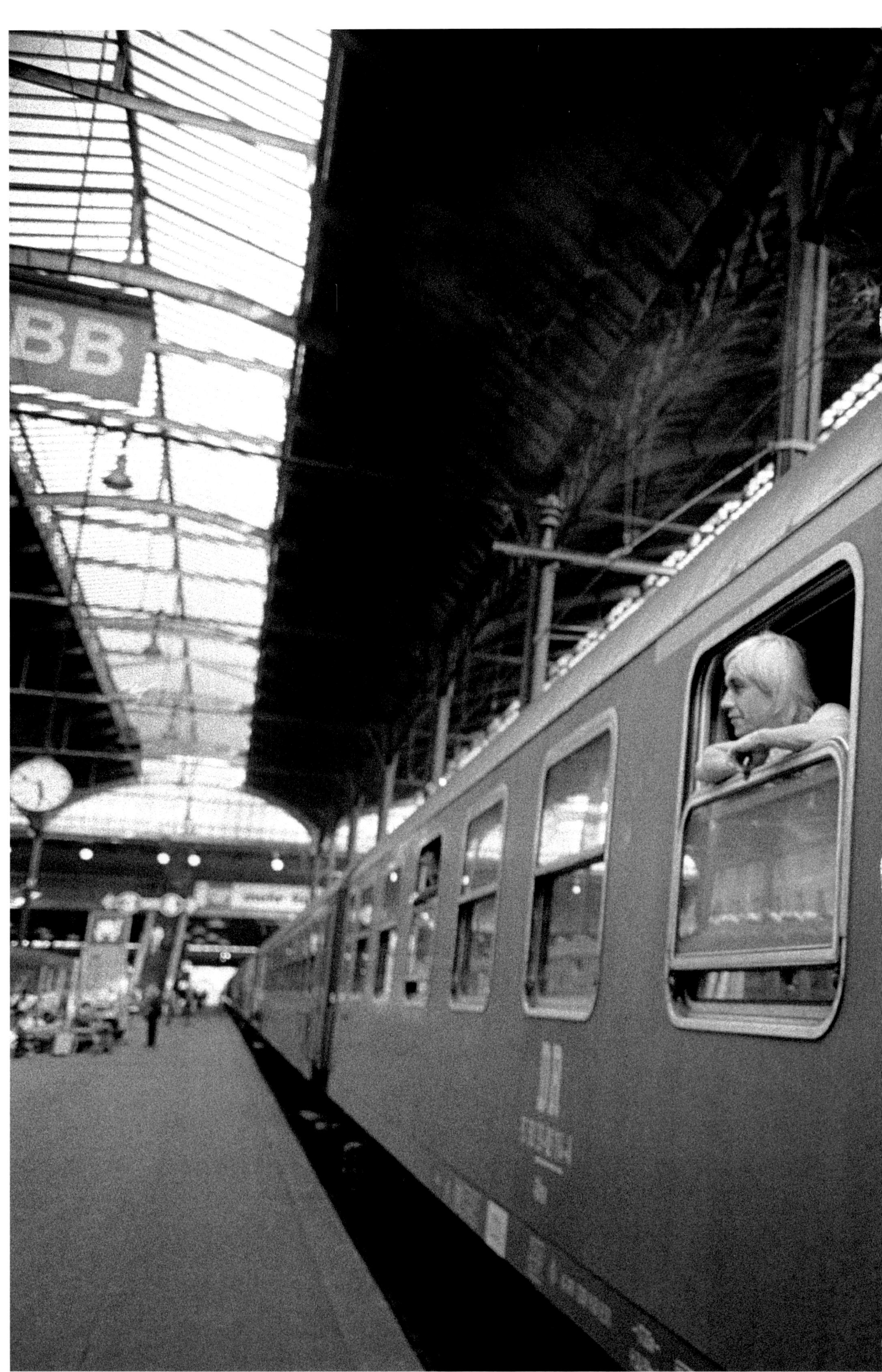

(Right) David, Pat, and Iggy look out the window of their train as they prepare to depart Basel, Switzerland for Moscow, Russia.
(Previous page) David rolls a cigarette as the train rolls through eastern Europe en route to Moscow.

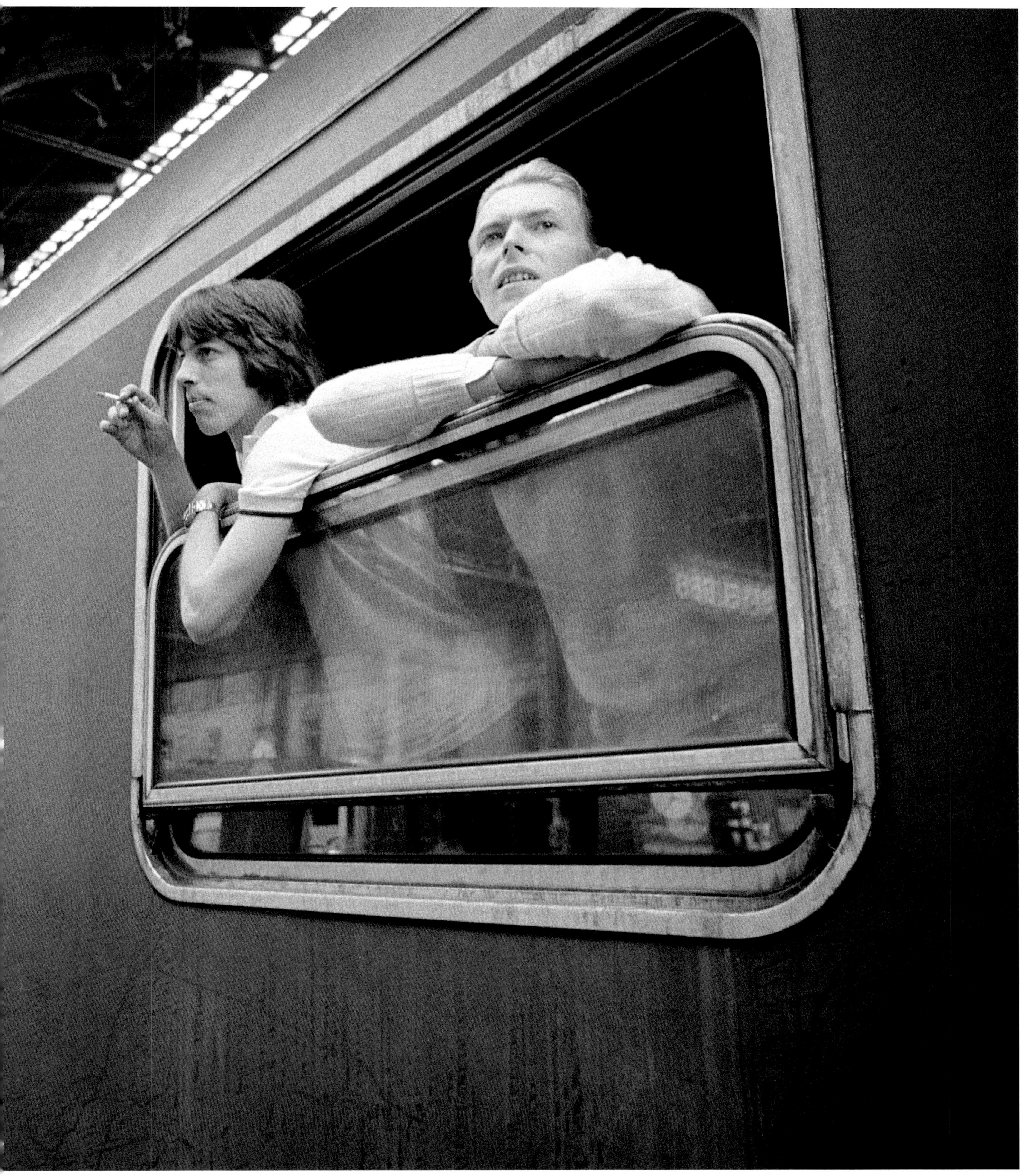

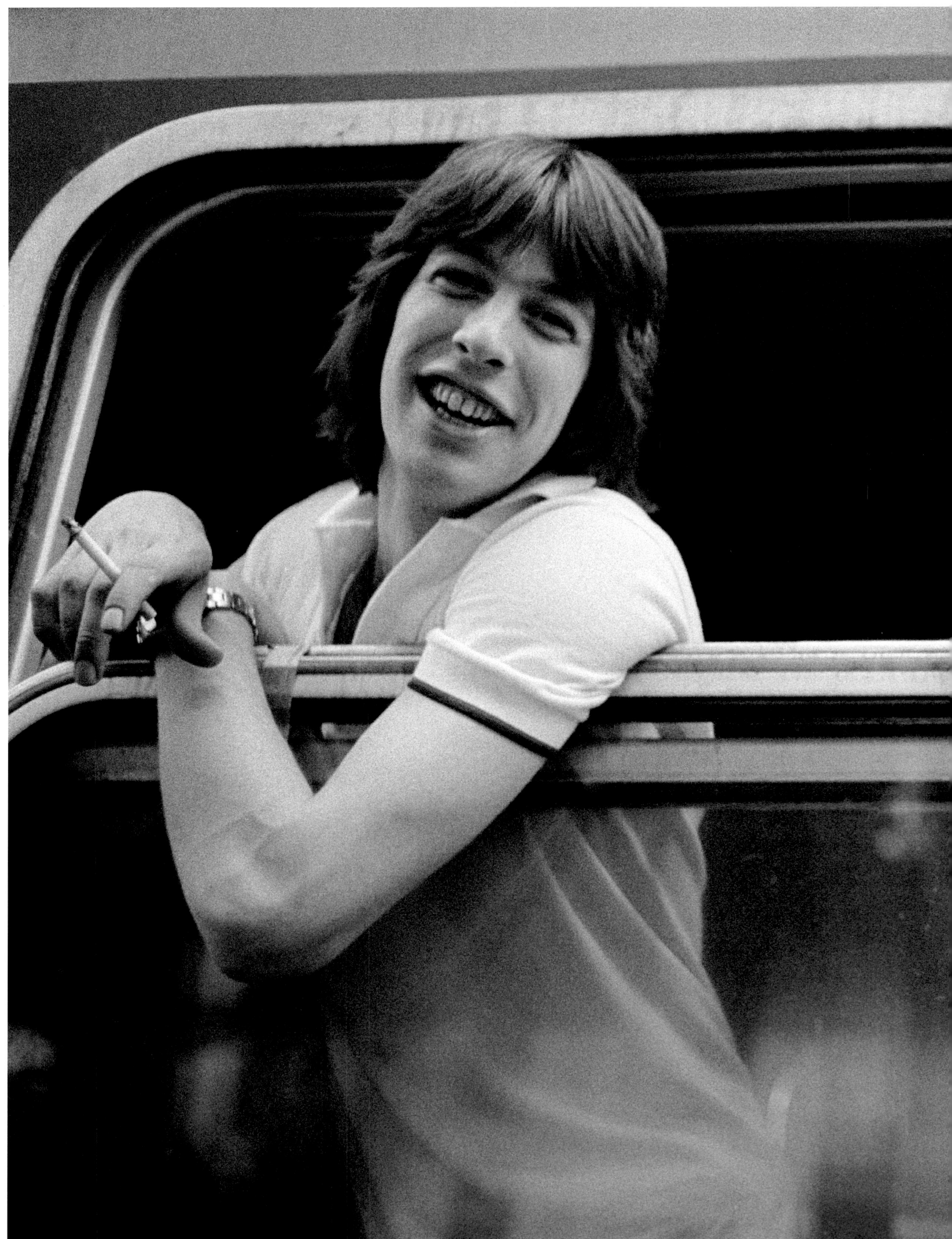

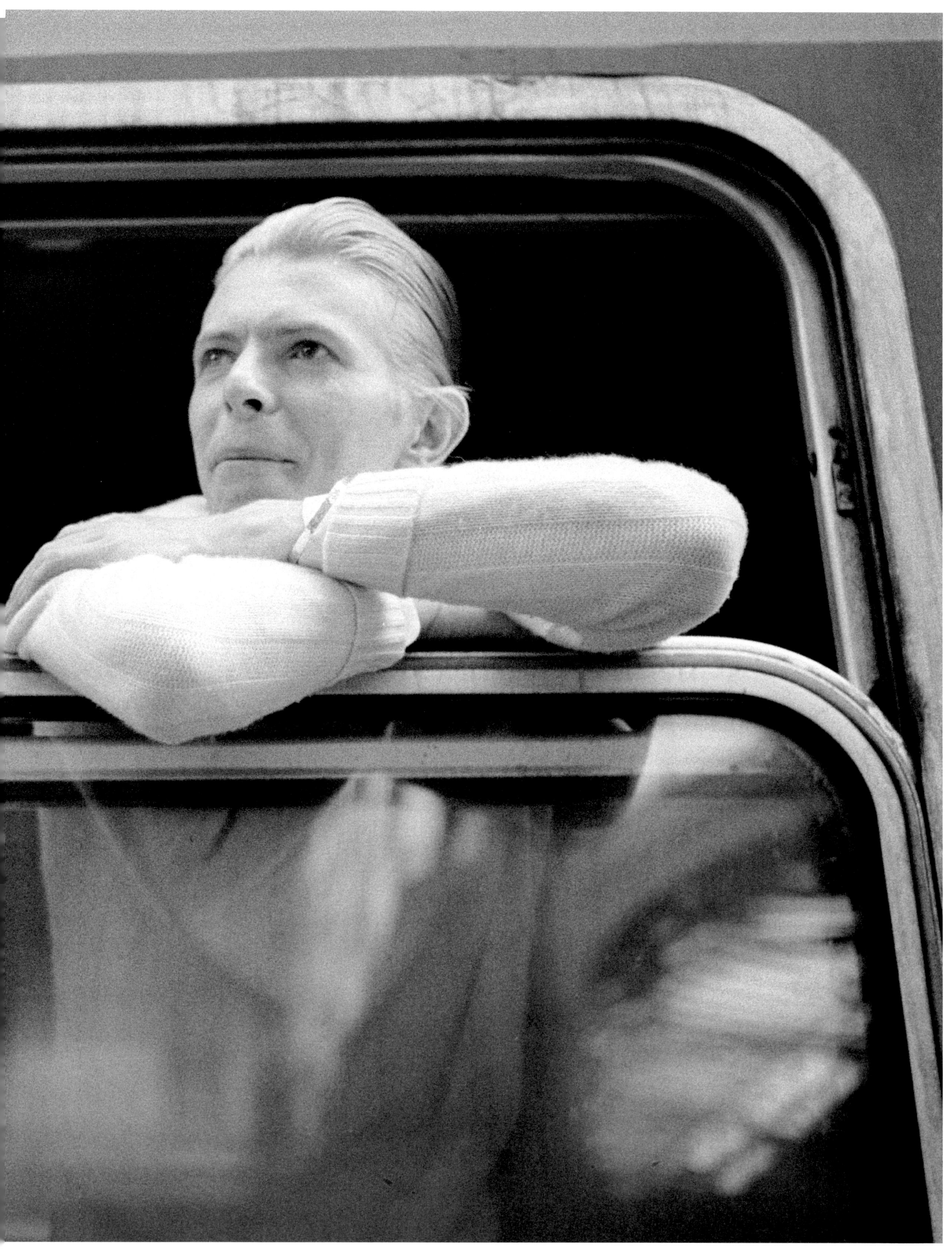

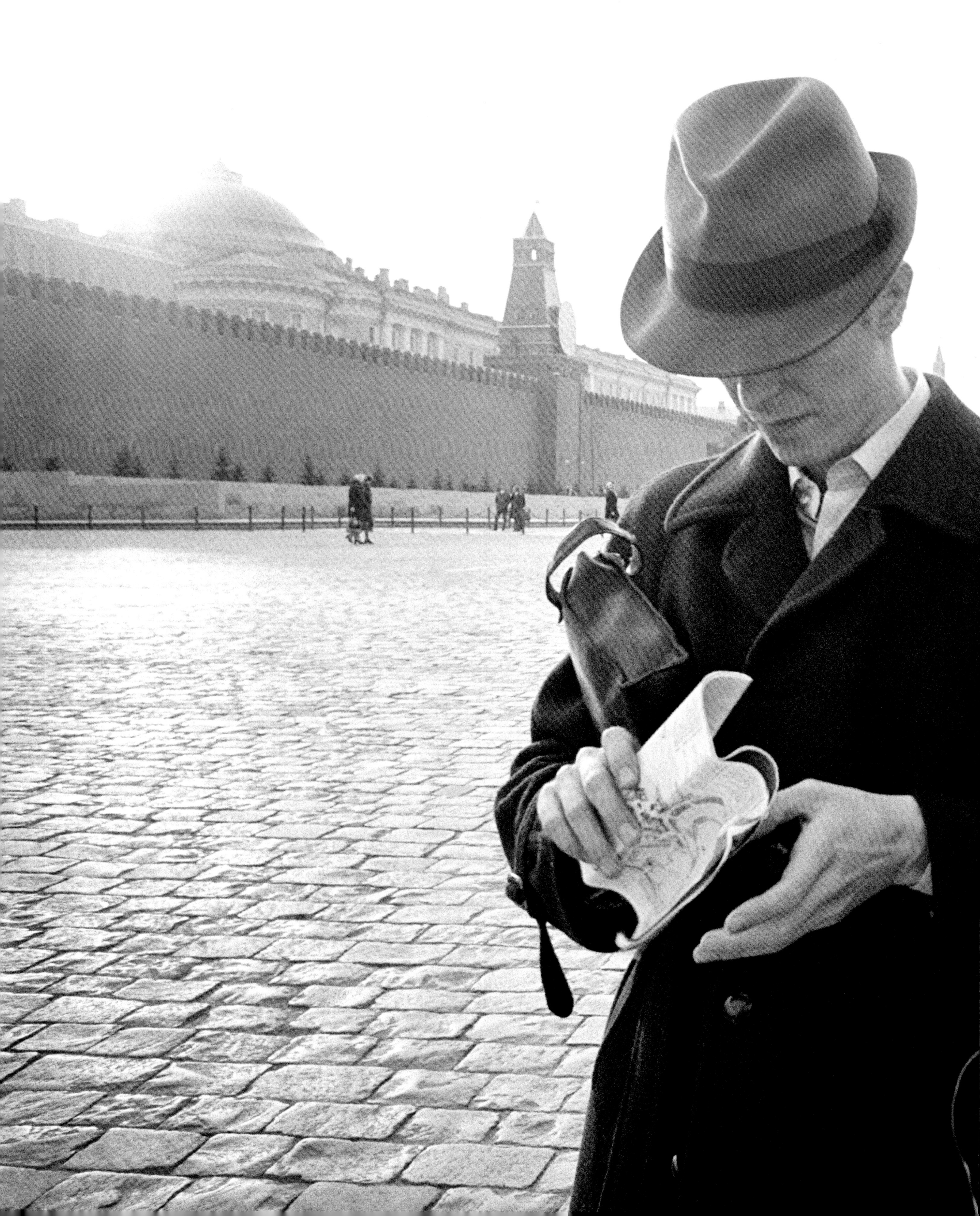

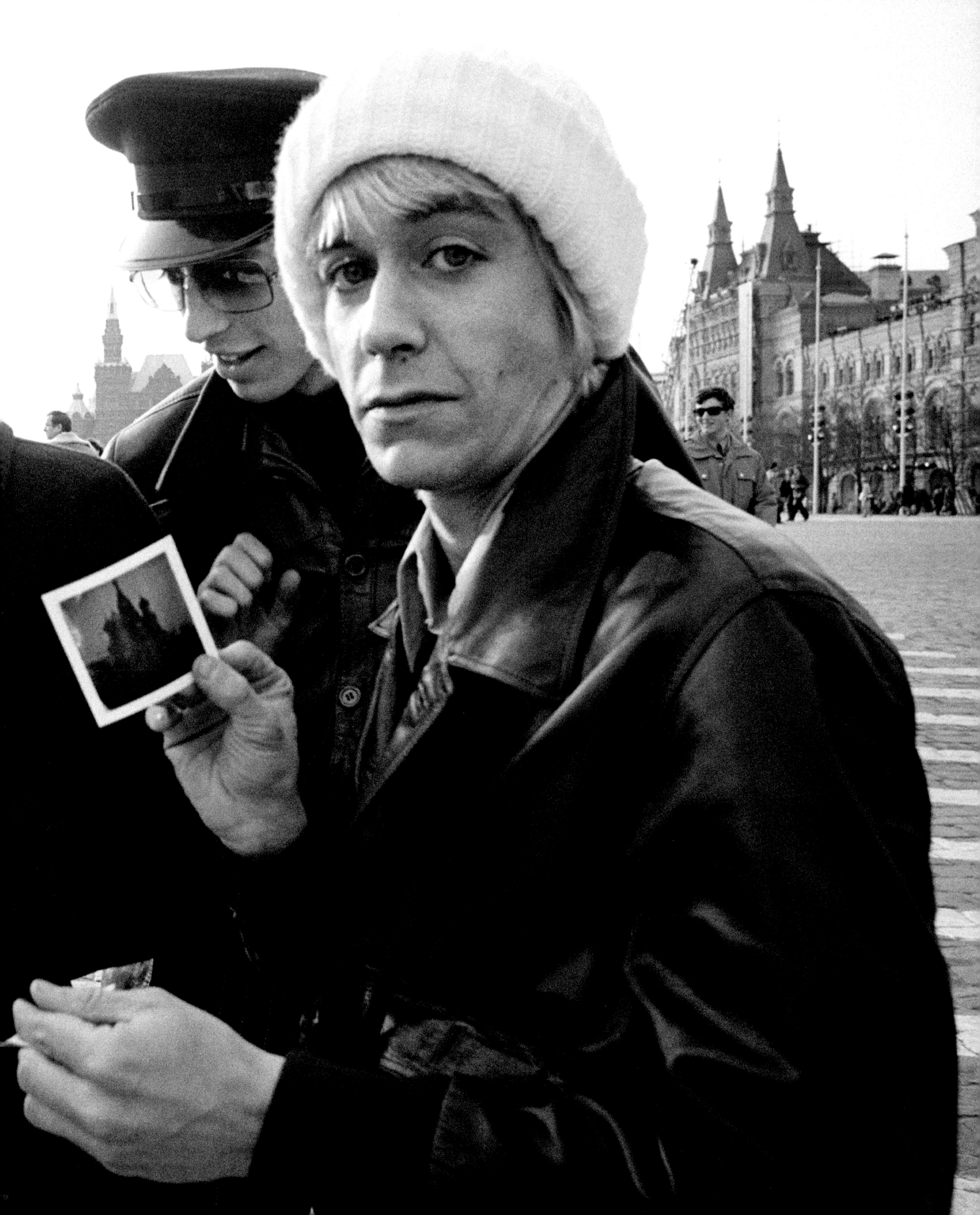

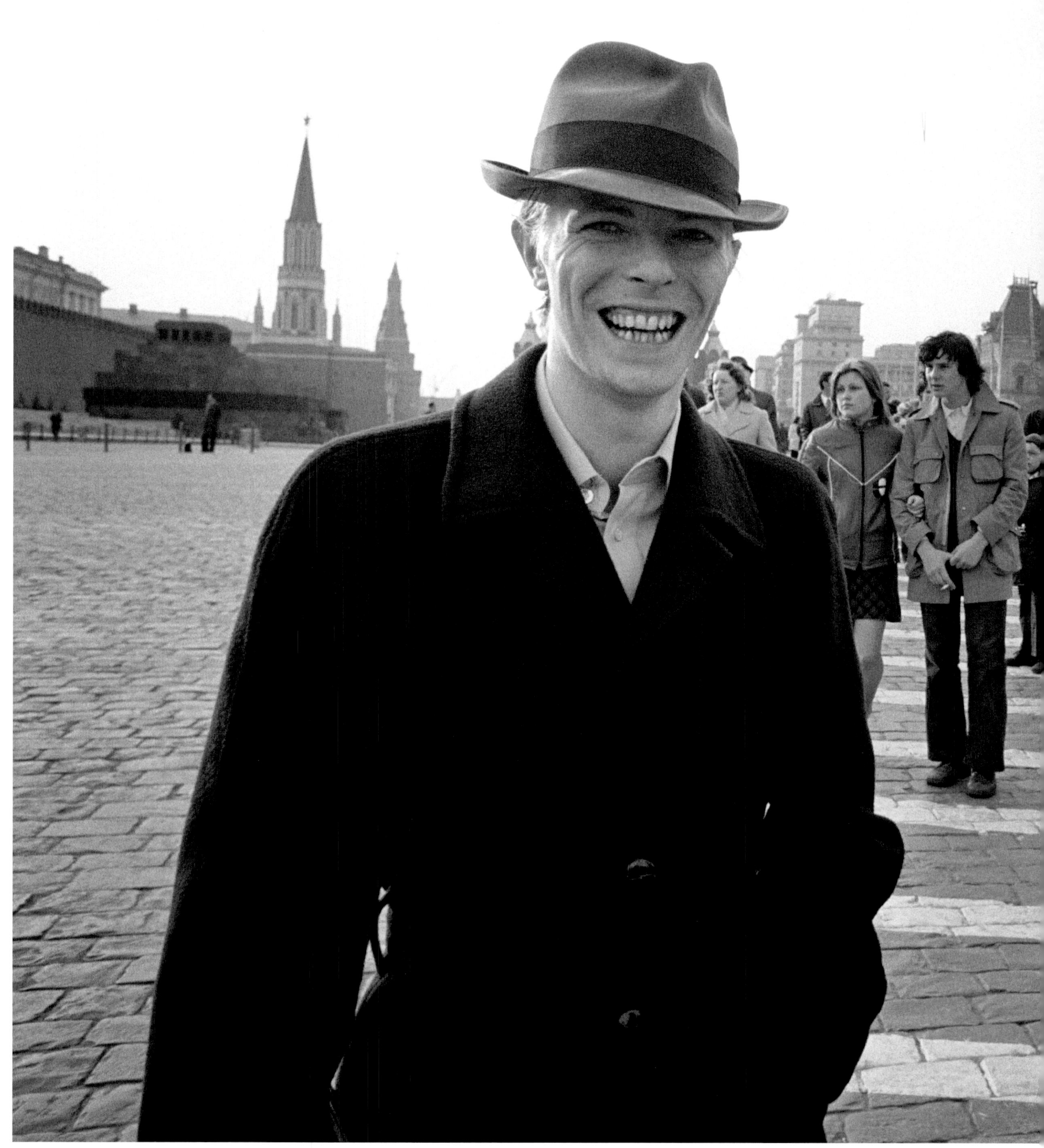

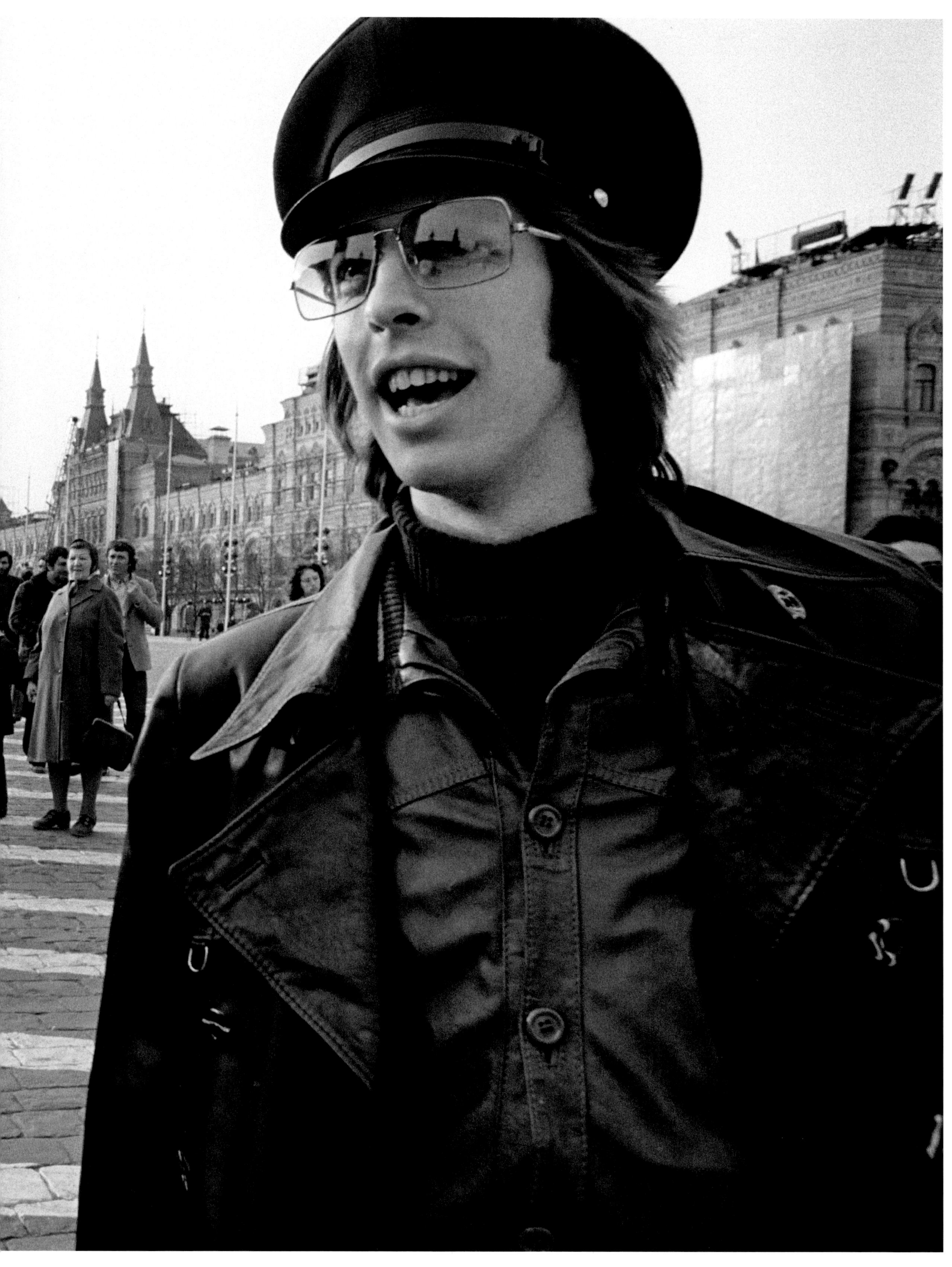

"THE GUY THAT TOOK US OFF THE TRAIN. THAT CAME INTO OUR COMPARTMENT.
WAS AN ALBINO KGB GUY. THAT SCARED THE PISS OUT OF US!" -ANDREW KENT

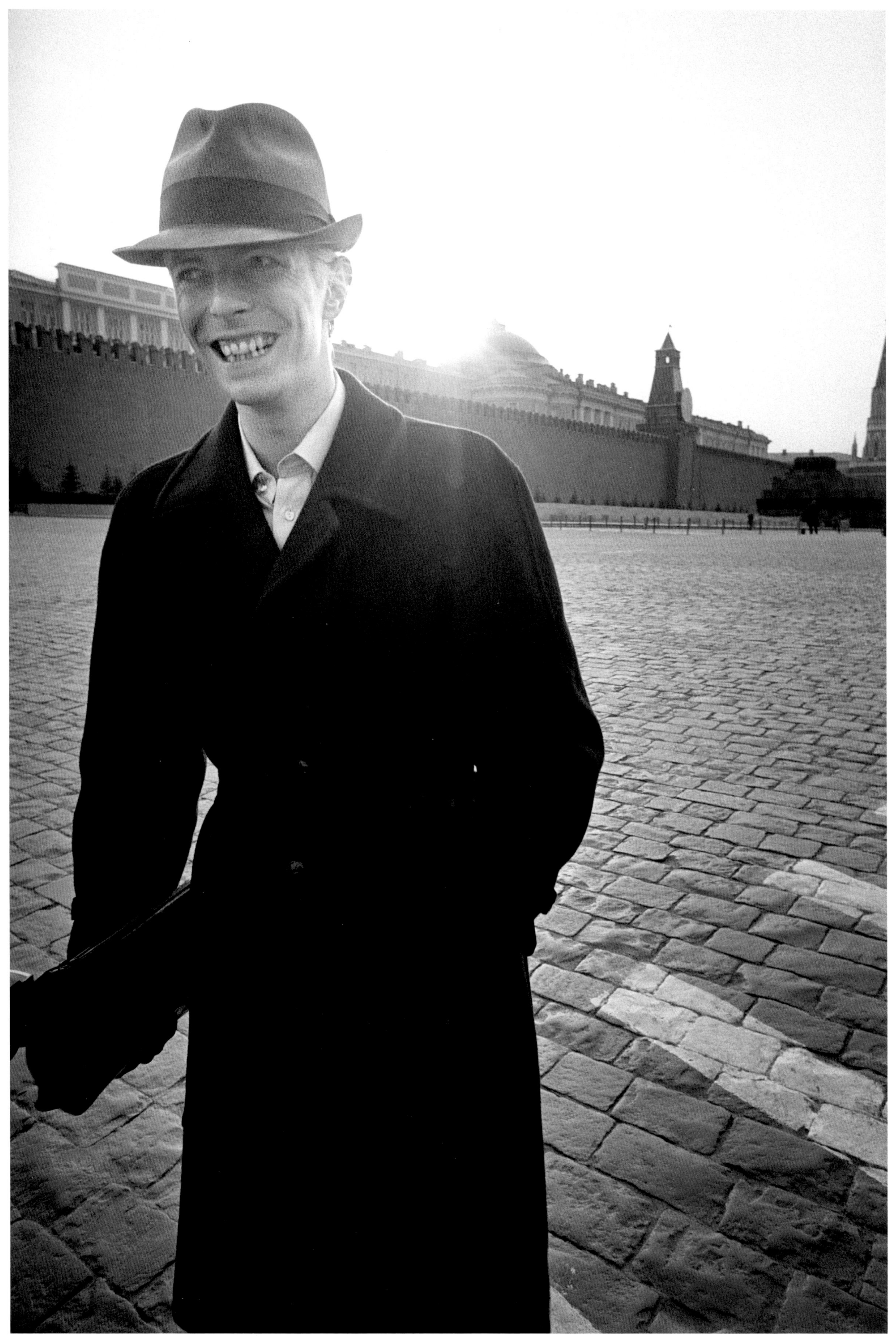

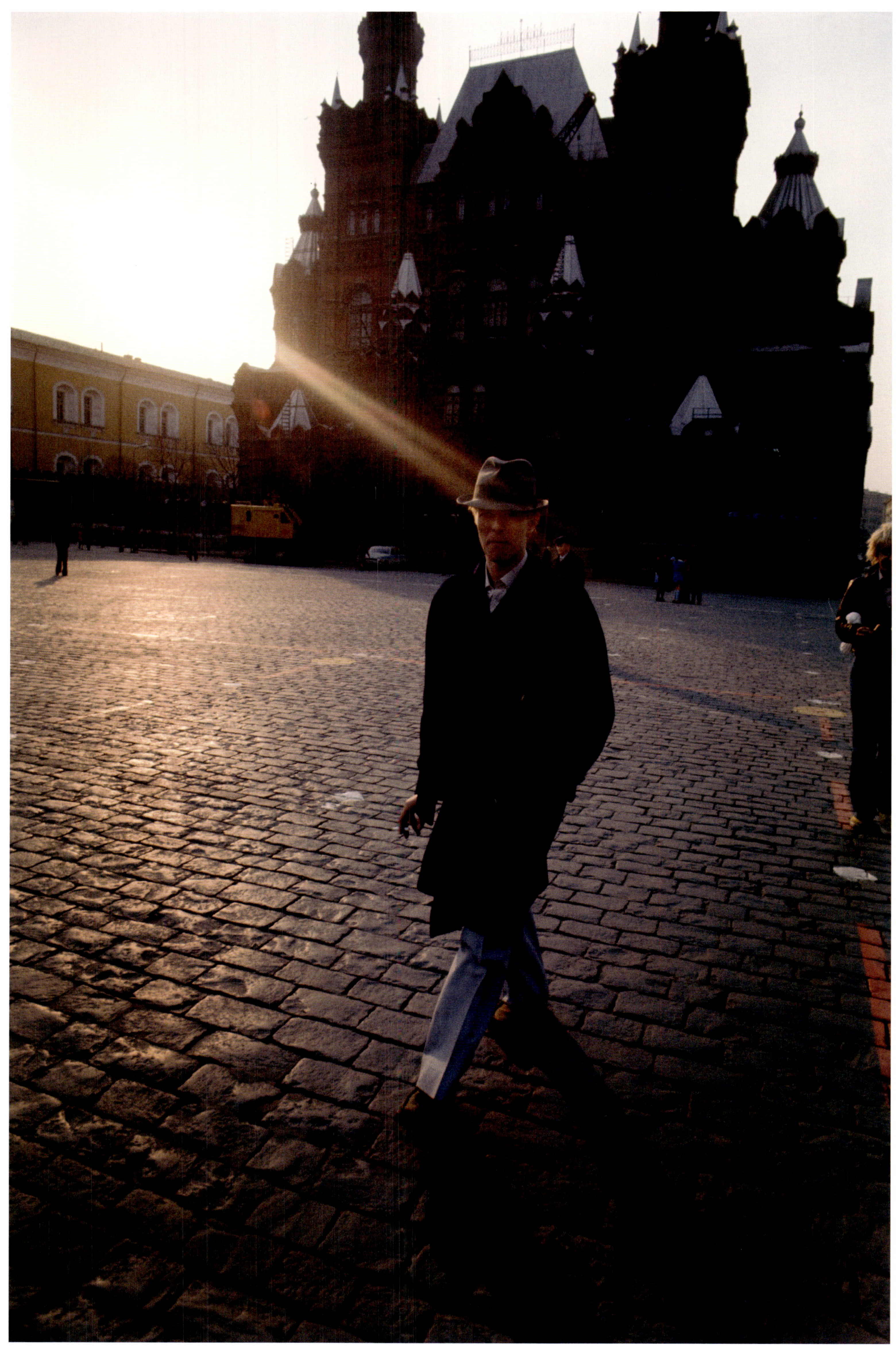

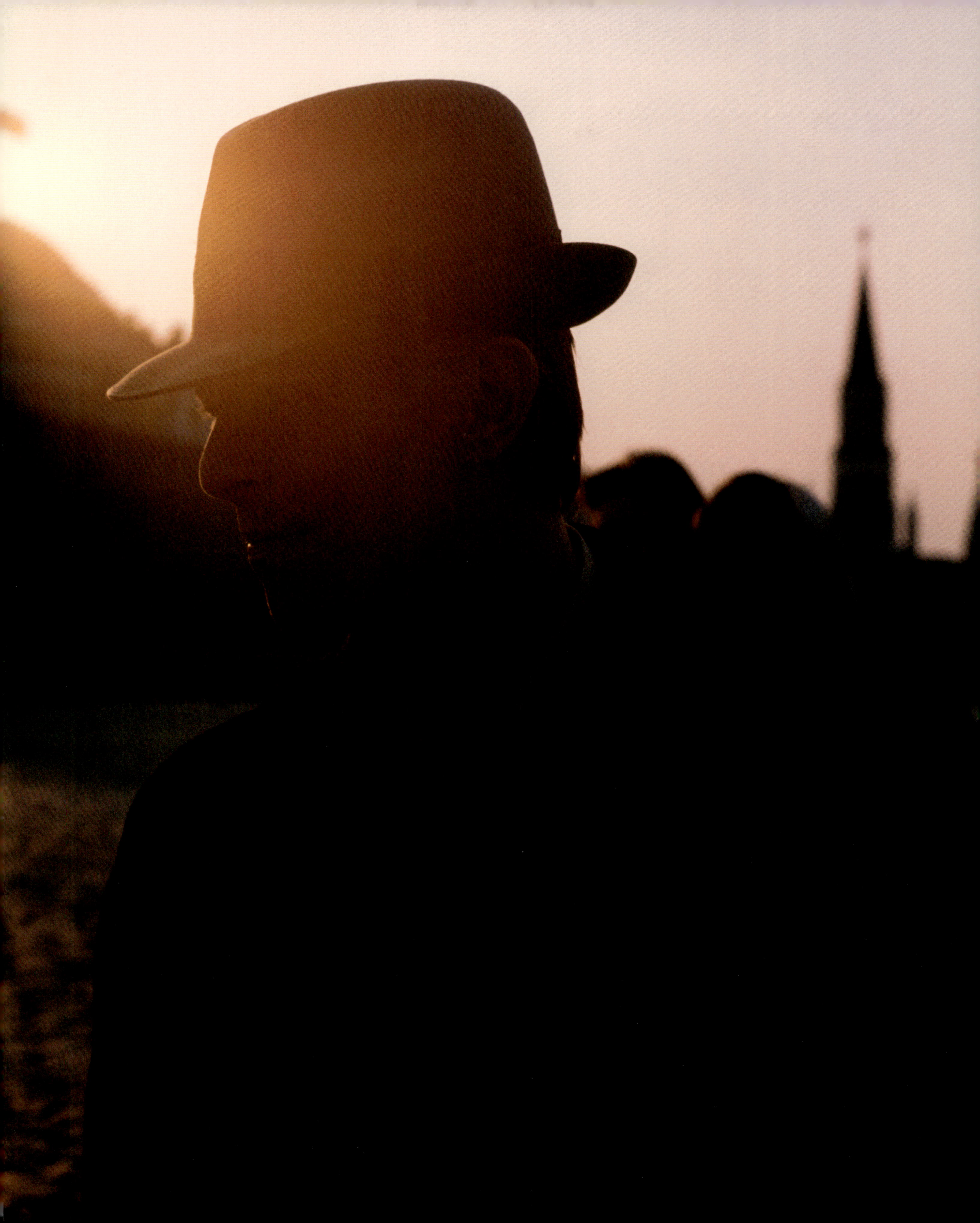

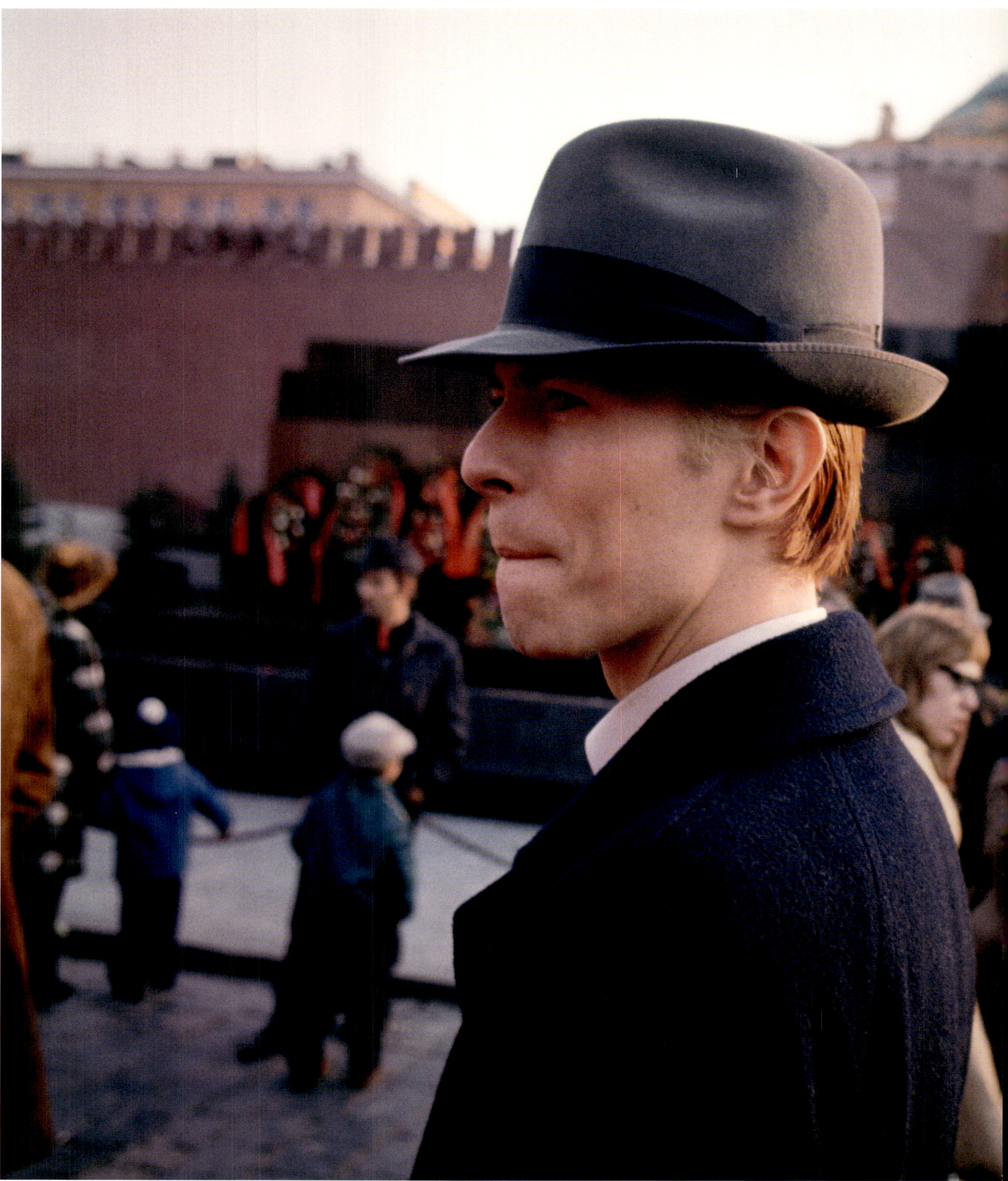

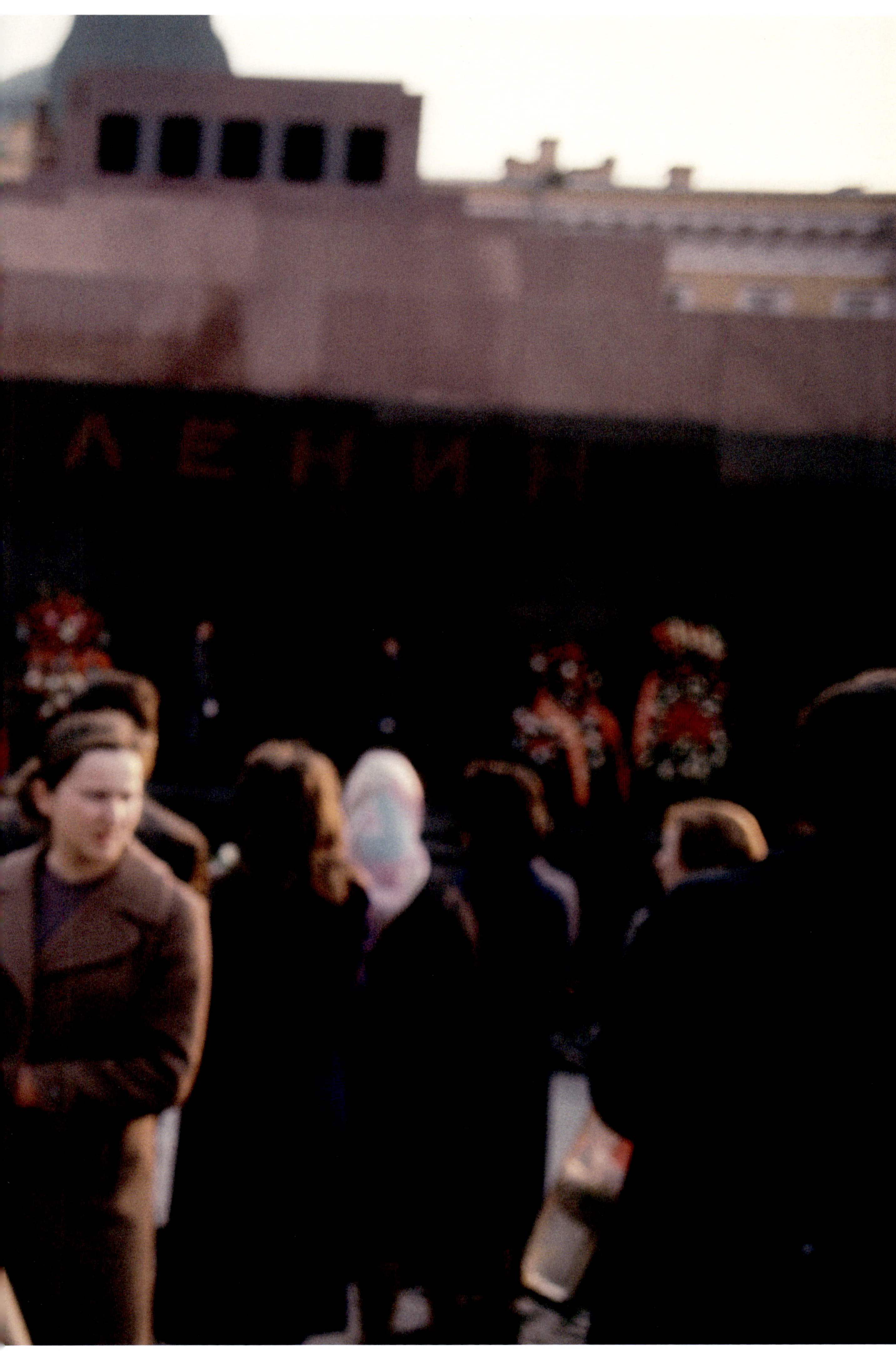

(Previous spread) David strolls about Moscow's Red Square, 1976.
(Left) David walks past the entrance to Lenin's tomb in Moscow.
(Next spread) David looks through a French magazine with a cover story on the Soviet Union on a train en route to Moscow.

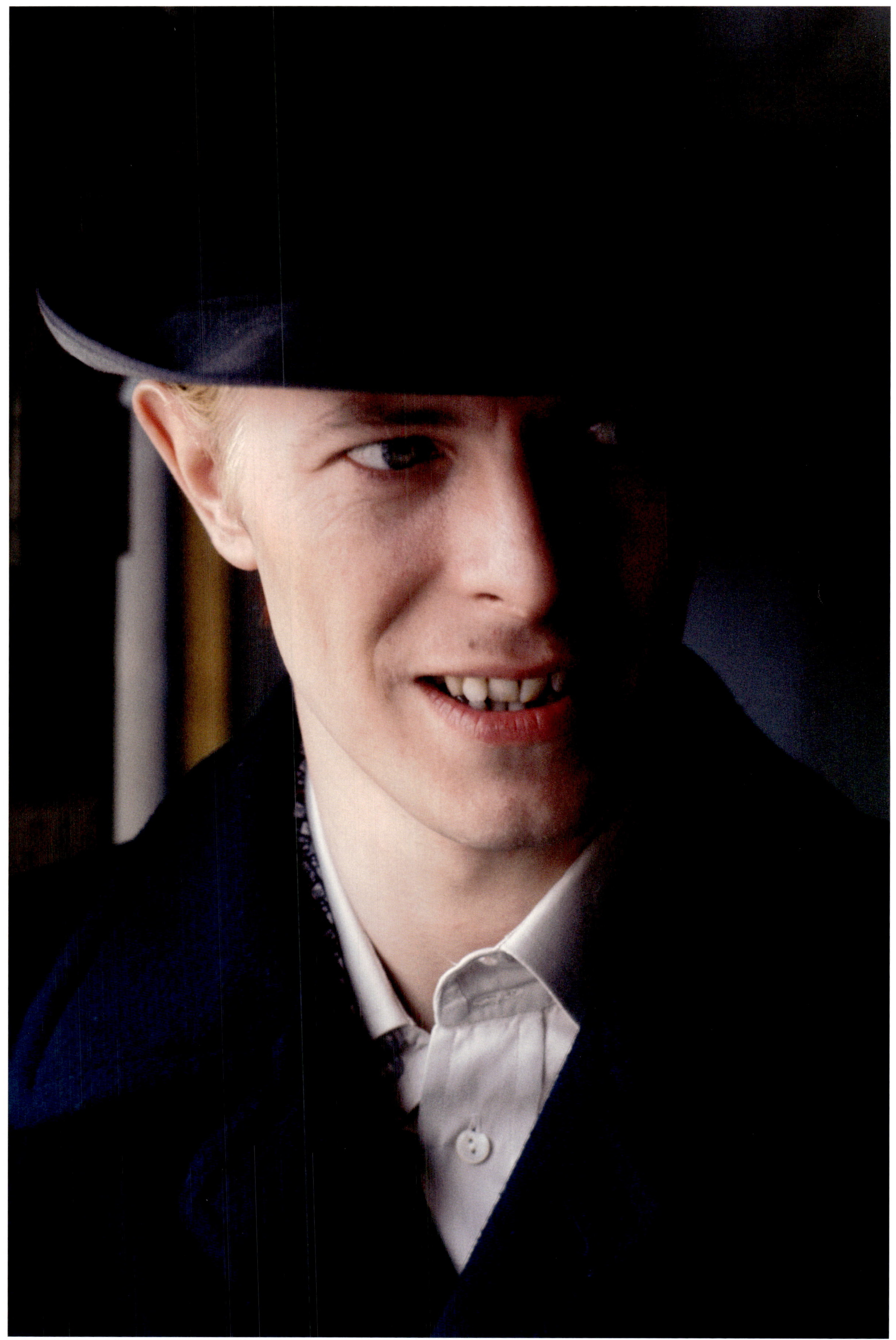

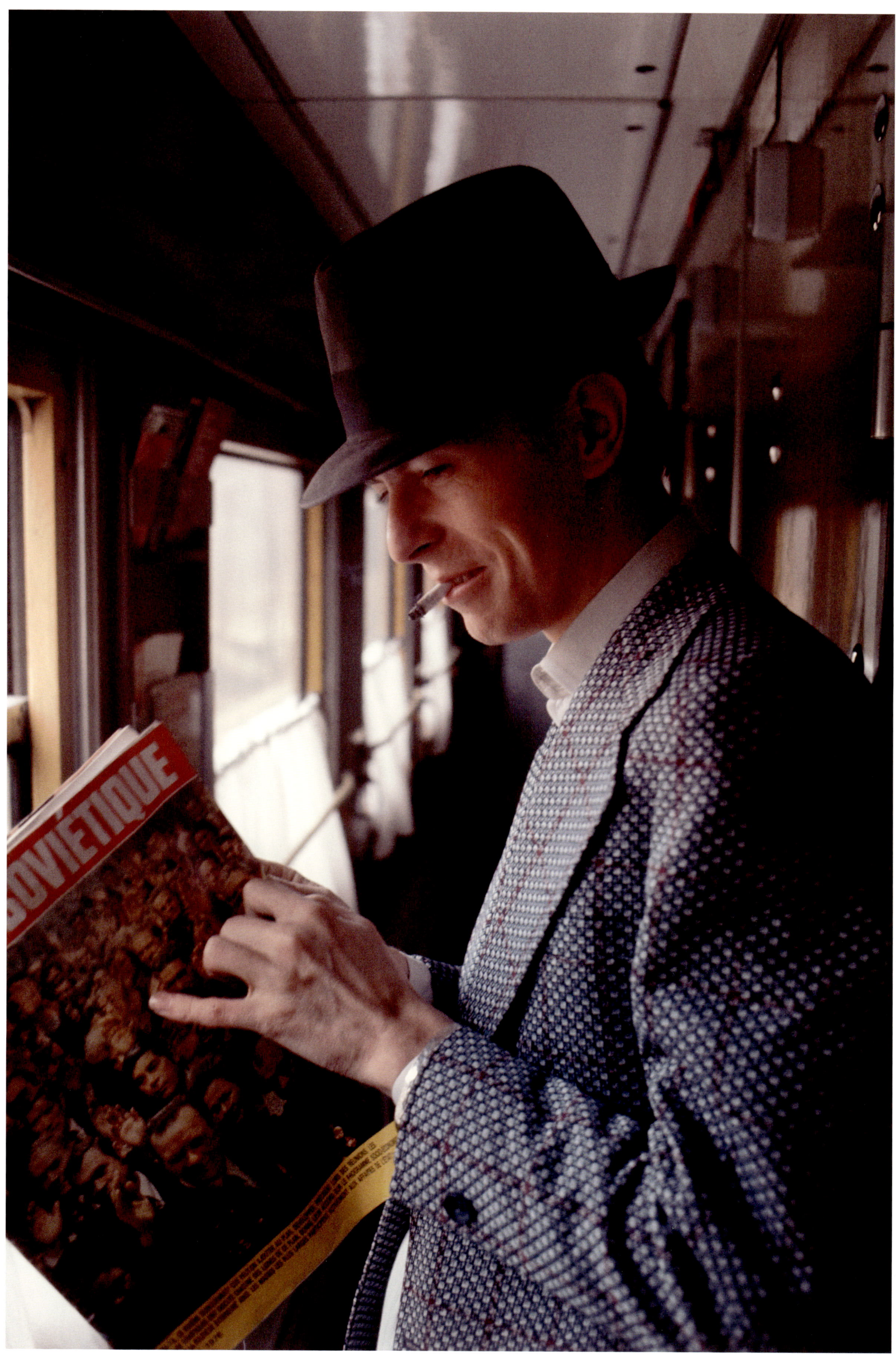

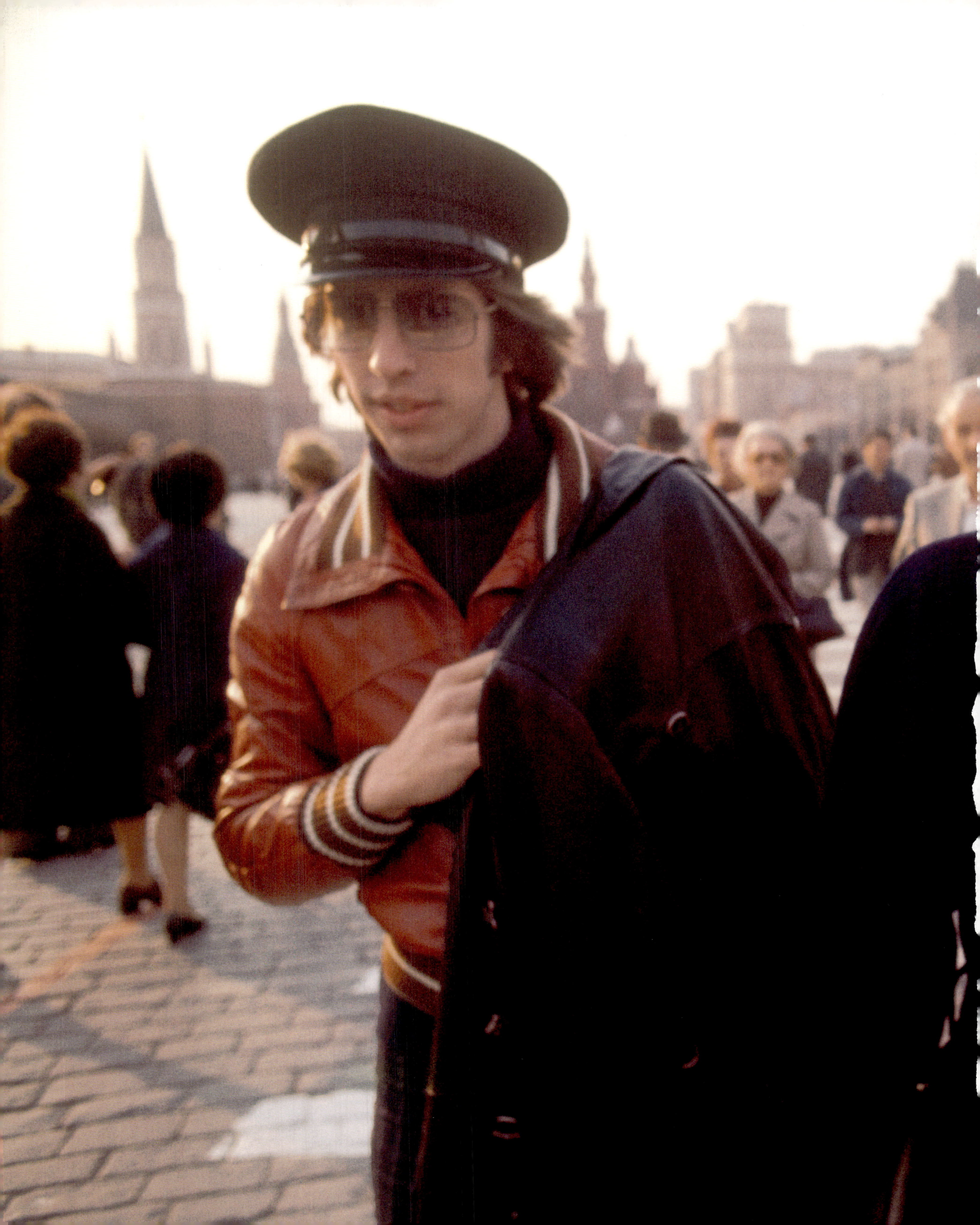

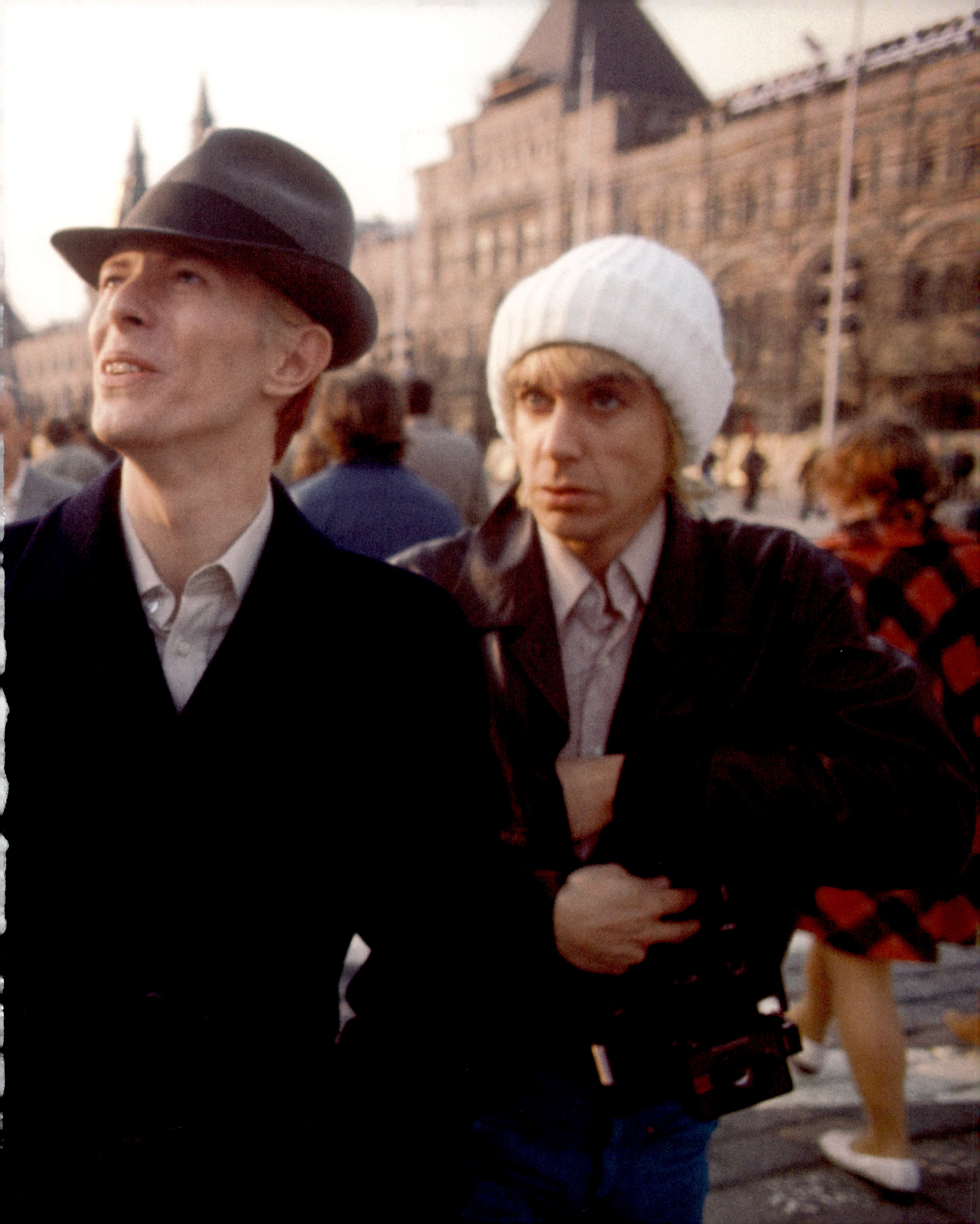

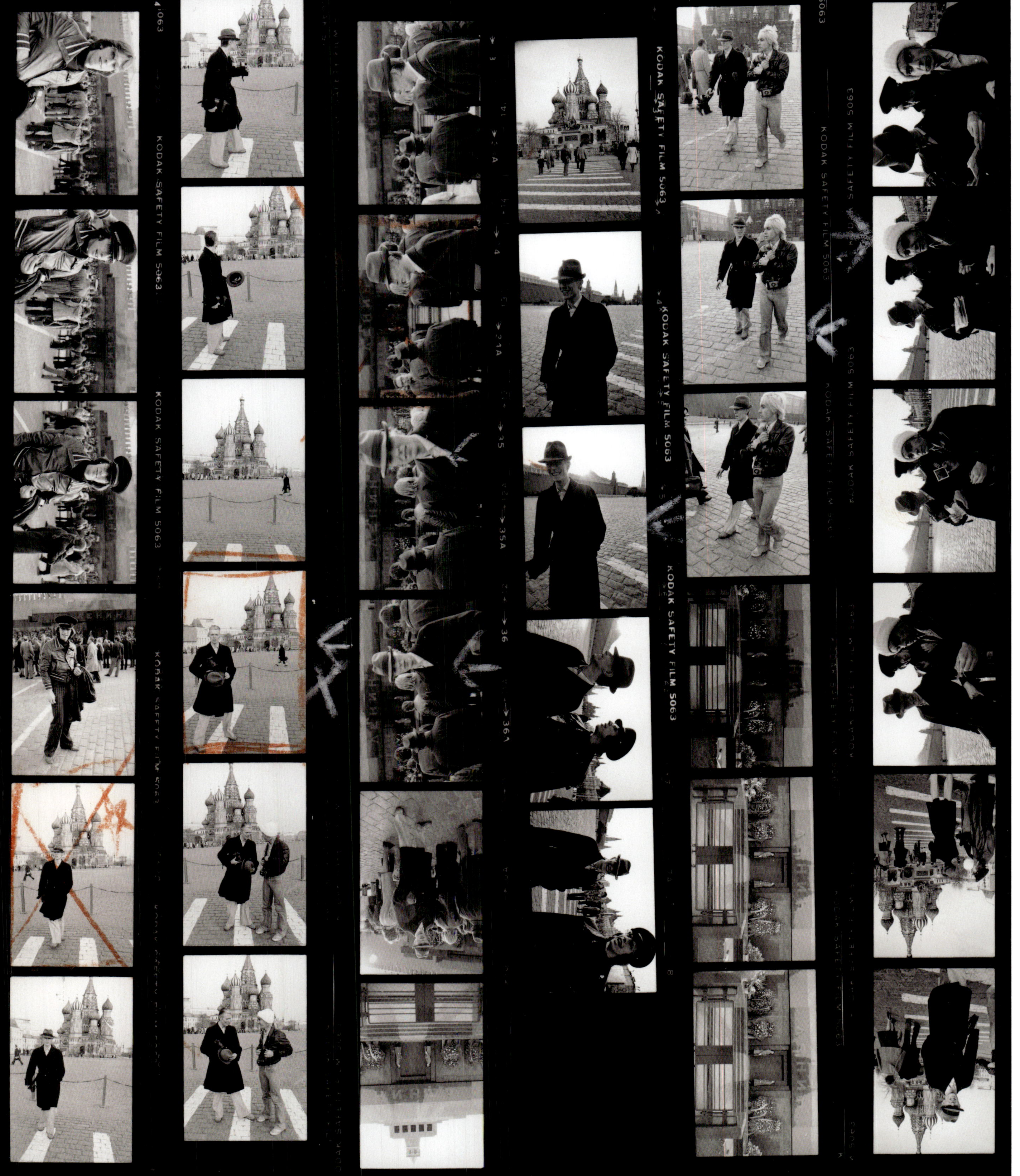

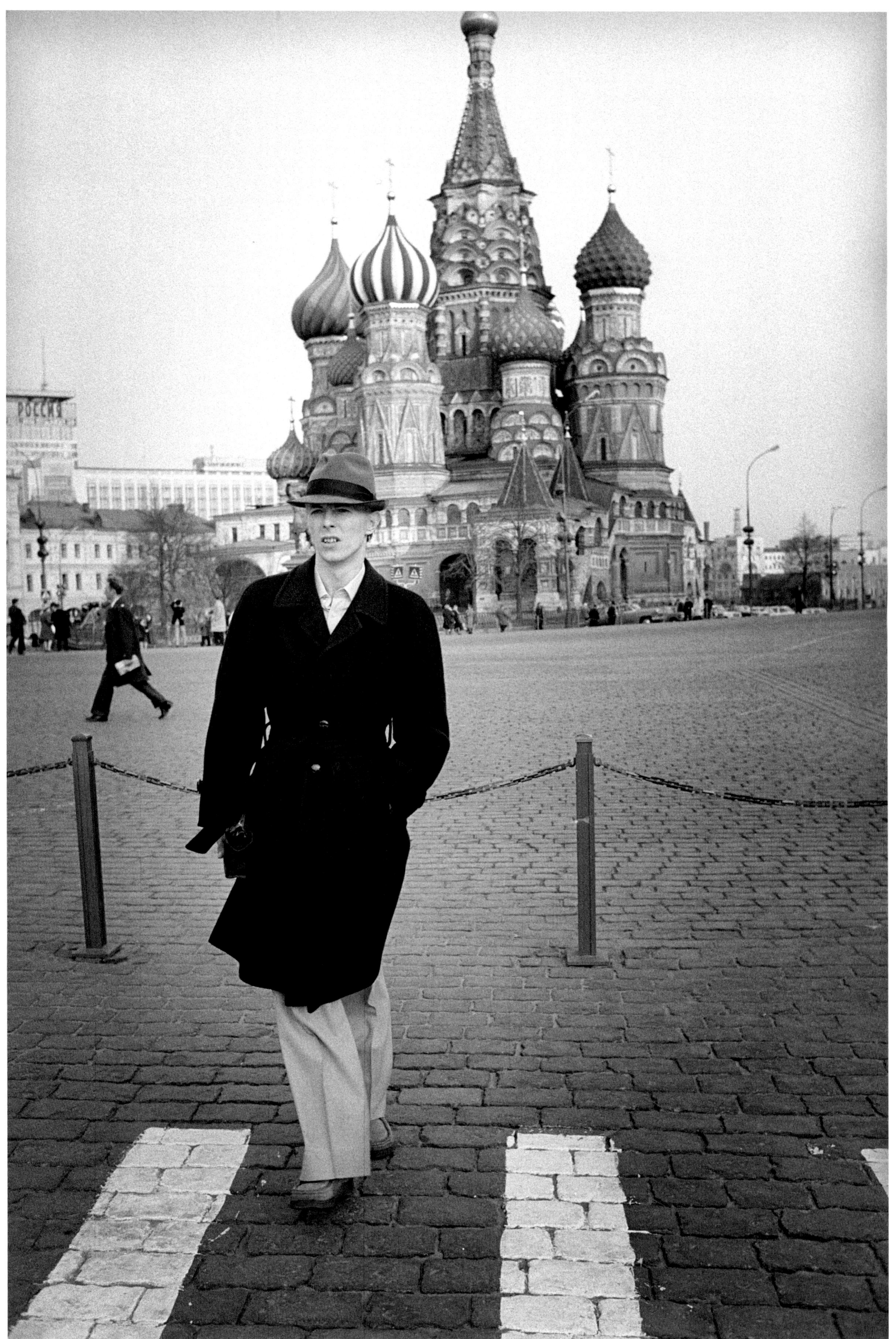

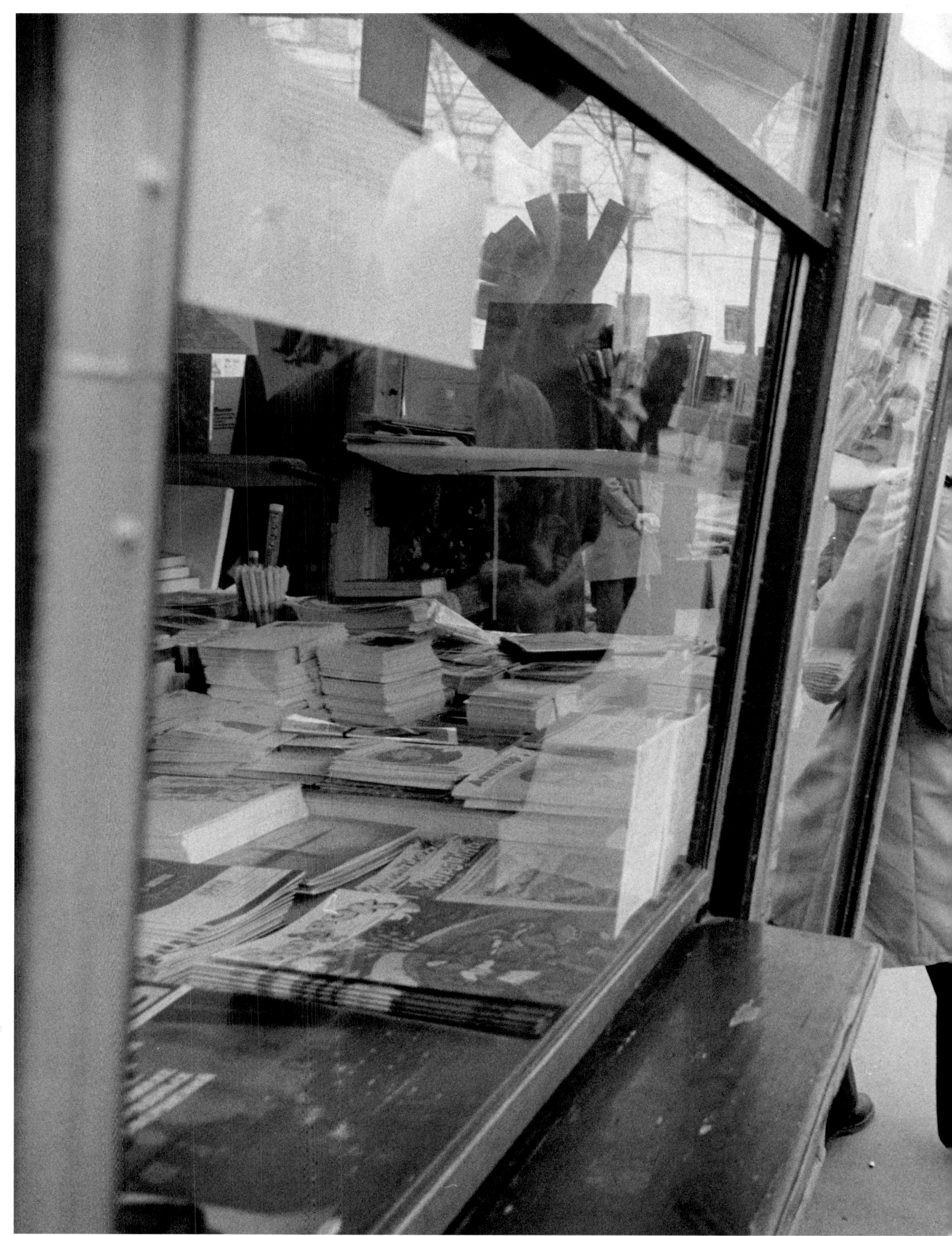

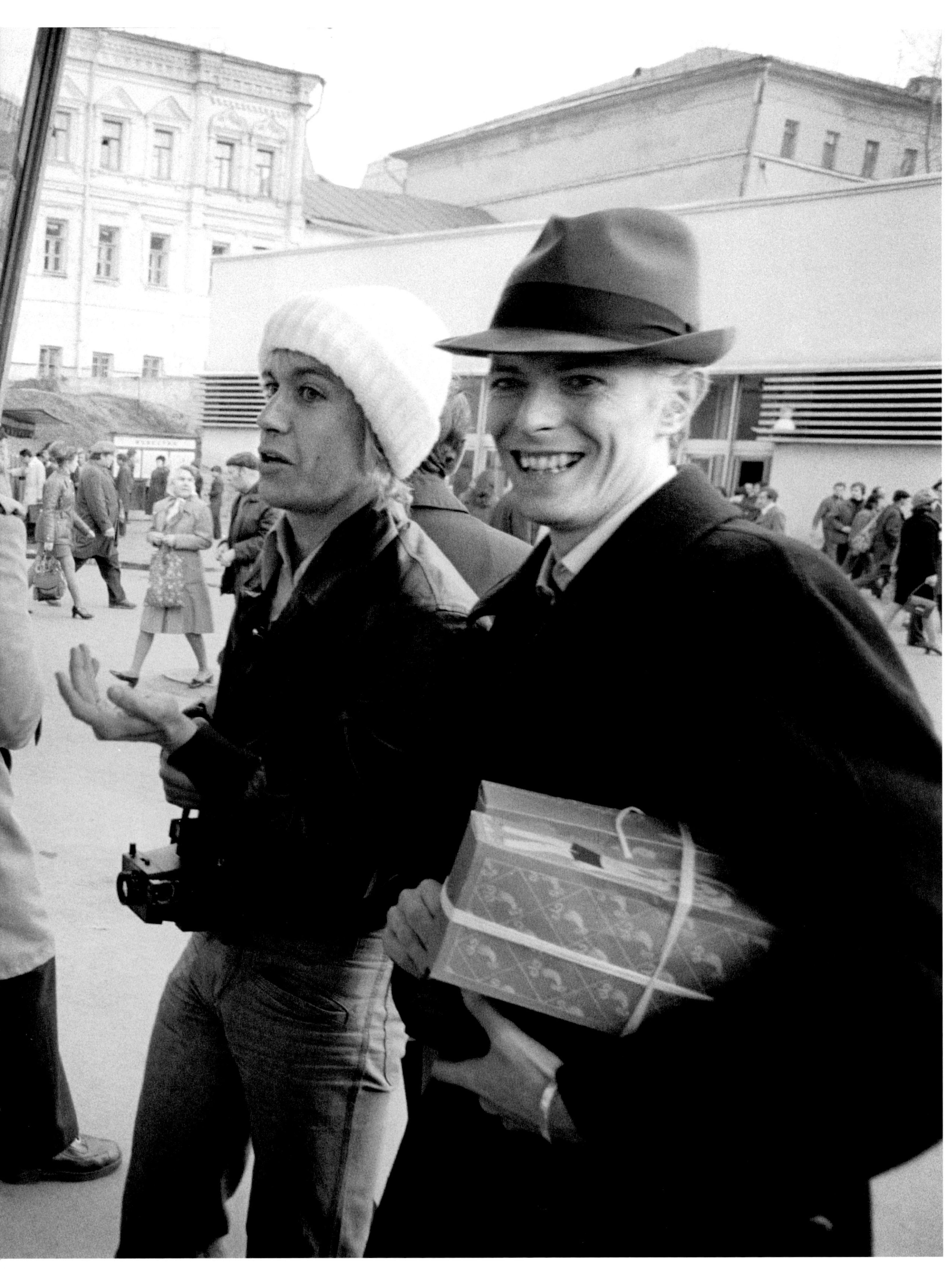

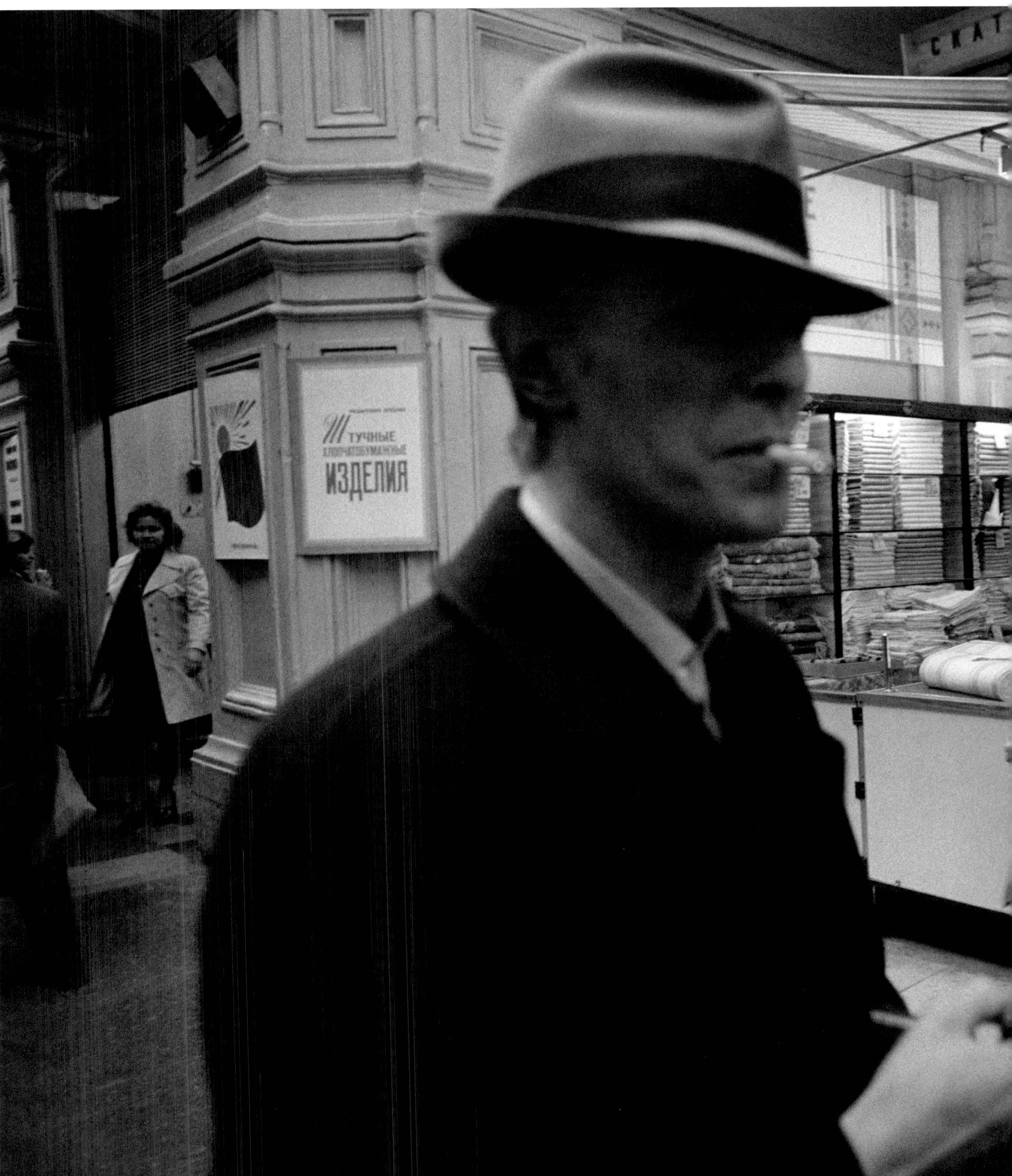

Штучные
хлопчатобумажные
ИЗДЕЛИЯ

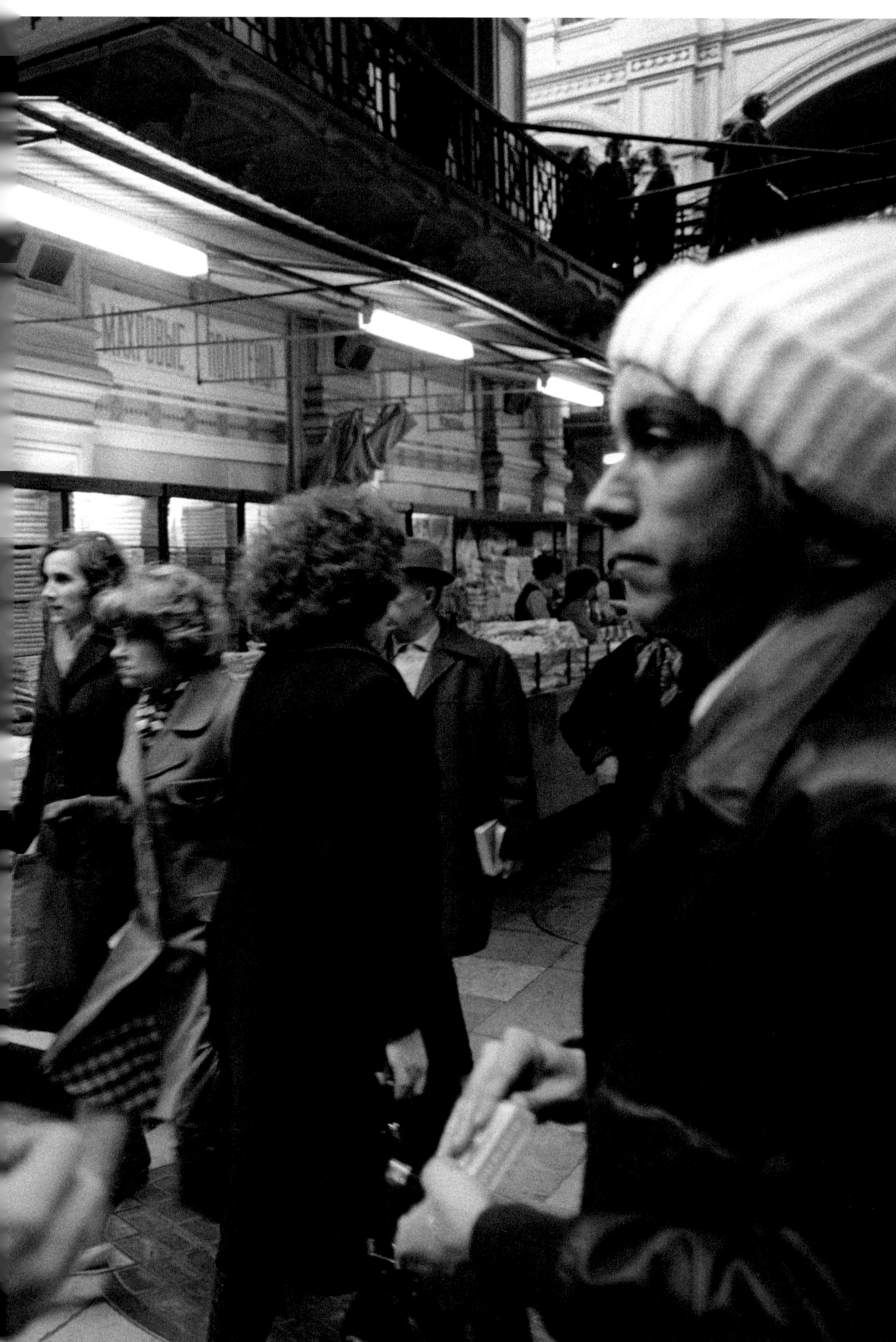

(Previous spread) David and Iggy stroll about Moscow's Red Square and do some shopping.
(Left) David and Iggy walk through a market in Moscow's Red Square.
(Next spread, left page) David enjoys a cigar prior to dinner in Moscow at the legendary Metropol Hall. The Metropol is famous as the location where the great Soviet poet Sergei Yesenin made a declaration of love to Isadora Duncan, Galina Vishnevskaya met her future husband Mstislav Rostropovich, one of the world's greatest cellists, and Michael Jackson once played the piano.

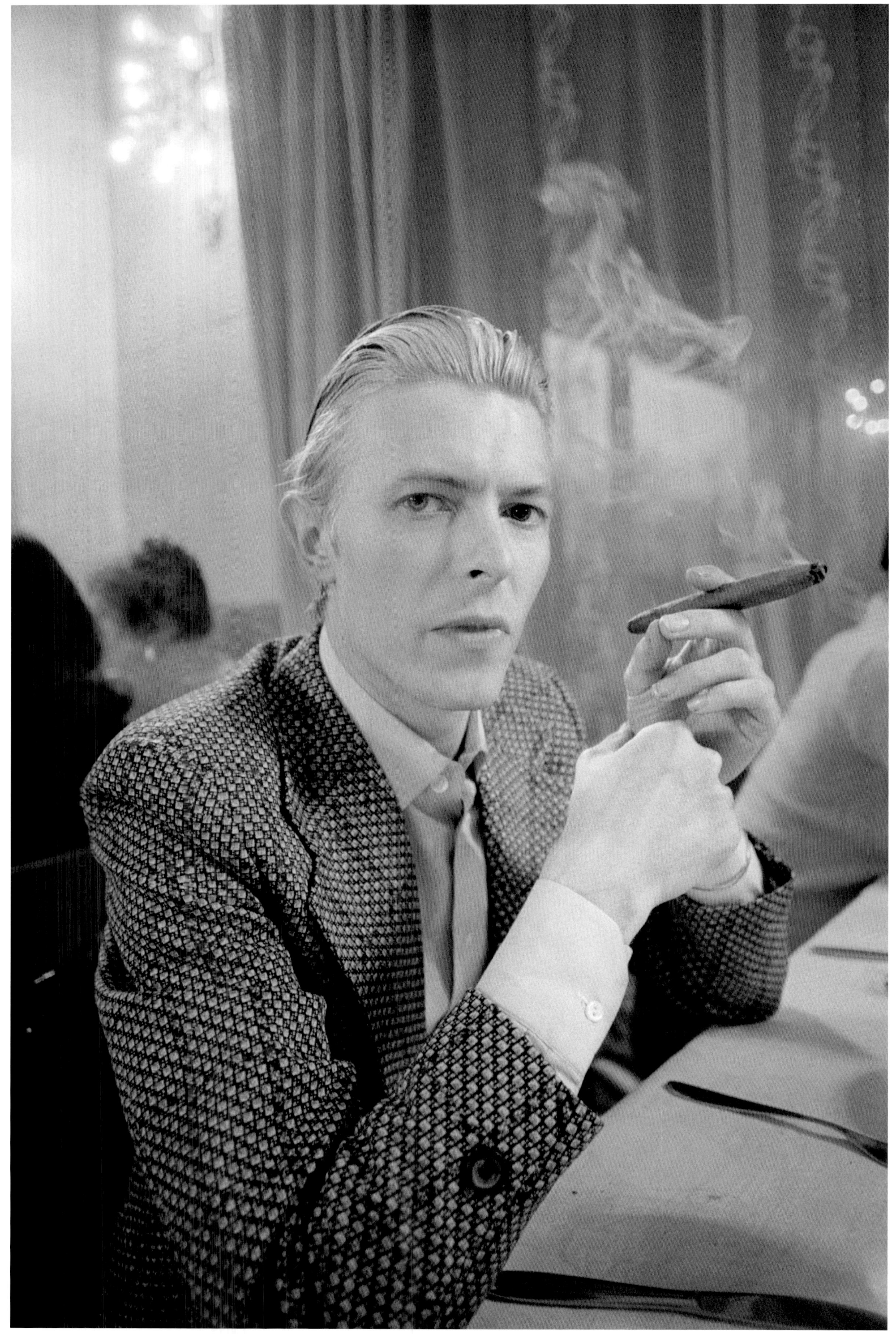

"SO WE GET ON THE TRAIN AND GET TO THE HELSINKI BORDER. DAVID AND IGGY GET STRIP-
SEARCHED. I GOT NOTHING AND I WAS THE ONE WHO HAD IT STASHED UNDER MY SEAT!"
-ANDREW KENT

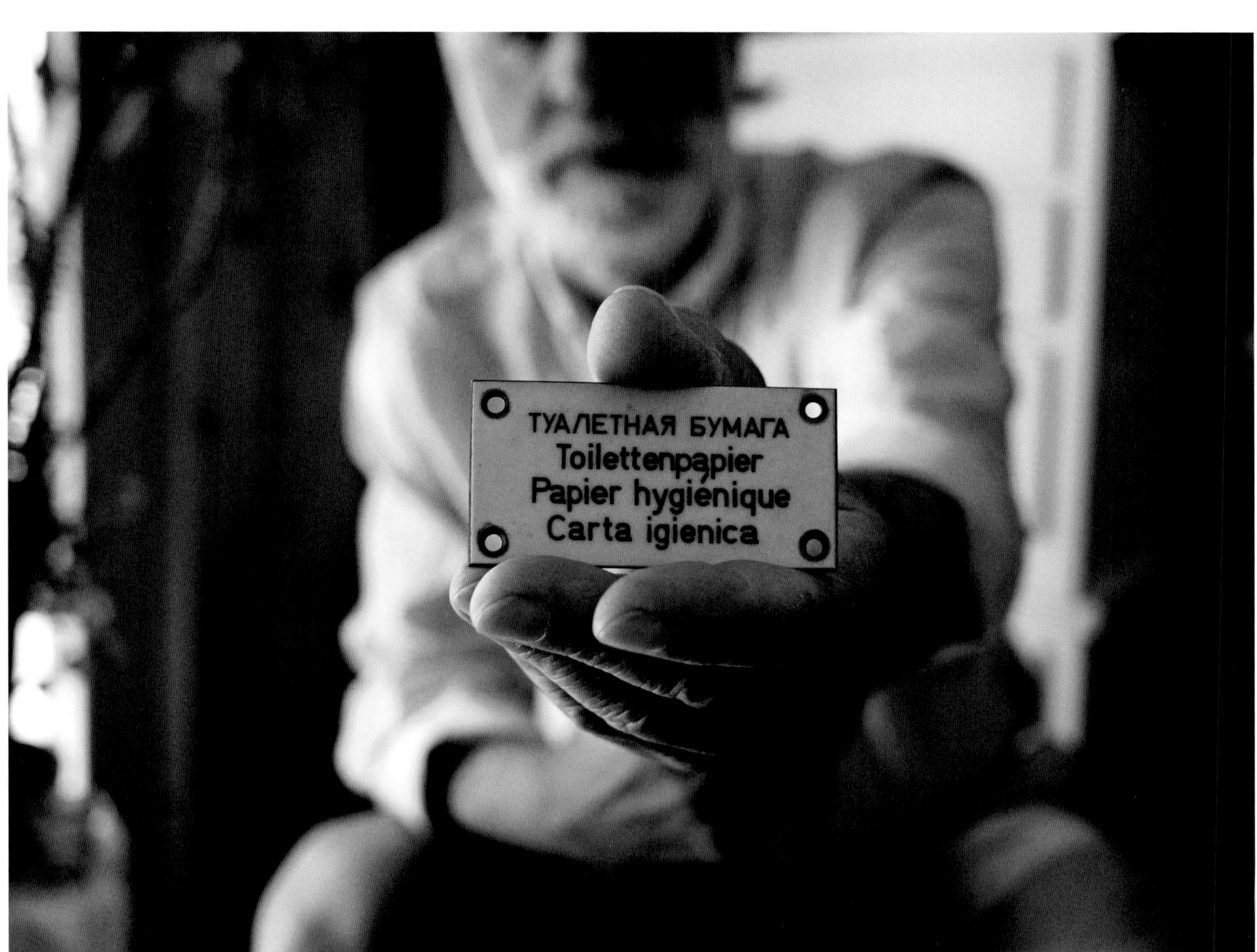
ТУАЛЕТНАЯ БУМАГА
Toilettenpapier
Papier hygiénique
Carta igienica

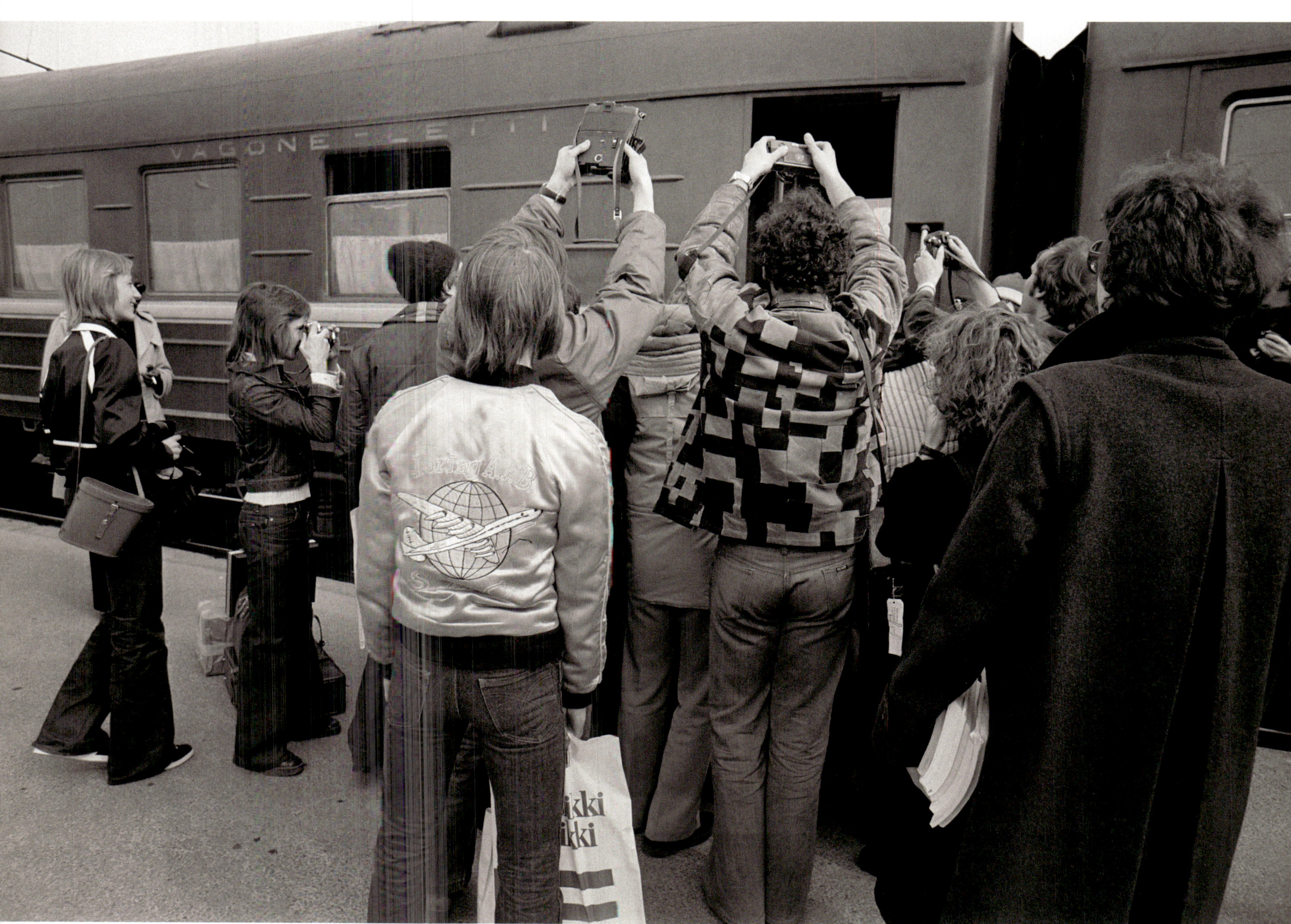

(Previous Page) Many years later in the comfort of his living room in Sun Valley Idaho, Kent displays the allegedly misappropriated bathroom plaque supposedly taken from the Soviet train.

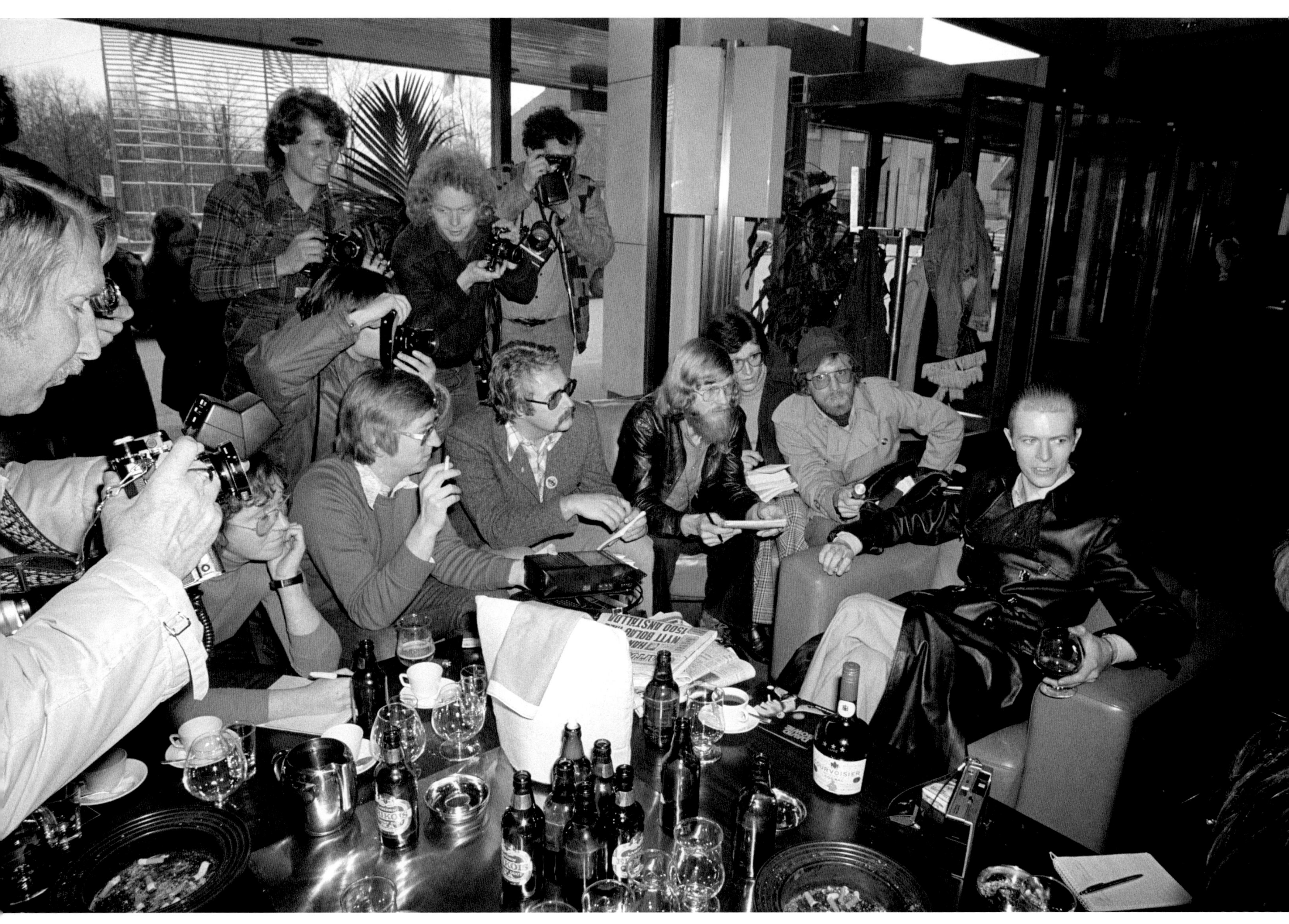

(Above) When David and his entourage of 4 finally returned to Helsinki, just one day later than scheduled, the press had been camped out at the hotel bar awaiting their eventual return.

(Left) Once word of David's arrival in Helsinki leaked to the media David's train was swarmed by European media.

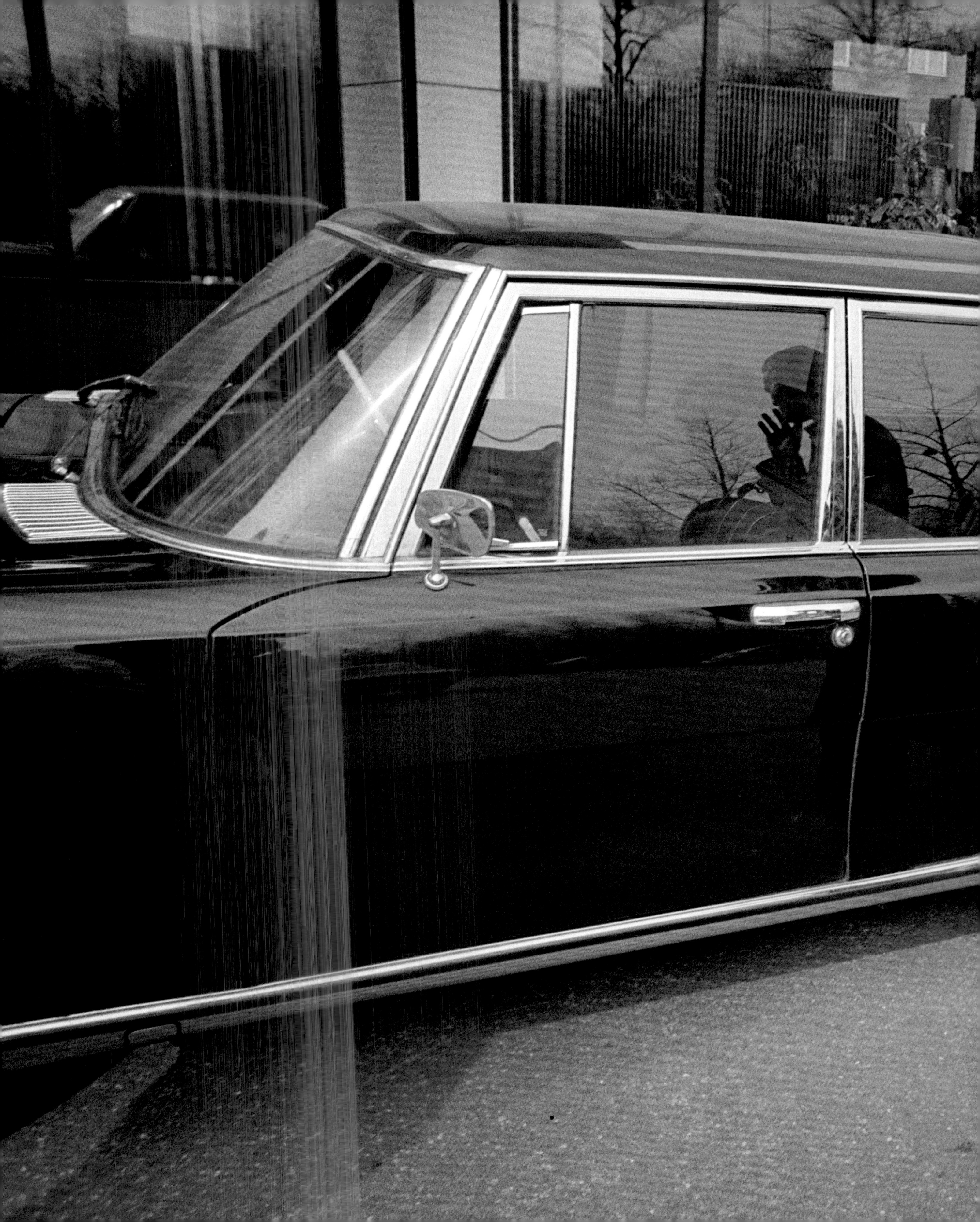

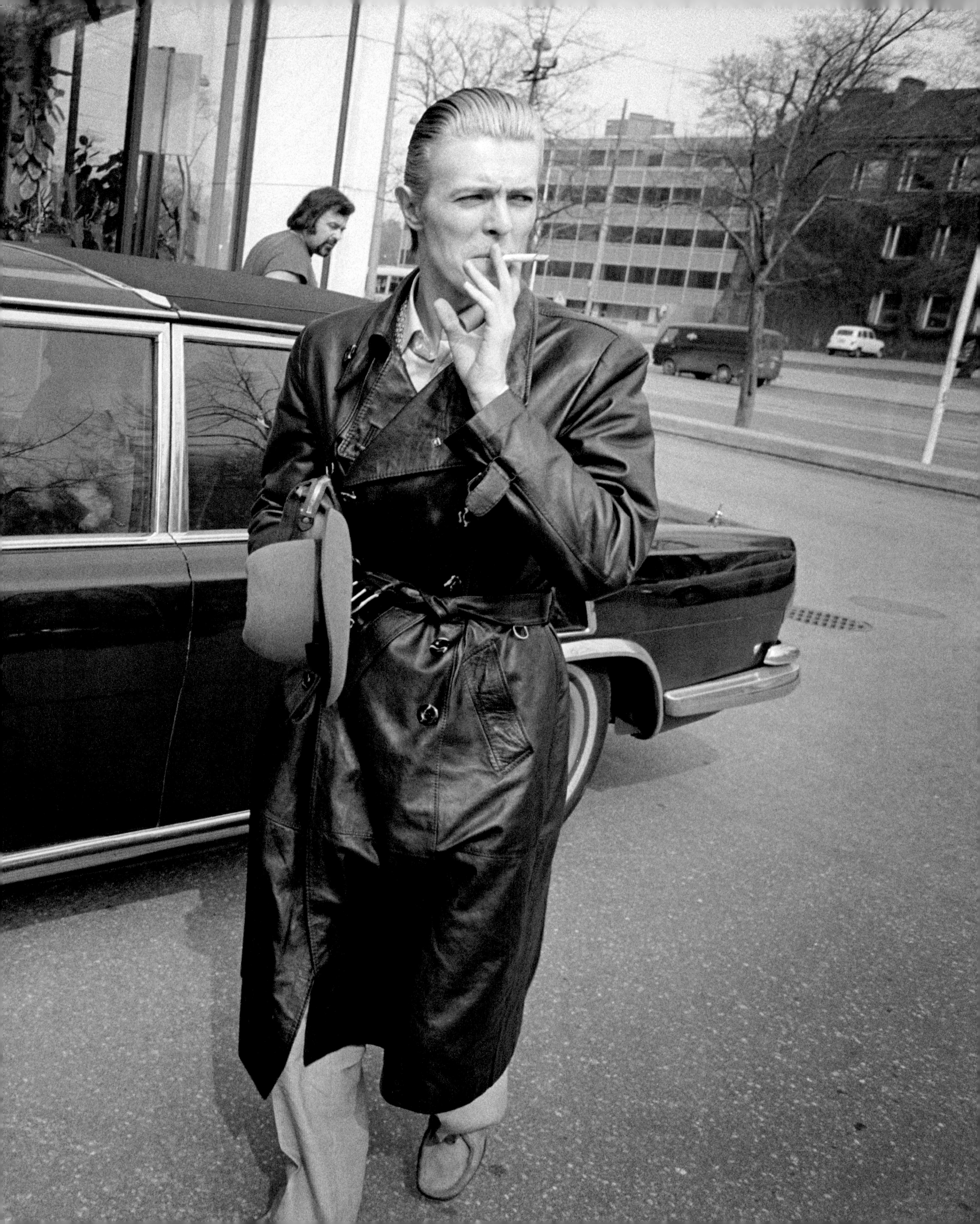

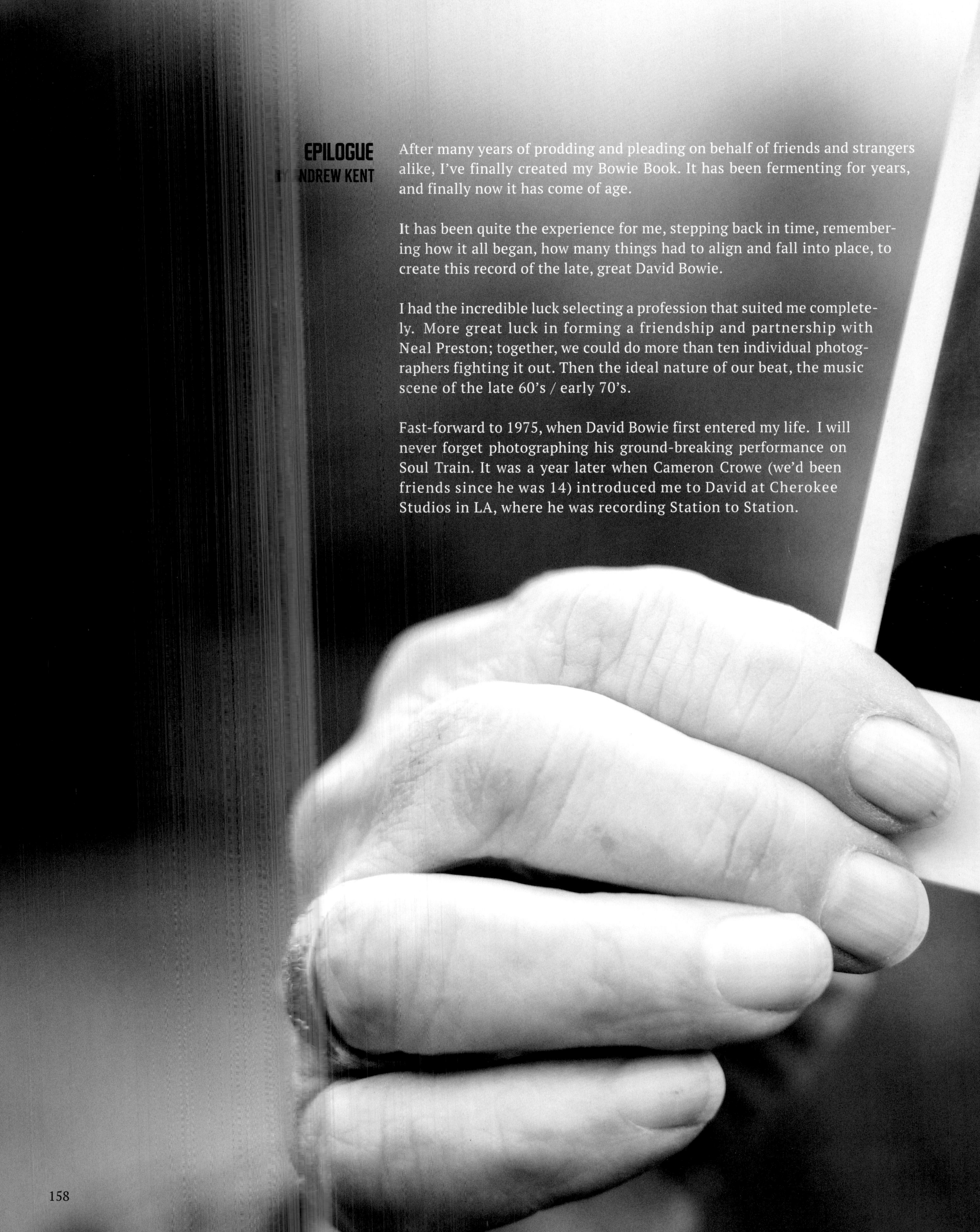

After many years of prodding and pleading on behalf of friends and strangers alike, I've finally created my Bowie Book. It has been fermenting for years, and finally now it has come of age.

It has been quite the experience for me, stepping back in time, remembering how it all began, how many things had to align and fall into place, to create this record of the late, great David Bowie.

I had the incredible luck selecting a profession that suited me completely. More great luck in forming a friendship and partnership with Neal Preston; together, we could do more than ten individual photographers fighting it out. Then the ideal nature of our beat, the music scene of the late 60's / early 70's.

Fast-forward to 1975, when David Bowie first entered my life. I will never forget photographing his ground-breaking performance on Soul Train. It was a year later when Cameron Crowe (we'd been friends since he was 14) introduced me to David at Cherokee Studios in LA, where he was recording Station to Station.

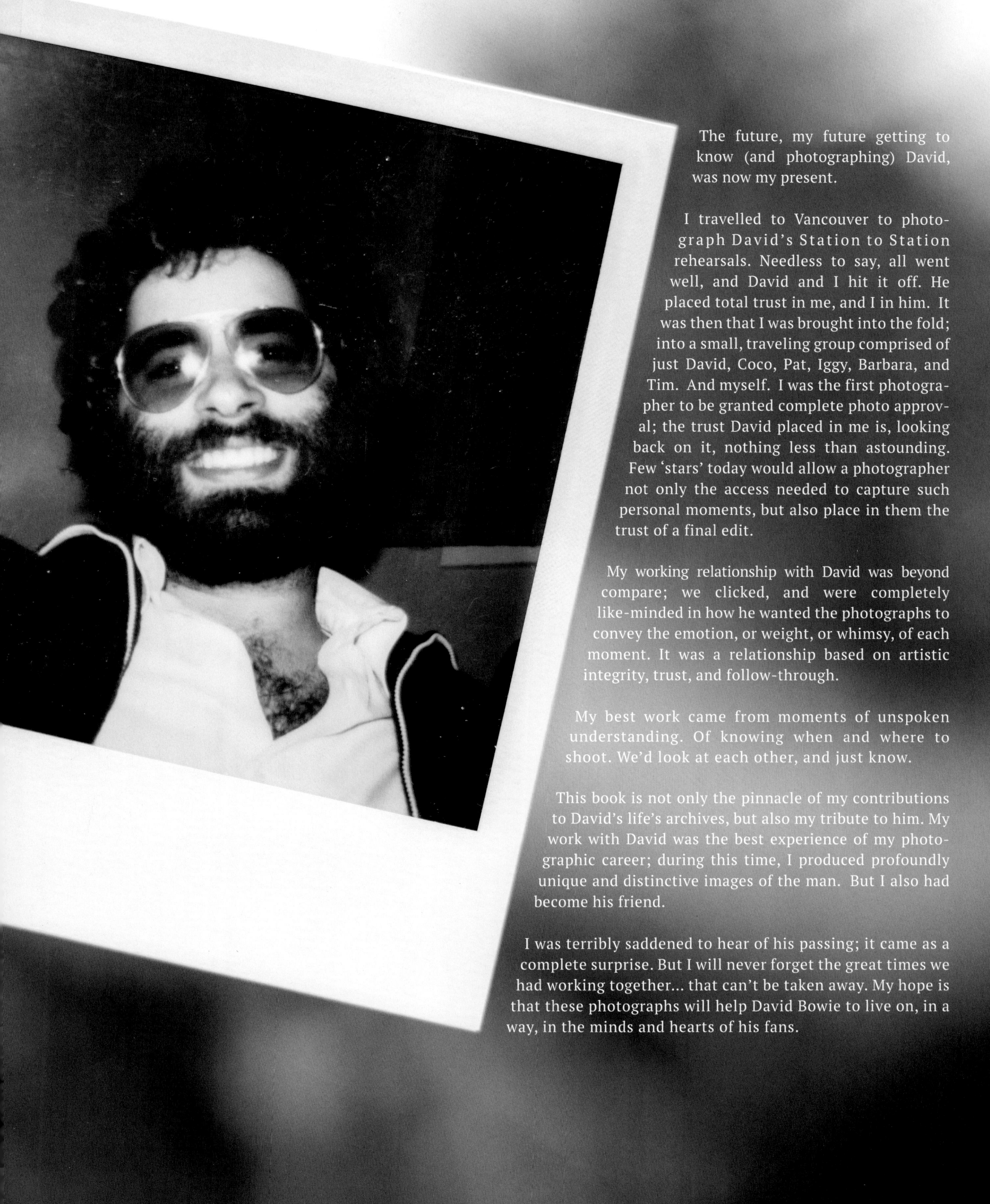

The future, my future getting to know (and photographing) David, was now my present.

I travelled to Vancouver to photograph David's Station to Station rehearsals. Needless to say, all went well, and David and I hit it off. He placed total trust in me, and I in him. It was then that I was brought into the fold; into a small, traveling group comprised of just David, Coco, Pat, Iggy, Barbara, and Tim. And myself. I was the first photographer to be granted complete photo approval; the trust David placed in me is, looking back on it, nothing less than astounding. Few 'stars' today would allow a photographer not only the access needed to capture such personal moments, but also place in them the trust of a final edit.

My working relationship with David was beyond compare; we clicked, and were completely like-minded in how he wanted the photographs to convey the emotion, or weight, or whimsy, of each moment. It was a relationship based on artistic integrity, trust, and follow-through.

My best work came from moments of unspoken understanding. Of knowing when and where to shoot. We'd look at each other, and just know.

This book is not only the pinnacle of my contributions to David's life's archives, but also my tribute to him. My work with David was the best experience of my photographic career; during this time, I produced profoundly unique and distinctive images of the man. But I also had become his friend.

I was terribly saddened to hear of his passing; it came as a complete surprise. But I will never forget the great times we had working together... that can't be taken away. My hope is that these photographs will help David Bowie to live on, in a way, in the minds and hearts of his fans.

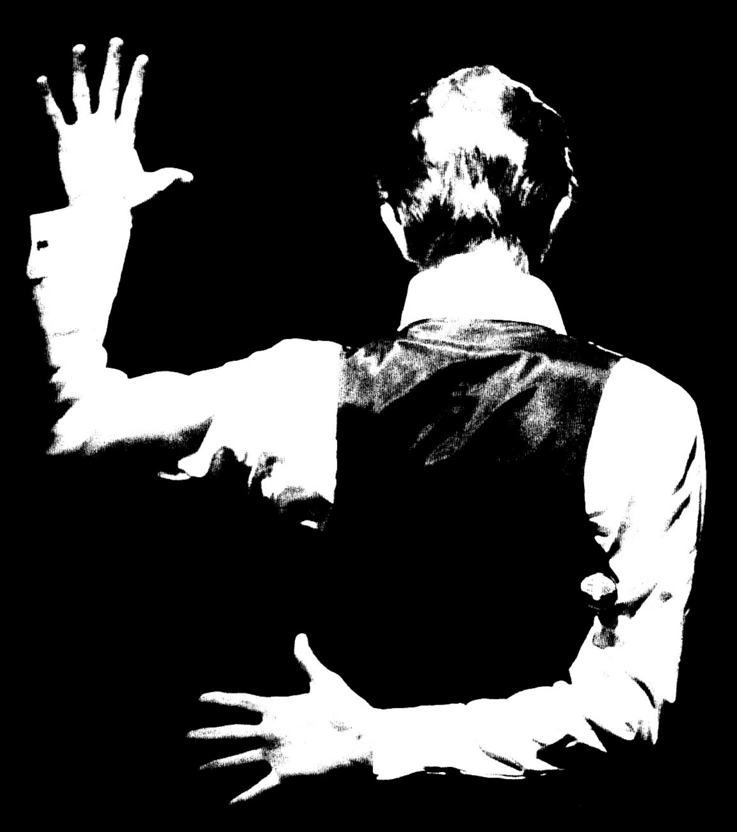

"THE MINUTE YOU KNOW YOU'RE ON SAFE GROUND, YOU'RE DEAD, YOU'RE FINISHED. IT'S OVER. THE LAST THING I WANT IS TO BE ESTABLISHED. I WANT TO GO TO BED EVERY NIGHT SAYING, "IF I NEVER WAKE AGAIN, I CERTAINLY WILL HAVE LIVED WHILE I WAS ALIVE." - DAVID BOWIE

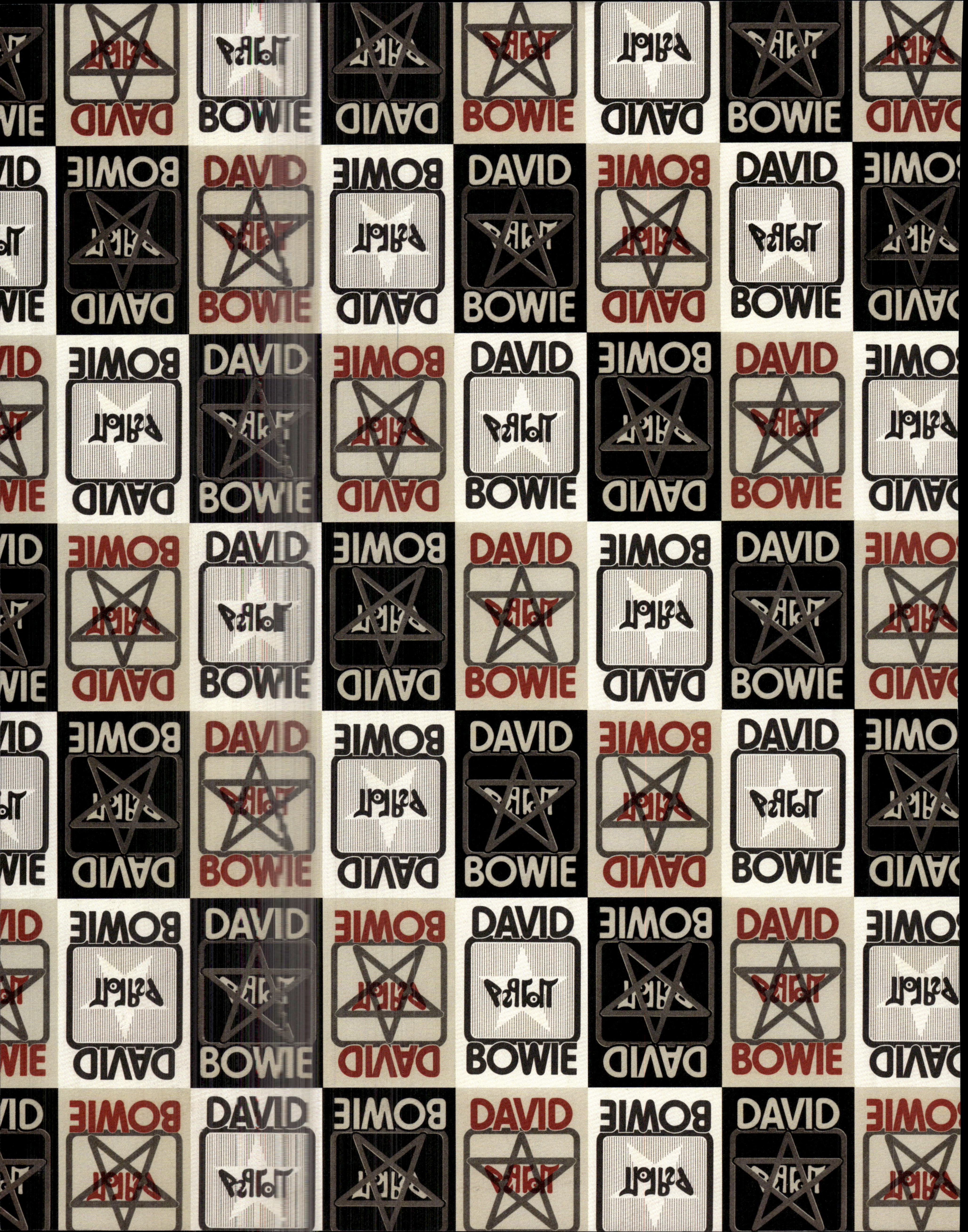